Rock and Romanticism

For the Record:
Lexington Studies in Rock and Popular Music

Series Editors:
Scott D. Calhoun, Cedarville University
Christopher Endrinal, Florida Gulf Coast University

For the Record: Lexington Studies in Rock and Popular Music features monographs and edited collections that examine topics relevant to the composition, consumption, and influence of the rock and popular music genres which have arisen starting in the 20th century in all nations and cultures. In the series, scholars approach these genres from music studies, cultural studies, and sociological studies frameworks, and may incorporate theories and methods from literary, philosophical, performance, and religious studies, in order to examine the wider significance of particular artists, subgenres, fandoms, or other music-related phenomena. Books in the series use as a starting point the understanding that as both products of our larger culture and driving forces within that wider culture, rock and popular music are worthy of critical study.

Advisory Board
Joshua Duchan, Wayne State University; David Easley, Oklahoma City University; Bryn Hughes, University of Miami; Greg McCandless, Full Sail University; Ann van der Merwe, Miami University; Meg Wilhoite

Titles in the Series

Rock and Romanticism: Blake, Wordsworth, and Rock from Dylan to U2, edited by James Rovira
The Beatles, Sgt. Pepper, and the Summer of Love: Roll Up for the Mystery Tour! edited by Kenneth Womack and Katheryn Cox
U2 Above, Across, and Beyond: Interdisciplinary Assessments, edited by Scott D. Calhoun

Rock and Romanticism

Blake, Wordsworth, and Rock from Dylan to U2

Edited by
James Rovira

LEXINGTON BOOKS
Lanham • Boulder • New York • London

Published by Lexington Books
An imprint of The Rowman & Littlefield Publishing Group, Inc.
4501 Forbes Boulevard, Suite 200, Lanham, Maryland 20706
www.rowman.com

Unit A, Whitacre Mews, 26-34 Stannary Street, London SE11 4AB

British Library Cataloguing in Publication Information Available

Library of Congress Cataloging-in-Publication Data

Names: Rovira, James.
Title: Rock and romanticism : Blake, Wordsworth, and rock from Dylan to U2 / edited by James Rovira.
Description: Lexington Books, [2018] | Series: For the record: Lexington studies in rock and popular music | Includes bibliographical references and index.
Identifiers: LCCN 2017055716 (print) | LCCN 2017056397 (ebook) | ISBN 9781498553841 (electronic) | ISBN 9781498553834 (cloth : alk. paper)
Subjects: LCSH: Music and literature. | Rock music—History and criticism. | Romanticism. | Blake, William, 1757-1827—Criticism and interpretation. | Wordsworth, William, 1770-1850—Criticism and interpretation.
Classification: LCC ML3849 (ebook) | LCC ML3849 .R63 2018 (print) | DDC 780/.0821—dc23 LC record available at https://lccn.loc.gov/2017055716

♾™ The paper used in this publication meets the minimum requirements of American National Standard for Information Sciences Permanence of Paper for Printed Library Materials, ANSI/NISO Z39.48-1992.

Printed in the United States of America

For my parents, for putting up with my music all of those years

Contents

Preface

I first met the rock photographer who provided the cover image, Taylor Fickes, when she and a co-worker at a Best Buy in Ohio helped me purchase a DSLR for my daughter Beka, who needed one for entry into an art program at the University of Central Florida. When I saw Taylor's rock photography online, I had an idea for a gallery exhibit devoted to Ohio rock and roll. From there, I thought I would pair that exhibit with a 200-level honors class devoted to music and literature, so I solicited ideas from the NASSR-L listserv, which is devoted to the study of Romantic literature. List members responded so enthusiastically that I decided to post a call for proposals (CFP) for an edited anthology devoted to exploring the intersections between rock and roll and Romanticism. I received fifty chapter proposals in response to that CFP. Out of those proposals, eleven essays and my introduction are published here.

I would like to first thank NASSR-L and its many generous members who made suggestions for my course, all of whom are listed on the *Rock and Romanticism* book blog.[1] I would also like to thank my contributors for making this project as enjoyable as I could hope, and I would like to thank the librarians at the Rock and Roll Hall of Fame Library and Archives for their professionalism, care, and generosity in their help with background research for this project and others that have not yet come to fruition. I would like to thank Associate Professor of Art and Diane Kidd Gallery Director Lee Fearnside for being a good friend and colleague as well as a great collaborator on our *Scars* exhibit and project, on the exhibit and talks related to Michael Phillips's work in *Blake in the Heartland*, and on the exhibit *Rock 'n' Roll in Ohio*.

NOTE

1. http://rockandromanticism.wordpress.com.

Introduction

Rock and Romanticism

James Rovira

When one of my undergraduate professors at Rollins College, Dr. Roy Star-
ling, introduced his class to British Romanticism, he did so by describing
what it was like for listeners when Bob Dylan plugged in his guitar at the
1965 Newport festival: electrifying, frightening, and transgressive. He didn't
mean to say at the time that Dylan was a Romantic poet, but that Wordsworth
was a rock star. He suggested that Wordsworth's poetry in the 1790s had an
effect similar to rock in the 1950s and 1960s and then over and over again in
subsequent decades. This comparison undoubtedly came readily to mind
because the influence of the English Romantics upon rock, especially since
the 1960s, is both pervasive and well known, with William Blake being the
greatest Romantic poet for the rock and roll generation. Musicians such as
Bob Dylan, the Fugs, and the Doors referred to his poetry in the 1960s,
Emerson, Lake & Palmer in the 1970s, Daniel Amos in the 1980s, Patti
Smith in the 1990s, the Martha Redbone Roots Project in 2012, U2's *Songs
of Innocence* in 2014, and U2 again in *Songs of Experience*, just released as
this book was going into production. Substantial work is devoted simply to
cataloging Blake in music.[1] This musical interest in Blake is unsurprising,
for Blake first sang his poems at informal social gatherings, drawing the
attention of musical scholars of his day who notated his original tunes.[2] But
Wordsworth and Coleridge make their appearances on rock albums as well,
and Wordsworth has as much representation as Blake in this volume, if not
slightly more. Since Bob Dylan's reception of the Nobel Prize in Literature
in 2016 seems to have placed beyond question rock's literary potential,[3] this
anthology seeks not only to demonstrate the influence of Romantic literature
on rock, which is already the subject of much attention, but to argue that rock

itself is a late-twentieth-century expression of Romanticism—an extension, continuation, partner, or doppelgänger of this eighteenth- and nineteenth-century phenomenon.

THEORIZING ROCK, HISTORICIZING ROMANTICISM

What is Romanticism? And what do I mean by calling rock a modern expression of Romanticism? When Mary Wollstonecraft used the phrase "romantic notions of honour" to describe one of two ways of motivating soldiers (the other being discipline and command) in her 1792 *Vindication of the Rights of Woman*, very few readers would have been confused by her use of the term "romantic" to refer to the values, traditions, or aesthetic of Medieval romance. Not long after, Byron would similarly use the word "romantic" to describe erotic relationships, Medieval romances, and contemporary works or even scenery that reminded him of a Medieval aesthetic. But in his 1820 response to an essay about *Manfred* that Goëthe published earlier that year, Byron registers a use of the term "Romantic" new to him, especially in relationship to English literature: "I perceive that in Germany, as well as in Italy, there is a great struggle about what they call 'Classical' and 'Romantic,'—terms which were not subjects of classification in England, at least when I left it four or five years ago." Byron dislikes this new use of the term "Romantic," especially when set in opposition to "Classical" authors whom Byron assumes to be Pope and Swift. So while he has no problem with the word "romantic" being used to describe a Medieval aesthetic or a structure of feeling, he objects to its use in a classification system for literature.

Despite Byron's distaste, the term "Romantic" as part of a classification system of European literature and art continued throughout the nineteenth century, though attempts to coherently define the term failed repeatedly. Ongoing concern about the meaning of the term "Romantic" manifested itself during the early twentieth century in an argument between Irving Babbitt and A. O. Lovejoy. This argument was initiated by Lovejoy's negative review of Babbitt's *Rousseau and Romanticism* (1919) published in the May 1920 issue of *Modern Language Notes* that eventually led to Lovejoy's now famous *PMLA* essay "On the Discrimination of Romanticisms" (1924). Lovejoy's opening remarks observe that his own work is being published one hundred years after "M.M. Dupuis and Cotonet . . . began an enterprise which was to cause them, as is recorded, 'twelve years of suffering,' and to end in disillusionment—the enterprise of discovering what Romanticism is, by collecting definitions and characterizations of it given by eminent authorities."[4] Summarizing uses of the term "Romantic" since then, Lovejoy arrives at the oft-quoted conclusion that the "word 'romantic' has come to mean so many things that, by itself, it means nothing. It has ceased to perform the function of a verbal sign."[5] As of the time of this writing we are approaching the one-hundredth anniversary of the publication of Lovejoy's essay, and it remains the most compelling and definitive statement of the problem: what exactly does the word "Romanticism" mean?

His challenge to make the word "Romanticism" a meaningful term in a classification system is twofold: first, to acknowledge the diversity of phenomena that fall under the umbrella of the word "Romanticism," and next, to make that umbrella a conceptually coherent entity, because once we acknowledge a variety of Romanticisms we imply the existence of a single entity that exists in a plurality of forms. A number of twentieth-century scholars attempted to meet Lovejoy's challenge, including René Welleck in 1949 and then Morse Peckham in 1970, who argued that Lovejoy met his own challenge in the concluding chapters of *The Great Chain of Being* (1936). Romanticism is organicism in Peckham's opinion, a single construct expressed in "positive" and "negative" modes that comfortably house the constellation of attributes typically associated with Romanticism. None of these definitions has been convincing enough to stick, however. By 1993, Stuart Curran in his introduction to the *Cambridge Companion to British Romanticism* would acknowledge Lovejoy's contribution and then affirm that due to the increasing sophistication of modes of historical and philosophical inquiry, "the problem of contemporary definition has been exacerbated—or perhaps rendered obsolete," along with the need to identify a single entity behind the plural form "Romanticisms."[6]

By that time, however, Robert Sayre and Michael Löwy had published "Figures of Romantic Anti-Capitalism" (1984) in *New German Critique*, which was subsequently republished in G. A. Rosso's and Daniel P. Watkins's *Spirits of Fire: English Romantic Writers and Contemporary Historical Methods* (1990). It appeared in this anthology alongside a number of essays applying Sayre's and Löwy's thesis, Michael Ferber's thorough critique of it, and their response to Ferber. Their work was later revised and expanded to book length in *Romanticism Against the Tide of Modernity* (2001).

Both their essay and book credit Lovejoy for his statement of the problem and then take as their starting point a definition of Romanticism derived from Lukács. Romanticism is "a critique of modernity, that is, of modern capitalist civilization, in the name of values and ideals drawn from the past (the precapitalist, premodern past)."[7] Or in shorter form, it is "opposition to capitalism in the name of pre-capitalist values."[8] They proceed to further define Romanticism as "an essential component of modern culture" that is a "collective mental structure" (*Weltanshauung*, or worldview) which is inextricably bound up with the Enlightenment, characterized by a sense of loss and a longing for unity, and focused on a subject that experiences this range of feelings in response to the interpellation of a capitalist subjectivity.[9]

This claim extends Lovejoy's significance to the twenty-first century by grasping both horns of his dilemma. On the first point, Romanticism as anti-capitalism in the name of pre-capitalist values is a conceptually coherent, single entity that is always subjectively felt but only sometimes politically conscious. On the second point, Sayre and Löwy present a diversity of Romanticisms under that big umbrella by developing a taxonomy of Romanticisms not based on nation of origin, as Lovejoy suggested, but one consisting of a variety of responses to capitalism: restitutionist, conservative, fascist, resigned, liberal, and revolutionary or utopian. The latter category is further subdivided into Jacobin-democratic, populist, utopian-humanist socialism, libertarian, and Marxist Romanticisms. Sayre's and Löwy's arguments underlie the work attempted by several, though not all, essays in this anthology,[10] but all essays assume that Romanticism continues into the present as an essential feature of modern culture and takes on a specific, musical transformation in the period following World War II.

I want to return briefly to Sayre's and Löwy's initial formulation of Romanticism as "opposition to capitalism in the name of pre-capitalist values" to emphasize the ways in which both components of their definition are equally stressed. If Romanticism were simply "opposition to capitalism," then it would be no more than a kind of proto-Marxism, which is perhaps why their 2001 restatement of their thesis modified this phrase to "opposition to modernity," even if that modernity is still capitalist in nature. It's important that we understand Sayre and Löwy are not thinking in terms of conscious support for one economic system versus another, but of subjective, emotional reactions to capitalist economies by those who live in them. These reactions can be viscerally negative or reactive even by those who benefit from and exploit the capitalist economy itself. While Löwy and Sayre assert that "Romanticism is one of Marx's and Engel's neglected sources, a source perhaps as important for their work as German neo-Hegelianism or French materialism,"[11] they are careful not to identify Romanticism with Marxism except as one specific variety in their taxonomy. They explain that Marx and Engels rejected longing for a pre-capitalist world as a reactionary tendency and "praised capitalism for having torn away the veils that had concealed exploitation in precapitalist societies" even while they "saw capitalism as a system that transforms every instance of economic progress into a public calamity."[12]

So while Marxism is anti-capitalist, it is not consistently anti-capitalist in the name of pre-capitalist values as Romanticism is: it is more often allied with Enlightenment emphases on reason, science, and progress. Romanticism is not simply opposition to the Enlightenment either, as Löwy and Sayre posit close enough interrelationships between Enlightenment and Romanticism that "certain forms of Romanticism manifest greater or lesser affinity with its enemy brother," Enlightenment.[13] In their view, Rousseau is the hinge figure between Romantic and Enlightenment thought. These "enemy brothers" are divided over the type of individual brought into being by a capitalist economy, so that "subjective individualism" is set against "numeric individualism"[14]: the Romantic individual is idealized as an existentially defined part of an organic whole while the Enlightenment individual is a data point in a mechanistic universe, a demographic, and later, a *consumer*. Therefore, Romanticism's true opposite would be Enlightenment theorized by instrumental reason in the service of capitalism.

Since Romanticism is "opposition to capitalism in the name of pre-capitalist values," it requires only capitalism to bring it into being, so that pre-capitalist economies could give rise to pre-Romantic responses, and Romanticism might last for as long as capitalism does. When Romanticism is defined not as an era but as a response to historical conditions in a condition/response model, the observation that popular songwriters from the early 1960s to the present drew so often and so consistently from Wordsworth, Coleridge, and Blake should seem not so much coincidental as expected. Rock musicians found in the Romantic poets kindred spirits or fellow travelers because these musicians were, like the poets, Romantics. There are also historically grounded reasons for defining rock musicians as Romantics, since eighteenth- and nineteenth-century European Romanticisms developed in conditions similar to the twentieth century after the end of World War II. Pervasive industrialism, widespread global trade, and the spread of European colonial enterprises earlier in the eighteenth century led to increasing conflicts around the globe and in Europe, culminating in political revolutions in the Americas and in France that were followed by almost continuous pan-European warfare from 1792 to 1815.

Similarly, the twentieth century saw two world wars followed by the rise of global capitalism and its partner, global communism. David Pichaske's *A Generation in Motion: Popular Culture and Music in the Sixties* describes post–World War II America in the 1950s as about "the unnatural prolongation of World War II heroism and mindset."[15] Pichaske suggests, somewhat stereotypically, but perhaps not inaccurately, that US victory in World War II made war, which was not fought on the soil of the continental US, and its associated military-style subservience seem like too-easy solutions for all social problems: "Let's make war on racism, bigotry, the Biggees, hippies . . . "[16] This mindset reacted very negatively to the U.S.S.R.'s launch of the Sputnik and entrance into space before the U.S.: "American generals, their egos bruised and their nerves jangled by the greatest of international upsets . . . thrash my ass in a mad race to bury the Ruskies beneath dollars, programs, and cerebrums."[17] Global capitalism and communism were both embodied by the rise of the United States and the Soviet Union as world superpowers, so by the onset of the 1950s, Europe, Russia, and the United

States were all poised for an emotionally intense, libidinally potent form of Romantic anti-capitalism: rock and roll.

What I think is diminished in Löwy's and Sayre's taxonomy of Romanticisms is a necessary emphasis on Romanticism as an aesthetic vehicle for a structure of feeling primary to any conceptual commitments. Their emphasis on the conceptual aspects of Romanticism may be a vulnerability of their ambition to develop a definition of Romanticism that applies equally to music, literature, art, political science, philosophy, religion, and other fields. Because they define Romanticism first and foremost as a "worldview" or a "collective mental structure" that manifests itself as a "series of themes" that are "logically related," their presentation privileges the conceptual over the affective.[18] Löwy and Sayre do explain this mental structure in terms of its affective components, placing them at the center of their thought: Romanticism in all of its manifestations is a "hostility towards present reality" that is "heavily charged with emotion."[19] It is characterized by a sense of loss and a longing for unity. But Löwy and Sayre ultimately base their taxonomy not on affective responses but on the subject's "relation to capitalism" that "brings together the political, the economic, and the social,"[20] which backgrounds the affective and elides the individual.

It is one thing to say that Romanticism is primarily a mental structure with a specific kind of emotional core and then to focus one's discussion on the mental structure. It is yet another to say that Romanticism is primarily a series of affective responses that we attempt, after the fact, to structure conceptually, even if we accept that these affective responses are all consciously or unconsciously some kind of reaction to capitalism. This examination of rock as a variety of late twentieth-century Romanticism allows for a possible reconsideration of the relationships among the affective and conceptual components of Löwy's and Sayre's theory of Romanticism. Blake and Wordsworth, in other words, might speak back to Löwy and Sayre through Bob Dylan, Leonard Cohen, and Kurt Cobain. What would happen if the conceptual and the affective were more equally engaged in a dialectic with one another rather than the conceptual subordinating the affective to its own taxonomy?

PREDECESSORS AND CHAPTER SUMMARIES

Herbert London's "American Romantics: Old and New" asserts in a 1969 study of the Beat poets and Bob Dylan that "the modern hippie movement is merely the most recent manifestation of an old romantic tradition in the United States."[21] However, this anthology's most significant predecessor is Robert Pattison's *The Triumph of Vulgarity: Rock Music in the Mirror of Romanticism* (1987). Pattison's monograph anticipates this one in its discussion of Romantic Satanism, largely accepting received definitions of Romanticism and then applying them to his subject with an emphasis on vulgarity as the valorization of the common over the elite: Romantic Satanism in rock is the triumph of the common person. Published in 1987, however, it cannot have anticipated developments in music or in scholarship on Romanticism since then. Keir Keightley's "Reconsidering Rock" writes a Modernism/ Romanticism dichotomy over rock music of the 1960s and later, asserting that both "Romanticism and Modernism challenged the emergence of industrial, urban capitalism, and both celebrated the author, artist, or musician as a privileged representative of an authentic, individual self," distinguishing between the two by associating Romanticism with the pastoral and Modernism with the urban.[22] Keightley further associates Romanticism with organicism and the valuation of the "pre-industrial past" while Modernism is associated with "shock effects and radical experimentation . . . [so that] the true artist must break with the past."[23] As a result, authenticity in rock is conceptualized very differently in Romantic and Modernist modes. The field of scholarship covering rock and Romanticism is otherwise currently dominated by individual studies of musicians and literary figures appearing in a variety of journals, background or influence studies, or popular culture approaches that cover more than just music. For example, William Blake and music has recently been considered in Steve Clark, Tristanne Connolly, and Jason Whittaker's *Blake 2.0: William Blake in Twentieth-Century Art, Music and Culture* (2012), which has five essays on Blake and music: one on Blake and Dylan, one on Blake and the Doors, one encyclopedic essay about musical adaptations, and an essay on echoes of Blake in 1990s' music. Jason Whittaker's essay on *Jerusalem* from 1979–2009 does work parallel to the kind of work being carried out here, so that the essays that follow have the potential to significantly extend the range of scholarship on this topic.

As we turn from literature to music, we will see that "rock" is every bit as contradictory and difficult to define as the word Romanticism. Because using the term "rock" in reference to popular music from the late 1940s through the early 2000s is problematic, each essay will be allowed to define rock or its subgenres for itself: I will not attempt to define them all here. Most contributors, however, are writing about artists who fall within the groupings of musical styles originating in the 1960s and 1970s known as "classic rock." The following list represents the rock figures covered by every essay but two in this anthology: The Beatles, Bob Dylan, Mick Jagger, Leonard Cohen, Jackson Browne, Rush, U2, Kurt Cobain and grunge, Blackberry Smoke, and Martha Redbone. Of this list, Martha Redbone performs within the musical traditions of folk, blues, Native American chant, and Southern gospel, combinations popular since the 1960s and with precedents in 1970s Native American rock bands such as Redbone and Blackfoot. Grunge is a direct musical brainchild of 1970s rock, influenced by punk and, before that, by musicians like Neil Young, Led Zeppelin, and The Who. Of the two musical outliers in this anthology, one deeply engages the triangle of Wordsworth, contemporary poetry, and twenty-first-century pop, hip-hop, and rap, while the second adds a continental European contribution to our study by exploring the interrelationships between Italian Romanticism and Piero Ciampi, an Italian musician and songwriter popular during the 1960s and 1970s.

Contributors have been asked to theorize or historicize their subjects in a way that places rock music in a coherent dialog with Romantic-era art and literature, contributing to a consideration of the boundaries or definitions of "Romanticism" as a literary and artistic mode while also considering the implications of chronological, national, social, sexual, ethnic, and economic difference. Many contributors employ Löwy's and Sayre's *Romanticism Against the Tide of Modernity* as a means of theorizing Romanticism in a trans-historical and cross-cultural manner, but overall these essays take a variety of approaches to their subjects while still privileging thematic definitions of Romanticism over mere periodization, exploring Romanticism as a constellation of themes that tend to aggregate around similar historical and cultural conditions. The one concept that I think all essays have in common is a sense of repetition: they see the past repeated in the present, similar conditions giving rise to similar responses, which perhaps validates historical approaches to Romanticism that require only a similarity of conditions to give rise to a similarity of responses. Chapters informally fall into three subdivisions organized around the major Romantic figures engaged here. An initial chapter engaging Shelley and the Rolling Stones is followed by four chapters about Blake and different figures in rock. The next chapter engages Wordsworth and Coleridge and is then followed by four chapters about Wordsworth. The last chapter covers Italian Romanticism and 1960s' Italian music, serving as a fitting end to this collection by providing a reflective point of both similarity to and distance from English Romanticism.

Luke Walker's "Tangled Up in Blake: The Triangular Relationship among Dylan, Blake, and the Beats," surveys the history of Blake's influence on Dylan and Dylan's borrowing, acknowledged or not, of Blake over the course of Dylan's career. Explaining Dylan's reticence to acknowledge Blake in the light of accusations of plagiarism or the attempt to reduce Dylan to his sources, Walker engages in careful groundwork designed to isolate and explain the various sources by which Dylan may have come to be influenced by Blake in the 1960s, an influence that resurfaced in the 1990s and then again in very late albums such as *Tempest*.

"Romanticism in the Park: Mick Jagger Reading Shelley" by Jaaneke van der Leest studies the implications of Mick Jagger reading portions of *Adonais* at the Hyde Park concert held just days after the death of Rolling Stones's founder Brian Jones. Van der Leest explains Jagger's view of his relationship with Jones as a case parallel to Shelley mourning his newly found potential friend, potential rival, and potential peer John Keats in the poem *Adonais*. Contextualizing this event within England's 1960s' rock culture and the internal politics of the Rolling Stones that led up to Brian Jones's ouster, this chapter explores the tensions and contradictions inherent in the existence of professional rivalry and professional jealousy among people engaged in art forms revolutionary in nature and intent.

Douglas Root's "William Blake: The Romantic Alternative" argues that grunge rock figures such as Kurt Cobain are poets parallel with William Blake though living in different ages. While their aesthetics differed greatly, both Blake and grunge musicians were engaged in a project of conscious and deliberate dissociation from the work of their predecessors. In their thinking, each narrowed the options for relationships with their poetic predecessors to being either stupidly imitative or deliberately progressive. Root further argues that both were steeped in a working-class ethic, grunge inventing the Northeastern lumberjack version of post-urban authenticity in the late 1980s and early 1990s, and that both were engaged in a reaction to and escape from urban decay that was exacerbated by disillusionment with the possibility or authenticity of escape. Both were anti-capitalist, particularly pushing against industrialism and consumerist culture, and both were iconoclasts, grunge breaking with 1970s' punk and classic rock in a way comparable to Blake breaking with his eighteenth-century predecessors.

Nicole Lobdell in "Digging at the Roots: Martha Redbone's *The Garden of Love: Songs of William Blake*" conducts a song by song analysis of Martha Redbone's Roots Project's *The Garden of Love: Songs of William Blake*. Redbone and her band set a selection of William Blake's poems to American folk music, the blues, Native American chants, and Southern gospel to explore not only Redbone's own "personal heritage and musical roots but also a collective musical history between Blake's England and Redbone's America." In doing so, Redbone either creates, invokes, or discovers what Lobdell calls "Appalachian Romanticism" and engages "Blake's poetry through memory, eulogizing what has been lost to time and progress, and celebrating, through sound and lyric, what remains." Lobdell demonstrates how Appalachia shares musical, cultural, and socioeconomic roots with Blake's England, and how Redbone's reaching out to Blake overcomes the temporal and geographic displacement between the two figures to discover how their art "originates from a common inspirational source."

"'Tangle of Matter and Ghost': U2, Leonard Cohen, and Blakean Romanticism" by Lisa Crafton triangulates Blake's, Cohen's, and U2's songwriting to illustrate how each artist represents, responds to, and addresses different life stages as they engage themes such as "social and cultural protest, the conflation of erotic/spiritual love, and the representation of the rupture of that symbiosis, especially in the poetic treatment of Judas, Yahweh, and Jesus." Life stage writing, therefore, is demonstrated in Crafton's chapter to be a vehicle for sociopolitical critique. Critique is simultaneously and alternatively inwardly and outwardly directed: politics are the outward manifestation of inwardly present "mind-forg'd manacles" and politics are the external force forging those manacles from the start. Blake's answer to this quandary, a Romantic response repeated by Leornard Cohen and then by U2 through both Blake and Cohen, is to address the mind first through imaginative vision.

This book's engagement with Wordsworth begins with the essay "The Inner Revolution(s) of Wordsworth and the Beatles" by David Boocker. Boocker argues that the Beatles's *Sgt. Pepper's Lonely Hearts Club Band* and William Wordsworth's *Lyrical Ballads* are significant parallel cases in which both come forward during times of intense social change to participate in an agenda for change, but both do so by advocating for an inner or psychological transformation or reform. This desire for inner transformation, according to Boocker, is motivated by expressions of social and personal despair and the observation of suffering in ways consistent with Sayre and Löwy's description of "resigned Romanticism."

"'When the Light that's Lost within Us Reaches the Sky': Jackson Browne's Romantic Vision" by Gary Tandy evaluates Jackson Browne's music against the taxonomy provided by Löwy and Sayre to argue that Browne is indeed a twentieth-century American Romantic poet. Exploring the themes of rejection of contemporary society, nostalgia for paradise lost, and a vision of paradise regained, Tandy sees in Browne's musical career alternations between revolutionary and utopian Romantic anti-capitalisms. Browne rejects current socio-economic structures in his longing for a lost world, but at the same time actively advocates for change through a clearly defined agenda that he seeks to see materially and politically realized in his lifetime. Tandy's compelling comparisons of Browne's work to Wordsworth's not only support his argument that Browne is a Romantic poet, but point out significant influence and identify Browne as an American reinvention of Wordsworth.

David S. Hogsette's "'Swimming Against the Stream': Rush's Romantic Critique of their Modern Age" engages Rush's early-career individualism through lenses provided by Marilyn Butler and Löwy and Sayre to analyze the features of Rush's critique of modernity. Hogsette argues that "Rush's Romantic vision encourages audiences to reflect personally upon the music's critical messages and to act locally within one's community while also recognizing the true challenges of the individual's ability to change the self and society within commercialized modernity." Defending Rush against charges of being conservative, reactionary, or even fascist, Hogsette argues that Rush's individualism follows the Romantic paradigm of being a critique of modernity, one characterized by nostalgia as a form of critique. Hogsette ultimately argues that over the course of Rush's four decades-long career the band's outlook and lyrics have reflected a transformation from one Romanticism in Löwy's and Sayre's taxonomy to another, moving from revolutionary or utopian Romanticism to restititutionist to resigned at different stages in their aesthetic and musical development.

"Wordsworth's 'Michael,' the Georgic, and Blackberry Smoke" by Ronald D. Morrison begins by more precisely defining Wordsworth's "Michael" as exemplary of georgic rather than pastoral conventions in the light of more recent ecocritical perspectives. Having done so, he then illustrates how the music of Blackberry Smoke, a contemporary country or southern rock band, appropriates georgic conventions in a way parallel to Wordsworth's "Michael." Both Wordsworth and Blackberry Smoke address "lingering problems that have plagued farming communities for two centuries or more: burdensome mortgages, the out-migration of rural young people, the loss of family farms, and the steady erosion of traditional rural customs and values." Additionally, both Wordsworth's "Michael" and the music of Blackberry Smoke similarly engage Evangelical tropes and rhetorical strategies to comment on rural and agricultural life and religion. Ultimately, both the band and the poet are allowed to comment on one another's engagement with rural communities, with rural religion, and with the specificities of place through their similar appropriation of georgic conventions.

Rachel Feder in "Wordsworth on the Radio" takes a unique approach to the subject of this volume by putting herself in a third position commenting on contemporary poets' responses to current music within a framework of temporality and deferment established by Wordsworth's *Prelude*. Beginning with Locke's concept of infinity as an endless extension of numbers, his application of that thought to the human mind, and his presentation of the mind's existence as an endless accretion of experience, she observes in Wordsworth's *Prelude* a growth of the poet's mind one image and one blank verse line at a time. The refusal of closure provided by Wordsworth's use of blank verse, however, allows the moments or "spots of time" recorded in Wordworth's poetry to continue into the future and so, by extension, into the present. From that starting point, she considers the implications of Brandon Brown's *Top 40* (2014) invoking Wordsworth in its poetry while it responds to Lana Del Rey, Amanda Bynes, Miley Cyrus, Taylor Swift, Justin Timberlake, and Daft Punk. Lauren Ireland's collection of epistolary prose poems, *Dear Lil Wayne* (2014), similarly "pleads for time and creates time, using poetry to activate everyday time travel." Sarah Blake's poems in *Mr. West* (2015) create a similar effect in their engagement with the music of Kanye West. Feder argues that Sarah Blake's poems stretch time in a Wordsworthian way by considering how celebrity is an alternate form of memory, a "different way to consume memory" as the memories of these musicians come to us externally through their music rather than internally through our own experience. Feder ultimately argues that displacing time and memory in this way allows Sarah Blake to engage Holocaust memory with Kanye's music through the medium of her own poetry, and that her act of doing so is a "neo-Romantic formation" first initiated by Wordsworth's _Prelude_.

Lorenzo Sorbo's "The '_Scapigliatura_' and _Poétes Maudits_ in the Songs of Piero Ciampi (1934–1980)" engages Italian Romanticism, its critics, and its reinvention in the 1960s and 1970s in the music of Piero Ciampi. After defining traditional Italian Romanticism as "moralizing and patriotic" and later Italian Romanticism as "languid and sentimental," Sorbo describes the rise of a new kind of Romanticism in the later nineteenth century called the _Scapigliatura_. This group took its name from French Bohemians of the earlier nineteenth century. Its members were critical of previous Italian Romanticisms and attempted to modernize Italian letters through the influence of European and American literature by figures such as Poe and Baudelaire. Sorbo then proceeds to identify the Italian singer/songwriter Piero Ciampi as clearly working in the tradition of the _Scapigliatura_, both in his life and in his lyrics, so that Ciampi represents a restatement or reinvention of late nineteenth-century Italian Romanticism, one that resonates with British and European Romanticisms of previous periods.

Portions of this introduction appear in James Rovira, Rock and Romanticism: Post-Punk, Goth, and Metal as Dark Romanticisms, _2017, Palgrave Macmillan, reproduced with permission of Palgrave Macmillan._

NOTES

1. Donald Fitch, _Blake Set to Music: A Bibliography of Musical Settings of the Poems and Prose of William Blake_ (Berkeley, CA: University of California Press, 1989). Full text available online at http://www.ucpress.edu/op.php?isbn=9780520097346. Supplement published 2001 at _BIQ_ 35, no. 2 (Fall 2001), http://bq.blakearchive.org/35.2.fitch. See also G. E. Bentley, Jr.'s review of volume 5 of _Blake Set to Music_ in _BiQ_ 30, no. 1 (Summer 1996), http://bq.blakearchive.org/30.1.bentley and Ashanka Kumari's thesis, "Adding to _Blake Set to Music:_ A Bibliography," at http://digitalcommons.unl.edu/cgi/viewcontent.cgi?article=1092&context=englishdiss. All URLs last accessed Jan. 4, 2017.

2. See G. E. Bentley, Jr., _Blake Records_, 2nd ed. (New Haven: Yale University Press, 2004): ". . . and though according to his confession, he was entirely unacquainted with the science of music, his ear was so good, that his tunes were sometimes most singularly beautiful, and were noted down by musical professors" (120–121).

3. David Pichaske's _Beowulf to Beatles: Approaches to Poetry_ (1972) sets rock lyrics alongside more traditionally anthologized poems to illustrate a variety of poetic terms and genres. His introduction somewhat contradictorily asserts that the treatment of rock lyrics as poetry is met with "laughter and unqualified ridicule" in the "halls of academia" while also asserting that there "now exists a substantial and growing body of what we might call rock criticism," and that it is "fashionable to quote rock, to 'study' rock, to criticize rock as one would criticize new volumes of poetry or new symphonic performances" (xxv). The situation appears to be that Dylan was regularly discussed in periodicals such as the _Saturday Evening Post, Atlantic,_ and _New Republic_ at the time of Pichaske's writing (New York: The Free Press, 1972). The 1973 edition of the _Norton Introduction to Literature_ anthologized the lyrics of "Mr. Tambourine Man," attributing them to Bob Dylan, and peer reviewed articles about Bob

Dylan begin appearing in the late 1960s. One of the earliest, Herbert London's "American Romantics: Old and New" asserts that "the modern hippie movement is merely the most recent manifestation of an old romantic tradition in the United States," *Colorado Quarterly* 18, no. 1 (1969), 5–20.

4. Arthur O. Lovejoy, "On the Discrimination of Romanticisms," *PMLA* 39, no. 2 (June 1924), 229.

5. Ibid., 232.

6. Stuart Curran, ed. *The Cambridge Companion to British Romanticism*, 2nd ed. (Cambridge: Cambridge University Press, 2010), xiii.

7. Michael Löwy and Robert Sayre. *Romanticism Against the Tide of Modernity* (Durham: Duke University Press, 2001), 17.

8. Robert Sayre and Michael Löwy, "Figures of Romantic Anti-Capitalism," *New German Critique* 32 (Spring/Summer 1984), 46. Note that references to the article will be "Sayre and Löwy" while references to the book will be "Löwy and Sayre."

9. Ibid., 51.

10. Most essays make some reference to Löwy and Sayre, a few relying on them extensively, which will bring into focus a diversity of readings of this text as well.

11. Löwy and Sayre, 90.

12. Ibid., 89.

13. Ibid., 56.

14. Ibid., 25.

15. David Pichaske, *A Generation in Motion: Popular Music and Culture in the Sixties* (New York: Schirmer Books, 1979), 3.

16. Ibid., 2.

17. Ibid., 7.

18. Ibid., 54.

19. Ibid.

20. Ibid., 60.

21. Herbert London, "American Romantics: Old and New," *Colorado Quarterly* 18, no. 1 (1969), 5–20.

22. Keir Keightley, "Reconsidering Rock," in *The Cambridge Companion to Pop and Rock*, eds. Simon Frith, Will Straw, and John Street (London: Cambridge University Press, 2011), 135.

23. Ibid., 136.

BIBLIOGRAPHY

Bentley, Jr., G. E. *Blake Records*, 2nd ed. New Haven: Yale University Press, 2004.

———. Rev. of *Blake Set to Music* in *Blake: An Illustrated Quarterly* 30, no. 1 (Summer 1996): http://bq.blakearchive.org/30.1.bentley.

Curran, Stuart, ed. *The Cambridge Companion to British Romanticism*, 2nd ed. Cambridge: Cambridge University Press, 2010.

Fitch, Donald. *Blake Set to Music: A Bibliography of Musical Settings of the Poems and Prose of William Blake.* Berkeley, CA: University of California Press, 1989.

———. "*Blake Set to Music*: Supplement 2001." *Blake: An Illustrated Quarterly* 35, no. 2 (Fall 2001): http://bq.blakearchive.org/35.2.fitch.

Keightley, Keir. "Reconsidering Rock." In *The Cambridge Companion to Pop and Rock*, edited by Simon Frith, Will Straw, and John Street, 109–142. London: Cambridge University Press, 2011.

Kumari, Ashanka. "Adding to Blake Set to Music: A Bibliography." Ph.D. diss., University of Nebraska, Lincoln, 2014. http://digitalcommons.unl.edu/cgi/viewcontent.cgi?article=1092& context=englishdiss.

London, Herbert. "American Romantics: Old and New." *Colorado Quarterly* 18, no. 1 (1969): 5–20.

Lovejoy, Arthur O. "On the Discrimination of Romanticisms." *PMLA* 39, no. 2 (June 1924): 229–253.

Löwy, Michael, and Robert Sayre. *Romanticism Against the Tide of Modernity*. Durham: Duke University Press, 2001.

Peckham, Morse. *The Triumph of Romanticism*. Columbia, SC: University of South Carolina Press, 1970.

Pichaske, David. *A Generation in Motion: Popular Music and Culture in the Sixties*. New York: Schirmer Books, 1979.

Rosso, G. A. and Daniel P. Watkins, eds. *Spirits of Fire: English Romantic Writers and Contemporary Historical Methods*. Madison, NJ: Fairleigh Dickinson University Press, 1990.

Sayre, Robert, and Michael Löwy. "Figures of Romantic Anti-Capitalism." *New German Critique* 32 (Spring/Summer 1984): 42–92.

Welleck, René. "The Concept of 'Romanticism' in Literary History I. The Term 'Romantic' and Its Derivatives." *Comparative Literature* 1, no. 1 (Winter, 1949): 1–23.

———. "The Concept of 'Romanticism' in Literary History II. The Unity of European Romanticism. *Comparative Literature* 1, no. 2 (Spring, 1949): 147–172."

Welleck, René and Austin Warren. *Theory of Literature*. New York: Harcourt, Brace, and Co., 1949.

Chapter One

Tangled Up in Blake

The Triangular Relationship among Dylan, Blake, and the Beats

Luke Walker

During a televised press conference in 1965, Bob Dylan was asked, "Do you think of yourself primarily as a singer or a poet?" In answer, Dylan famously quipped that he thought of himself "more as a song and dance man, y'know."[1] While the heavily ironic evasiveness of the response is typical of Dylan's 1960s' interview style, I will argue in this essay that his unwillingness to engage with this particular question can also be understood as the product of a complex set of personal and cultural anxieties relating to influence and canonicity, Romanticism and counterculture, Beat poetry and rock music, and that these interlinked anxieties provide the key contexts for Dylan's relationship with the poetry of William Blake.

I also want to suggest that the same anxieties are evident in another, more absurd question posed to Dylan later in the same press conference by the Beat poet and 1960s' countercultural icon Allen Ginsberg: "Do you think there will ever be a time when you'll be hung as a thief?" To this more unexpected question from his friend and mentor, Dylan simply responded, "You weren't supposed to say that."[2] This evasive approach to questions of influence, appropriation, canonicity, and self-definition has been particularly evident on occasions when Dylan has been asked more specifically about the influence of William Blake, a figure who by the mid-1960s had attained a talismanic status within the alternative textual canons of the Beat movement and 1960s' counterculture, largely due to tireless evangelizing on his behalf by Allen Ginsberg.[3]

1

Despite Dylan's continued efforts at avoidance and obfuscation, the "singer or poet" question was not left behind in the 1960s, but has resurfaced in recent years with increased frequency and to increased public attention. In 2003 Christopher Ricks did much to reignite the issue with the publication of *Dylan's Visions of Sin*, which provides close readings of Dylan's lyrics and draws parallels with the work of various poets from the high canon of English literature, including Blake and other Romantics.[4] The following year, the debate was given fresh fuel when Dylan himself published his (possibly partly fictional) memoir *Chronicles: Volume One*, along with an updated edition (the first in several decades) of his collected *Lyrics*.[5] Notably, even when Dylan was actually awarded the Nobel Prize in Literature in 2016, this did little to settle the matter of his literary status, not least because of his own ambivalent response to the award.

In seeking to investigate the links between Dylan and Blake, this chapter therefore becomes part of a long debate, one which Dylan himself has alternately fueled and warned against. I do not make any claim to bring this debate to an end, but perhaps, by bringing increased attention to the historical circumstances in which works by Dylan and by Blake have been produced and received, the terms of the debate can at least be advanced.

BLAKE'S MUSIC

Although Blake, as far as we know, was never asked to choose between the roles of poet and singer as Dylan was, it would have been a valid question. Arguably he could indeed be categorized not only as a poet, engraver, printmaker, and painter, but also as a songwriter and singer; this aspect of Blake's work should be apparent from the title of his best-known work, *Songs of Innocence and of Experience*, but is nonetheless often overlooked. The lyrical form of that collection is emphasized through the content of the first poem or song, the "Introduction" to *Innocence* ("Piping down the valleys wild. . . "), which features a narrator who, at the request of an angelic child, firstly pipes, then sings, and finally writes down his songs (which the reader must assume are the songs of Blake's collection itself), thus providing a model of poetic composition which begins with non-vocal music, continues with oral poetry or song, and ends with written literature.[6] There is also good evidence that Blake composed or improvised tunes to accompany at least some of his works; several contemporary accounts describe Blake singing his songs or poems, and he is even said to have died "Singing of the things he saw in Heaven."[7]

These original musical contexts of Blake's own work, combined with the general importance of Blake to 1960s' counterculture, make it unsurprising that Blake should have a deep influence on the popular music associated with the period. Blakean references are found in the work of a diverse range of 1960s' musicians and groups, including The Doors, Led Zeppelin, Van Morrison, The Fugs, and Patti Smith, and in 1970 Allen Ginsberg himself released an album of his settings of Blake, entitled *Songs of Innocence and Experience by William Blake, tuned by Allen Ginsberg*.[8] Meanwhile, in the case of Dylan, song titles such as "Gates of Eden" (1965), "Golden Loom" (1975),[9] and "Every Grain of Sand" (1981) have ensured that Blake's influence on Dylan has long been taken for granted by fans, popular music writers, and literary scholars. Arguably, however, the oft-stated connection between these two poet-songwriters has too rarely been subjected to rigorous critical analysis.[10] Thus the opening pages of the *Cambridge Companion to Bob Dylan* assert that "Bob Dylan is the spiritual twin of the English Romantic poet William Blake," but the remainder of the volume leaves this bold claim entirely unsupported.[11]

"THE BELLS OF WILLIAM BLAKE"

Dylan's earliest Blake reference occurs in a work which appears on his third album, *The Times They Are A-Changin'* (1964).[12] Significantly however, this work is not a song, but a long poem entitled "11 Outlined Epitaphs," whose stanzas are spread across the reverse of the album cover and continue on an insert within the album.[13] Perhaps because it is not a song, it has been very little written about, either in relation to its Blake connections or otherwise. However, it is noteworthy not only for the fact that it contains Dylan's earliest reference to Blake, but also because—somewhat remarkably given the assumed closeness of the connection between Blake and Dylan—this work remains the only mention of Blake's name in all of Dylan's published written output: his lyrics, album liner notes, poems, the "novel" *Tarantula*, and the memoir *Chronicles*; as we will see shortly, Dylan has verbally referred to Blake in a number of interviews.

Dylan's relationship with his influences represents the major theme of "11 Outlined Epitaphs," but even in this poem Dylan's approach to the issue seems conflicted; he identifies himself as "a thief of thoughts" who has "built an' rebuilt / upon what is waitin'," but insists that this does not make him "a stealer of souls." Suze Rotolo, Dylan's highly literate girlfriend of the early 1960s (who was responsible for introducing him to the work of Brecht, Byron, and possibly Blake)[14] has described how "[a]ccusations of plagiarism would always be a ball and chain on Dylan's career as a songwriter, but especially so in the early years."[15] However, if the "ball and chain" of such accusations provides the context for Dylan's ambiguous and defensive self-characterization in the early part of "11 Outlined Epitaphs," it is noteworthy that later in the poem Dylan's approach seems to change, as he proudly and openly lists his musical and literary influences. The eclectic list he produces ranges from Brecht and Yevtushenko to Pete Seeger, Miles Davis, and numerous others, each of them represented by a synechdochic characterization of their work, significantly including—separated by just a few lines—the "love songs of Allen Ginsberg" and "the bells of William Blake."

Setting aside for now the question of why Blake might be associated with "bells," I want to draw attention to the pairing of Blake and Ginsberg in this early work of Dylan's. While Dylan's admiration for the writing of Ginsberg and other Beats predated the beginning of his musical career,[16] it is significant that his composition of "11 Outlined Epitaphs" (and his first written mention of Blake) coincided with the first meeting between himself and Ginsberg in December 1963.[17]

"GATES OF EDEN ARE NAMED IN ALBION AGAIN"

Just as the work of the Beats had a powerful impact on Dylan's life and writing, so too was the first encounter with Dylan and his music an important event for Ginsberg. Recalling later how he had first heard recordings of Dylan's music just weeks before he met Dylan himself, Ginsberg claimed that he had wept tears of joy when he recognized that the lyrics of "A Hard Rain's A-Gonna Fall" represented the passing on of the Beat torch to a younger generation.[18] However, there is also evidence that Ginsberg's highly emotional reaction to Dylan's song may have included a certain anxiety at what he recognized as an ending of the "Beat era," or its transformation into something new; when he met Dylan in person shortly afterwards, he turned down Dylan's invitation to accompany him to his next concert, fearful that he "might become his slave or something, his mascot."[19]

As a committed Blakean, Ginsberg was also quick to comment on the connections between Dylan's work and Blake's. While in England with Dylan in 1965, Ginsberg heard Dylan's new song "Gates of Eden," and instantly noted its Blakean title and lyrics, which he drew attention to in his own poem "Who Be Kind To" (1965).[20] In Ginsberg's poem, the music of Dylan and the Beatles is seen as heralding the arrival of the 1960s in Britain, which Ginsberg represents as a re-awakening of Blake's mythical figures of Jerusalem and Albion: "Liverpool Minstrels . . . / raise up their joyful voices and guitars in electric Afric hurrah for Jerusalem– / . . . and Gates of Eden are named in Albion again."[21]

On several occasions in the early 1970s (though not during the earlier recording sessions for his Blake album), Ginsberg was able to persuade Dylan to accompany him on guitar while Ginsberg sang his arrangements of Blake's songs, and footage of Ginsberg singing Blake's "Nurse's Song" is included in Dylan's epic experimental film *Renaldo and Clara* (1978), where he plays a character billed simply as "The Father."[22] This is suggestive of his real-life role as something of a father figure not only to Dylan but also to 1960s' counterculture as a whole.[23] It therefore seems appropriate that he should be featured in Dylan's film singing Blake, whose work he was so instrumental in weaving into the fabric of the 1960s.

Ginsberg played a similar role in an earlier Dylan film, *Don't Look Back* (1967), D. A. Pennebaker's documentary of Dylan's 1965 tour of England (during which Ginsberg had first heard "Gates of Eden"). Throughout the film's opening sequence, which is the famous video of "Subterranean Homesick Blues," Ginsberg can be seen hovering in the background while Dylan stands in the alley behind London's Savoy Hotel holding up placards bearing the keywords of the song. Ginsberg's visual appearance in the video, sporting his trademark 1960s' full beard and leaning on a staff, references and reinforces his role as 1960s' father figure.[24] More specifically however, as Sean Wilentz has noted, Ginsberg's appearance in the "Subterranean Homesick Blues" video makes him look "like a Blakean Jewish prophet."[25]

Ginsberg was not the only Beat poet to latch on to the Blakean references in "Gates of Eden." Michael McClure, who like Ginsberg had a lifelong fascination with Blake, and who later became close not only to Dylan but also to the more overtly Blake-influenced band The Doors, tells a story which perfectly illustrates the complex dynamic between Dylan and the Beats, with its mutual anxieties of influence and its strong Blakean connection. McClure remembers his initial resistance to listening to Dylan's songs: "I absolutely did not want to hear Dylan. I imagined, without admitting it to myself, that Dylan was a threat to poetry—or to my poetry. I sensed that a new mode of poetry, or rebirth of an old one, might replace my mode."[26] When in 1965 he was finally persuaded to listen to Dylan's music, his emotional response was remarkably similar to Ginsberg's: "The next thing I knew I was crying. It was 'Gates of Eden.'"[27] Like Ginsberg, listening to this song immediately made him think of Blake, and even induced in McClure an experience which paralleled Ginsberg's own 1948 "Blake vision" (during which Ginsberg had famously heard Blake's disembodied voice speak to him). McClure recalls: "I had the idea that I was hallucinating, that it was William Blake's voice coming out of the walls. . . Then I went back to those people who had tried to get me to listen [to Dylan] and I told them that I thought the revolution had begun." However, when McClure met Dylan in person shortly afterwards and told him about the Blakean experience that "Gates of Eden" had induced in him, Dylan responded by declaring that he himself "had not read Blake and did not know the poetry," something that McClure understandably found "hard to believe."[28] Dylan also made similar statements about Blake to Ginsberg around this time. Indeed, according to Ginsberg, part of the initial impetus for his own project of setting Blake's *Songs of Innocence and of Experience* to music was that "Dylan said that he didn't like Blake, so I thought this would be an interesting way of laying Blake on him."[29]

"RELATIONSHIPS OF OWNERSHIP / THEY WHISPER IN THE WINGS"

One way to explain the clear contradictions between, on the one hand, the negative statements Dylan made about Blake to Ginsberg and McClure in the mid-1960s and, on the other hand, the interest in Blake which is apparent in "11 Outlined Epitaphs" and "Gates of Eden," would be simply to refer to the contrary and quixotic public persona that Dylan began to adopt around this time in response to his growing fame. However, it is significant that Dylan's evasive and contradictory comments about Blake were made not to some "square" interviewer, but privately to Beat poets who had become his friends and to whom he also owed a longstanding debt of influence, as both he and they acknowledged. We can therefore see such comments as born out of the specific anxieties that formed part of the complex dynamic of literary exchange between Dylan and the Beats, in which, as Dylan sings in "Gates of Eden," "Relationships of ownership / They whisper in the wings."[30] Blake in the 1960s in some ways "belonged" to Ginsberg and other Beats like McClure, and Dylan seemed reluctant to admit that he had "borrowed" him. Likewise, Ginsberg was alert to the danger that he himself might become a "slave or something" to the younger poet and singer whose Blakean lyrics and energy he so admired, while McClure initially feared that Dylan's "new mode of poetry . . . might replace my mode," before finally hearing Dylan as "William Blake's voice coming out of the walls."

This three-way dynamic of influence among Dylan, Blake, and the Beats, and the tensions within it, can be further illustrated through a very literal textual borrowing, that of a whole manuscript. In 1972 Ginsberg finally published his early lyric poems under the Blakean title *The Gates of Wrath*. These poems mainly date from around the time of Ginsberg's 1948 Blake vision, with titles such as "On Reading William Blake's 'The Sick Rose'" and "Vision 1948"; they are also somewhat imitative of the style of Blake's own lyric poetry. At the end of the 1972 collection, Ginsberg included a note ("Hindsight") explaining that he had originally sent the manuscript to a publisher in England in the early 1950s who had apparently lost it: "I had no complete copy till 1968 when old typescript was returned thru poet Bob Dylan—it passed into his hands years earlier."[31] The story is intriguing and mysterious. Ginsberg's brief note suggests that the poems had been in Dylan's possession for some time (since "years earlier") and yet by 1968 Dylan and Ginsberg had already been good friends for around five years, during which time Dylan had never returned them or seemingly even mentioned them to his mentor.

There are several points to be made about this story. First, it seems possible, as Nelson Hilton has suggested, that at least some of Blake's earlier influence on Dylan may have come second-hand, via these unpublished Ginsberg poems, although Dylan would also have had plenty of other opportunities to be influenced by Blake more directly.[32] Second, however, Dylan's mysterious acquisition and long-term loan of Ginsberg's manuscript has uncomfortable similarities with his more infamous habit of stealing interesting-looking records from friends' record collections.[33] Furthermore, the borrowing of these poems provides us with an additional context within which to understand the strange question that Ginsberg posed to Dylan during the 1965 press conference: "Do you think there will ever be a time when you'll be hung as a thief?" I am not suggesting that Ginsberg's question related specifically to the *Gates of Wrath* manuscript (although Ginsberg's note seems to suggest that the manuscript may well have already been in Dylan's possession by that time), or that Ginsberg did not primarily mean his question as some kind of in-joke or wind-up, but rather that there are underlying tensions concerning borrowing, stealing, and literary influence which are revealed in this incident.[34] In this context, it is noteworthy, given Dylan's unease at the persistent question of whether he should be defined as "a singer or a poet," that Ginsberg pointedly names him in this "Hindsight" as "poet Bob Dylan." Ginsberg's insistence that his friend be defined as a poet—with the level of literary seriousness this implies—is of course complimentary, but it can also be seen as part of an ongoing attempt by Ginsberg to integrate Dylan (and the 1960s' rock music for which he is a signifier) into the earlier canons of Beat poetry and Blakean Romanticism.[35]

Thus, I want to argue that among the interlinked canons of Romanticism, Beat writing, and rock music, the process and direction of appropriation and definition is not as straightforward as it may at first appear. Carrie Noland has written of the two-way "relations of influence" between Rimbaud and punk music, while Edward Larrissy, in his introduction to the collection *Romanticism and Postmodernism*, describes the "multiple temporality" of Blake, in which his meaning (and that of Romanticism more generally) is defined by the ongoing cycles of posthumous reception, so that "[f]rom the point of view of the study of reception Blake is a late nineteenth-century and twentieth-century poet . . . not a poet of the Romantic period."[36] As we have seen, Ginsberg was alert to the danger that he might become a "slave" to Dylan, not just because of Dylan's personal magnetism, but also in the sense of being appropriated as a "mascot" by him and by the 1960s' music culture he represented. Dylan, however, who has himself spent much of his career attempting to avoid becoming a "slave" to his fans' definition of him, was surely also alert to Ginsberg's project of appropriating *him* for the Beats and for Blake. As Sean Wilentz writes, "In one sense, Ginsberg was anointing Dylan; in another, he was making sure nobody forgot how Dylan was really an extension of himself, Kerouac, and the other Beats. Once a salesman, always a salesman."[37] Wilentz is here referencing the fact that Ginsberg spent the first half of the 1950s working for advertising and market research companies, learning skills he would later put to use not only promoting his own writing and that of his friends, but also selling less tangible goods such as the concept of "Beat" itself, and later many of the concepts and tropes out of which 1960s' counterculture was formed, including the work of his "guru" William Blake.

It is also significant that according to Ginsberg's note in *The Gates of Wrath*, the return of his own early lyric poems, combined with his deepening friendship with Dylan, actually inspired Ginsberg's interest in recording and writing songs. This preoccupation led not only to the release of Ginsberg's 1970 album of Blake songs, but also to shifts in his poetic practice in the decades that followed; Ginsberg now hoped "to write a poem or song with words that are so inevitable that people will be able to use it all the time—like Dylan or Blake."[38] Once again, we can identify a complex, cyclical dynamic of influence existing between Dylan and the Beats, moreover one that clearly involves Blake. In the liner notes to his Blake album, Ginsberg again linked Blake and Dylan, expressing the hope that "musical articulation of Blake's poetry will . . . provide an eternal poesy standard by which to measure sublimity and sincerity in contemporary masters such as Bob Dylan."[39] Just as we can detect complex anxieties surrounding appropriation and borrowing within Ginsberg's apparently complimentary reference to "poet Bob Dylan" in the "Hindsight" note, so too can we see this reference to Dylan, printed on Ginsberg's album cover, as double-edged. On the one hand, Dylan is flatteringly described by his Beat mentor as a "contemporary master." But at the same time, Ginsberg is insisting that Dylan's poetry and song needs to be "measure[d]" or judged against the "eternal poesy standard" of his own spiritual mentor, William Blake.

So, given all of this, what should we make of Dylan's claims not to know or like Blake? Was it really necessary for Ginsberg to go about "laying Blake" on Dylan through his own Blake recordings in the late 1960s? Perhaps most importantly, can we find any evidence of Dylan reading Blake independently, rather than simply picking up Blakean fragments from Ginsberg or from the 1960s' countercultural milieu? The answer to the last question is yes: there is evidence that Dylan was in physical possession of Blake's poems, although it is perhaps significant that all such evidence dates from after 1965, the year he released the Blakean "Gates of Eden" while simultaneously insisting that he "had not read Blake and did not know the poetry." In 1966, Ginsberg made a gift to Dylan of a large box of poetry books, including a collection of Blake's works, for Dylan to read while he recovered from his motorcycle accident.[40] Coincidentally or not, Dylan's former neighbor, the painter Bruce Dorfman, has related how when he first got to know Dylan not long after the motorcycle accident, Dylan was avidly reading Blake, and even gave Dorfman "a handsome edition" of Blake's *Songs of Innocence and of Experience* as a Christmas present (presumably this was the 1954 Trianon Press full-color reproduction of *Songs*).[41] Perhaps the most significant evidence, however, is Dylan's response in a 1968 interview when asked if he had read Blake: "I have tried. Same with Dante and Rilke. I understand what's there, it's just that the connection sometimes does not connect . . . Blake did come up with some bold lines though . . ."[42]

If Dylan here comes across as something of a magpie, borrowing Blake's glittering "bold lines," this is of course typical of much 1960s' appropriation of Blake, for example the use of his aphorisms as graffiti on campus walls. However, it is important to remember that this is also one of the ways in which Blake has been read ever since his lifetime, when his friend Fuseli admitted that Blake was "damned good to steal from."[43] Furthermore, as Mike Goode argues in his seminal 2006 article "Blakespotting," such a reading practice is not necessarily un-Blakean, since "Blake's proverblike poetry actively encourages readers to appropriate and resituate its lines."[44] In fact, Goode provocatively and convincingly suggests, the ultimate "ambition" of Blake's fragmentary and quotable lines is to spread themselves organically through space and time like the "rhizomatic" forms celebrated by Deleuze and Guattari, until they are "directed towards everybody by everyone."[45] (Given Blake's importance to the Beats, an additional frame of reference here, not mentioned by Goode, would be William Burroughs's concept of the "word virus," as explored in his 1962 novel *The Ticket That Exploded* and elsewhere.) Thus one of the revolutionary properties of Blake's tactically deployed aphorisms is their ability to upset "relationships of ownership," so that it becomes unclear in which direction influence, appropriation, and "ownership" flows. If we further combine this with Edward Larrissy's paradoxical observation that Blake's posthumous reception means he is "not a poet of the Romantic period" (and in fact neither does the concept of "Romanticism" belong to the "Romantic period"), we can see that the personal anxieties of influence which haunt the relationships among Dylan, Blake, and the Beats are subsets of broader cultural anxieties and paradoxes concerning influence, definition, and canonicity. The meanings of Blake and of Romanticism are influenced and constituted by their later reception, just as they influence the work of Ginsberg, Dylan, and others.

"REPEAT QUOTATIONS / DRAW CONCLUSIONS"

I want to conclude by jumping forward from the 1960s to the so-called "late" period of Dylan's career, in which there is some evidence that Dylan's interest in Blake has returned and perhaps even strengthened. As I will show, the Blake of Dylan's late period may have escaped the specific set of anxieties of influence that I identified as existing between Dylan and the Beats, but Dylan's Blake is still caught up in the context of his 1960s' reception, and indeed within the more general context of the accusations of plagiarism which persistently haunted him.

In 1992, just as Dylan started to re-emerge from his years in the critical wilderness, he revealed in an interview that he was getting "back into reading the William Blake poems again. It seems like when you're young and you read 'em they don't have the effect on you that they do when you get older."[46] Then in 2012 (nearly fifty years after Dylan's first Blake reference in "11 Outlined Epitaphs") Dylan concluded his album *Tempest* with a song in which Blake is given a central role. Significantly, the song "Roll on John" is a meditation on mortality and "get[ting] older" but also an elegy for the 1960s themselves. While it has not yet had time to become part of the established critical "canon" of Blakean Dylan songs, "Roll on John" must now take its place at the heart of this canon, alongside "Gates of Eden" and "Every Grain of Sand," since it contains the longest and most overt Blake reference of any Dylan song. The highly allusive song is primarily a tribute to another 1960s' icon, John Lennon, and features quotations from several Beatles songs (particularly "A Day in the Life"), alongside references to Lennon's life and death. However, the song can also be interpreted as Dylan finally accepting his own status as countercultural icon and survivor of the 1960s; the song's elegiac tone encompasses more than just the figure of Lennon himself, and its unusually direct use of Blake's poetry seems to signify a new openness in Dylan's longstanding relationship with Blake as a literary icon of the period. At the same time, however, there are still a number of other tensions to be discovered within the song which involve questions of literary influence and problematic "relationships of ownership."

The song's Blakean element is already hinted at in its chorus, which contains the line "You burned so bright." Then in the final verse Dylan makes his borrowing explicit. "Tyger, tyger, burning bright," he sings, but before completing Blake's most famous opening couplet, Dylan switches his sources, singing the words "I pray the Lord my soul to keep." This line is borrowed not from Blake but from the traditional children's prayer "Now I lay me down to sleep," which was included in the most widely used American school textbook of the eighteenth century, *The New England Primer*. "In the forest of the night," Dylan continues, then finishes his quatrain with a line adapted from his other eighteenth-century source: "Cover him over, and let him sleep."[47]

This distinctive intertextual approach to Blake which Dylan adopts in "Roll on John" seems to suggest an awareness of the way in which Blake's *Songs* are influenced by (and in critical conversation with) eighteenth-century children's prayers and hymns.[48] Certainly, Dylan's new composite version of "The Tyger" continues Blake's deliberately unsettling dual vision of God as both "Tyger" and "Lamb." This effect is added to by Dylan's ambiguous use of pronouns in the verse quoted above, which further serves to suggest a conflation of the semi-mythical 1960s' figures of Lennon and Dylan themselves.

Although Ginsberg's various encounters with the Beatles provide a few very minor links between Lennon and Blake, there is no particularly obvious biographical or literary reason for Dylan to pair Blake and Lennon as he does so deliberately in "Roll on John"; perhaps surprisingly for a former art school student, Lennon does not seem to use Blake at all in his own work.[49] Blake's strong presence within Dylan's tribute to Lennon can therefore be read primarily as an invocation of Blake's own status as a presiding spirit of the 1960s.

Yet if Dylan now seems comfortable making more overt use of Blake in his work, there are still problematic aspects of Dylan's relationship with his sources in "Roll on John." While Dylan's "late period" albums—from *Time Out of Mind* (1997) onwards—have received widespread critical acclaim, the "[a]ccusations of plagiarism" that Suze Rotolo highlighted as a feature of Dylan's "early years" have also resurfaced in a new form in relation to the content of these late albums (and even his memoir *Chronicles*). With the help of internet search engines, it has become possible to prove that many of Dylan's recent songs are constructed as jigsaws of unacknowledged (some would say hidden) lines and phrases taken from a wide variety of other sources.[50] Even the title of the album *"Love and Theft"* (2001) is a quotation, apparently taken from the historian Eric Lott's 1993 study, *Love and Theft: Blackface Minstrelsy and the American Working Class*.[51] Yet while Dylan carefully places quotation marks around this album title, and the listener is obviously meant to notice the well-known lines from Blake and the Beatles in "Roll on John," most of his recent borrowings have been invisible, drawing on obscure and sometimes bizarre sources including a translated Japanese gangster memoir.[52] Thus David Yaffe refers to the "committee of muses" hovering behind Dylan's recent works, and notes that "[s]ometimes he alludes, but other times he plunders and buries."[53]

As well as the very obvious literary allusions in "Roll on John" to Blake's "The Tyger" and to the traditional prayer "Now I lay me down to sleep," the song is also typical of Dylan's later work in its reliance on a much more obscure "buried" literary source. Scott Warmuth, who in recent years has unearthed a wealth of fragmented literary sources on Dylan's "late" albums, has shown that "Roll on John" contains multiple lines and phrases all taken from the same short section of Robert Fagles's 1996 translation of Homer's *The Odyssey*, as do several other songs on *Tempest*.[54] Stripped of their original context, these lines are no longer recognizable as the work of Homer, or even his modern translator. Thus this late work of Dylan's emerges as a patchwork of Blake, the Beatles, and Homer, together of course with lines of Dylan's own invention.

While comparisons have been made between Dylan's patchwork technique and that of modernists such as T. S. Eliot,[55] the key difference is that many of Dylan's allusions are "buried," so untraceable without the help of internet search engines. Although Dylan is certainly familiar with the work of Eliot,[56] a better comparison for Dylan's recycling of an eclectic variety of literary material might be the "cut-up" composition technique employed by William Burroughs, and indeed Dylan refers admiringly to Burroughs and his cut-up method in a number of interviews.[57] Dylan's method is also a reminder that the textual contexts of the 1960s' counterculture are complex and sometimes unexpected; the presence of Blake in the work of Dylan and others is just one aspect of this literary counterculture where, as Dylan sings in "Love Minus Zero/No Limit," people "Read books, repeat quotations / Draw conclusions on the wall."

Nonetheless, while "Roll on John" seems to reveal a newly open quality in Dylan's relationship to Blake, we might question whether his direct quotation of what are probably Blake's most famous lines represents anything more than a decontextualized "plundering" of Blake, especially if we remember Dylan's revealing 1968 comment that "Blake did come up with some bold lines" but that "the connection sometimes does not connect."[58] Indeed, we might link this to the way in which Blake's most visible presence within 1960s' counterculture as a whole was via the widespread repetition and literal "Draw[ing] on the wall" of a relatively small number of his aphorisms, mostly taken from *The Marriage of Heaven and Hell*, such as "'The tygers of wrath are wiser than the horses of instruction" and "If the doors of perception were cleansed every thing would appear to man as it is: infinite."[59] How much of Blake's meaning remains in the famous opening lines of "The Tyger" when Dylan appropriates them in "Roll on John"?

As I have suggested, Dylan's pairing of the lines from "The Tyger" with an example of eighteenth-century children's verse suggests some contextual knowledge of the historical background and literary technique of Blake's *Songs*. We can also see "Roll on John" as a song that actually takes as one of its themes the 1960s themselves, evoked in part through the song's aphoristic use of Blake. Finally, however, I want to emphasize once again that taking the historicist approach to Blakean reception studies that is advocated and exemplified by Mike Goode in "Blakespotting," and which I have attempted to follow here, must lead us to recognize that the fundamental meaning of Blake is affected or even created by his radical 1960s' reception. This does not mean that we lose sight of the importance of the historical and political circumstances of his texts' original production, but rather that we appreciate how their latent potential is revealed in their later reception. Furthermore, Blake's characteristic use of proverbs, aphorisms, and what Dylan identified as his "bold lines" is the driving force behind the dissemination and appropriation of Blake's work. This has ensured that his work is not only read, but also reused, reactivated, reimagined, and even once again set to music in the work of Dylan and others, so that the "bells of William Blake" continue to ring out across the ages.

NOTES

1. "Television Press Conference, KQED (San Francisco), December 3, 1965," in *Dylan on Dylan: The Essential Interviews*, ed. Jonathan Cott (London: Hodder & Stoughton, 2006), 61–80 (62). Michael Gray used Dylan's answer as the title of his ever-expanding study of Dylan, currently in its third edition as *Song & Dance Man III: The Art of Bob Dylan* (London: Continuum, 2000).

2. Ibid., 63.

3. Ginsberg's role as 1960s' promoter of Blake is well known (as is the story of his 1948 "Blake vision"), but the extent and seriousness of his knowledge of Blake is still underappreciated. Alongside other work on this topic see Luke Walker, "Allen Ginsberg's Blakean Albion," *Comparative American Studies* 11, no. 3 (2013): 227–242.

4. Christopher Ricks, *Dylan's Visions of Sin* (London: Penguin, 2003).

5. Bob Dylan, *Chronicles: Volume One* (London: Simon & Schuster, 2004); Bob Dylan, *Lyrics: 1962–2001* (London: Simon & Schuster, 2004).

6. Whether deliberate or not, there are strong similarities between Dylan's "Mr. Tambourine Man" and this poem. Both feature a request to a musician—the "Piper" or the "Tambourine Man"—to play a song, and describe the ecstatic effects of that song (which is also the text itself) on the listener, who variously weeps "with joy to hear" or dances "beneath the diamond sky with one hand waving free."

7. See G. E. Bentley, *The Stranger from Paradise: A Biography of William Blake* (New Haven and London: Yale University Press, 2001), 74–75, 437–438.

8. An expanded version of Ginsberg's original Blake album is available on CD as *The Complete Songs of Innocence and Experience*, Omnivore OV-220, 2017, 2 compact discs.

9. An outtake from *Desire* (1975), "Golden Loom" was eventually released on *The Bootleg Series Volumes 1–3 (Rare & Unreleased) 1961–1991*, Columbia 47382, 1991, 3 compact discs. The lyrics are included within the *Desire* section of Dylan's *The Lyrics: 1961–2012* (New York: Simon & Schuster, 2016), 374.

10. From a Romanticist perspective, the most significant work so far on this topic is a chapter by Steve Clark and James Keery, "'Only the wings on his heels': Blake and Dylan," in *Blake 2.0: William Blake in Twentieth-Century Art, Music and Culture*, ed. Steve Clark, Tristanne Connolly, and Jason Whittaker (Basingstoke: Palgrave Macmillan, 2012), 209–229. Among the many popular music writers who have written on Dylan, the most detailed and useful references to Blake are made by Michael Gray; see for example the entry for Blake in Gray's *The Bob Dylan Encyclopedia* (London: Continuum, 2006), 51–54.

11. Kevin J. H. Dettmar, introduction to *The Cambridge Companion to Bob Dylan*, ed. Kevin J. H. Dettmar (Cambridge: Cambridge University Press, 2009), 1–14 (8).

12. Bob Dylan, *The Times They Are A-Changin'*, Columbia CS 8905, 1964, 33⅓ rpm.

13. Interestingly given the anxieties surrounding the question of Dylan's status as poet or singer, "11 Outlined Epitaphs" is excluded from *The Lyrics: 1961–2012*; it was earlier included in his *Writings and Drawings* (London: Jonathan Cape, 1973), 100–110, and in his *Lyrics: 1962–1985* (New York: Knopf, 1985), 106–116.

14. See Suze Rotolo, *A Freewheelin' Time: A Memoir of Greenwich Village in the 1960s* (London: Aurum Press, 2008), 172, 235, and Clark and Keery, "Blake and Dylan," 227n.

15. Rotolo, *A Freewheelin' Time*, 135.

16. See, for example, Dylan, *Chronicles*, 34.

17. On this first meeting between Dylan and Ginsberg, see Barry Miles, *Ginsberg: A Biography* (London: Viking, 1989), 333–334.

18. Interview with Ginsberg in Martin Scorsese's film *No Direction Home* (Hollywood, CA: Paramount, 2005), DVD. As Sean Wilentz notes, the significance of this event is made doubly apparent in the film by the fact that Ginsberg in the interview begins to choke up once again as he remembers his initial reaction to Dylan's music (Wilentz, *Bob Dylan in America* [London: Bodley Head, 2010], 320n).

19. Miles, *Ginsberg*, 333–334. According to poet Anne Waldman, during Dylan's 1975 Rolling Thunder tour (in which both Ginsberg and Waldman participated), the favorite joke was that "Ginsberg was Dylan's most dedicated groupie" (quoted in Wilentz, *Bob Dylan in America*, 76).

20. The song's links to Blake have been noted by many of those who have written on Dylan; for an interesting close reading by a Romanticist scholar see Nelson Hilton, "Waxed in Blake," *Blake: An Illustrated Quarterly* 43, no. 3 (2009): 110–111.

21. Allen Ginsberg, *Collected Poems: 1947–1997* (New York: HarperCollins, 2006), 368.

22. *Renaldo and Clara*, directed by Bob Dylan (theatrical release 1978, never officially released for home viewing).

23. As Wilentz suggests, by giving Ginsberg the role of "The Father" in *Renaldo and Clara*, Dylan was in effect casting him "as the patriarch of the entire hip cultural family" (*Bob Dylan in America*, 76.)

24. The fact that Ginsberg features on this video is often commented on simply as a marker of the closeness of his friendship with Dylan, with the underlying assumption that his inclusion in the background of the shot—engaged in animated conversation with Dylan's tour manager Bob Neuwirth and occasionally throwing his arms in the air in prophetic style—is more or less accidental. However, the fact that Ginsberg also appears, in exactly the same position on the screen, in an alternate take of the video shot on the same day in a different location, suggests that his inclusion was in fact very deliberate. ("'Subterranean Homesick Blues' Alternate Take," *Don't Look Back*, directed by D.A. Pennebaker (1967; New York: Sony BMG, 2007), DVD, 2 discs. Given Ginsberg's passion for Blakean pilgrimages (see Walker, "Allen Ginsberg's Blakean Albion"), he must surely also have known that the alley where "Subterranean Homesick Blues" was filmed is adjacent to the site of Blake's final residence, 3 Fountain Court, where in 1827 he died "Singing of the things he saw in Heaven."

25. Wilentz, *Bob Dylan in America*, 157.

26. Michael McClure, "Bob Dylan: The Poet's Poet," *Rolling Stone*, March 14, 1974, accessed February 28, 2014, http://www.rollingstone.com/music/news/bob-dylan-the-poets-poet-19740314. All quotations are from the unpaginated online version of this article.

27. Ibid.

28. Ibid.

29. Allen Ginsberg, *Deliberate Prose: Selected Essays 1952–1995*, ed. Bill Morgan (Harmondsworth: Penguin, 2000), 151.

30. Bob Dylan, "Gates of Eden," in *Lyrics: 1962–1985* (New York: Knopf, 1985), 174.

31. Allen Ginsberg, *The Gates of Wrath: Rhymed Poems, 1948–1952* (Bolinas, CA: Grey Fox Press, 1972), 56.

32. Hilton, "Waxed in Blake," 110–111.

33. See Robert Shelton, *No Direction Home: The Life and Music of Bob Dylan* (Cambridge, MA: Da Capo Press, 2003), 73–74, where Dylan's victims recall his behavior with a mixture of horror and admiration: "He had an unerring sense of what to take" (74).

34. It is also significant that this odd verbal exchange between Ginsberg and Dylan took place two days before Dylan joined Ginsberg, McClure, and other Beats for the so-called "Last Gathering of the Beats" photoshoot outside City Lights Bookshop in San Francisco, on December 5, 1965.

35. This dynamic is also illustrated by the fact that Ginsberg was one of those who first recommended Dylan for the Nobel Prize in Literature, 20 years before he was finally awarded the prize. Earlier still, in 1974, Ginsberg composed a poem addressed to Dylan, presciently entitled "A Poem for the Laurels You Win" (also known as "On Reading Dylan's Writings"), which contains the lines "Sincerest form of flattery / Is Imitation they say." Significantly however, the conceit of this poem is that it is Ginsberg imitating Dylan, rather than the other way around, as Ginsberg describes his own attempts to break his "long line down" in order to "write a song your way." See "Friday's Weekly Round-Up–290" on *The Allen Ginsberg Project* website, ed. Peter Hale, accessed November 20, 2016, http://allenginsberg.org/2016/10/fridays-weekly-round-up-290-2/.

36. Carrie Jaurès Noland, "Rimbaud and Patti Smith: Style as Social Deviance," *Critical Inquiry* 21, no. 3 (1995): 581–610, also reprinted in a revised form in Noland's *Poetry at Stake: Lyric Aesthetics and the Challenge of Technology* (Princeton, NJ: Princeton University Press, 1999); Edward Larrissy, introduction to *Romanticism and Postmodernism*, ed. Larrissy (Cambridge: Cambridge University Press, 1999), 1–12 (10).

37. Wilentz, *Bob Dylan in America*, 77. See also Richard E. Hishmeh, "Marketing Genius: The Friendship of Allen Ginsberg and Bob Dylan," *The Journal of American Culture* 29, no. 4 (2006): 395–405.

38. Michael Schumacher, *Dharma Lion: A Biography of Allen Ginsberg* (New York: St Martin's, 1992), 559.

39. Ginsberg, *Deliberate Prose*, 278–279.

40. Miles, *Ginsberg*, 391–392.

41. Howard Sounes, *Down the Highway: The Life of Bob Dylan* (London: Doubleday, 2001), 231.

42. "*Sing Out!* interview, 1968," in *Dylan on Dylan*, 113–138 (119). Ellipses in original interview.

43. John Beer, *William Blake: A Literary Life* (Basingstoke: Palgrave Macmillan, 2007), 149. Fuseli was presumably referring to Blake's artistic motifs rather than his poetry.

44. Mike Goode, "Blakespotting," *PMLA* 121, no. 3 (2006): 769–786 (776).

45. Ibid., 772.

46. Quoted in Clinton Heylin, *Still on the Road: The Songs of Bob Dylan, Vol. 2: 1974–2008* (London: Constable, 2010), 385. While Heylin's source for the quote is not entirely clear, he seems to suggest that it is from an interview Dylan gave in Australia in March 1992.

47. Dylan, *The Lyrics: 1961–2012*, 666–667. Confusingly, "Roll on John" shares its title with a traditional song which formed part of Dylan's early-1960s' repertoire.

48. Particularly good summaries of this important aspect of Blake's work are provided by Zachary Leader, *Reading Blake's Songs* (London: Routledge & Kegan Paul, 1981), 1–36, and by Heather Glen, *Vision and Disenchantment: Blake's Songs and Wordsworth's Lyrical Ballads* (Cambridge: Cambridge University Press, 1983), 8–32.

49. Ginsberg first met the Beatles in Dylan's London hotel room in 1965, where they spent what Ginsberg described as "a drunken night talking about pot and William Blake" (*The Letters of Allen Ginsberg*, ed. Bill Morgan [Cambridge, MA: Da Capo Press, 2008], 307). According to Barry Miles, however, this Blake conversation actually consisted of Ginsberg flirtatiously falling into Lennon's lap and asking his opinion of Blake, while Lennon pretended total ignorance of the subject, either in an attempt to escape Ginsberg's drunken advances or because of the general atmosphere of tension between Dylan and the Beatles (Miles, *Ginsberg*, 370). In 1971, Lennon and Ringo Starr joined Ginsberg in singing Blake's "Nurse's Song" at Lennon's birthday party (Schumacher, *Dharma Lion*, 556–557), and in 1976 Ginsberg gave Lennon cassettes of his Blake recordings (*The Letters of Allen Ginsberg*, 385.)

50. These issues are well summarized in Wilentz, *Bob Dylan in America*, 302–319, and in Martin Jacobi, "Bob Dylan and Collaboration," in *The Cambridge Companion to Bob Dylan*, 69–79.

51. Officially, "Mr. Dylan neither confirms nor denies a connection between the title of his album and the title of that book." But there is wide critical consensus that this is the case, and Lott's book relates to a period of American history in which Dylan has a strong interest (which also expresses itself on the songs of the album). See Eric Lott, "'Love and Theft' (2001)," in *The Cambridge Companion to Bob Dylan*, 167–173.

52. See Wilentz, *Bob Dylan in America*, 308–309.

53. David Yaffe, "Bob Dylan and the Anglo-American Tradition," in *The Cambridge Companion to Bob Dylan*, 15–27 (21).

54. Scott Warmuth, "A Tempest Commonplace," accessed March 4, 2014, http://www.pinterest.com/scottwarmuth/a-tempest-commonplace. Dylan's strong interest in *The Odyssey* is confirmed by the fact that it is one of three books he focuses on in detail in his Nobel Lecture ("Bob Dylan's Nobel Lecture," delivered June 2017, *The Swedish Academy* website, accessed July 4, 2017, http://www.svenskaakademien.se/en/nobel-lecture).

55. See, for example, Wilentz, *Bob Dylan in America*, 312–313.

56. In "Desolation Row" (1965), Dylan depicts "Ezra Pound and T. S. Eliot / Fighting in the captain's tower," while in *Chronicles* he tells us, "I liked T. S. Eliot. He was worth reading" (110).

57. See for example Cott, *Dylan on Dylan*, 45, 49, 87.

58. Ibid., 119.

59. William Blake, *The Marriage of Heaven and Hell*, in *The Complete Poetry and Prose of William Blake*, Newly Revised Edition, ed. David V. Erdman (Berkeley: University of California Press, 1982), 37, 39.

BIBLIOGRAPHY

Beer, John. *William Blake: A Literary Life*. Basingstoke: Palgrave Macmillan, 2007.

Bentley, G. E. *The Stranger from Paradise: A Biography of William Blake*. New Haven, CT: Yale University Press, 2001.

Blake, William. *The Marriage of Heaven and Hell*. In *The Complete Poetry and Prose of William Blake*, Newly Revised Edition, edited by David V. Erdman, 33–45. Berkeley, CA: University of California Press, 1982.

Clark, Steve, and James Keery. "'Only the wings on his heels': Blake and Dylan." In *Blake 2.0: William Blake in Twentieth-Century Art, Music and Culture*, edited by Steve Clark, Tristanne Connolly, and Jason Whittaker, 209–229. Basingstoke: Palgrave Macmillan, 2012.

Cott, Jonathan, ed. *Dylan on Dylan: The Essential Interviews*. London: Hodder & Stoughton, 2006.

Dettmar, Kevin J. H. *The Cambridge Companion to Bob Dylan*. Cambridge: Cambridge University Press, 2009.

Don't Look Back. Directed by D.A. Pennebaker. 1967. New York: Sony BMG, 2007. DVD (2 discs.)

Dylan, Bob. *Chronicles: Volume One*. London: Simon & Schuster, 2004.

———. "Gates of Eden." In *Lyrics: 1962–1985*. New York: Knopf, 1985.

———. *Lyrics: 1962–1985*. New York: Knopf, 1985.

———. *Lyrics: 1962–2001*. London: Simon & Schuster, 2004.

———. "Nobel Lecture." Delivered June 2017. *The Swedish Academy* website, accessed July 4, 2017. http://www.svenskaakademien.se/en/nobel-lecture.

———. *The Bootleg Series Volumes 1–3 (Rare & Unreleased) 1961–1991*, Columbia 47382, 1991, 3 compact discs.

———. *The Lyrics: 1961–2012*. New York: Simon & Schuster, 2016.

———. *The Times They Are A-Changin'*, Columbia CS 8905, 1964, 33⅓ rpm.

———. *Writings and Drawings*. London: Jonathan Cape, 1973.

Ginsberg, Allen. *Collected Poems: 1947–1997*. New York: HarperCollins, 2006.

———. *Deliberate Prose: Selected Essays 1952–1995*, edited by Bill Morgan. Harmondsworth: Penguin, 2000.

———. *The Complete Songs of Innocence and Experience*. Omnivore OV-220, 2017, 2 compact discs. Expanded edition of *Songs of Innocence and Experience*, originally released in 1970.

———. *The Gates of Wrath: Rhymed Poems, 1948–1952*. Bolinas, CA: Grey Fox Press, 1972.

———. *The Letters of Allen Ginsberg*, edited by Bill Morgan. Cambridge, MA: Da Capo Press, 2008.

Glen, Heather. *Vision and Disenchantment: Blake's Songs and Wordsworth's Lyrical Ballads*. Cambridge: Cambridge University Press, 1983.

Goode, Mike. "Blakespotting." *PMLA* 121, no. 3 (2006): 769–786.

Gray, Michael. *Song & Dance Man III: The Art of Bob Dylan*. London: Continuum, 2000.

———. *The Bob Dylan Encyclopedia*. London: Continuum, 2006.

Hale, Peter. "Friday's Weekly Round-Up–290." *The Allen Ginsberg Project* website, accessed November 20, 2016, http://allenginsberg.org/2016/10/fridays-weekly-round-up-290–2/.

Heylin, Clinton. *Still on the Road: The Songs of Bob Dylan, Vol. 2: 1974–2008*. London: Constable, 2010.

Hilton, Nelson. "Waxed in Blake." *Blake: An Illustrated Quarterly* 43, no. 3 (2009): 110–111.

Hishmeh, Richard E. "Marketing Genius: The Friendship of Allen Ginsberg and Bob Dylan." *The Journal of American Culture* 29, no. 4 (2006): 395–405.

Jacobi, Martin. "Bob Dylan and Collaboration." In *The Cambridge Companion to Bob Dylan*, edited by Kevin J. H. Dettmar, 69–79. Cambridge: Cambridge University Press, 2009.

Larrissy, Edward. *Romanticism and Postmodernism*. Cambridge: Cambridge University Press, 1999.

Leader, Zachary. *Reading Blake's Songs*. London: Routledge & Kegan Paul, 1981.

Lott, Eric. "'Love and Theft' (2001)." In *The Cambridge Companion to Bob Dylan*, edited by Kevin J. H. Dettmar, 167–173. Cambridge: Cambridge University Press, 2009.

McClure, Michael. "Bob Dylan: The Poet's Poet." *Rolling Stone*, March 14, 1974, accessed February 28, 2014, http://www.rollingstone.com/music/news/bob-dylan-the-poets-poet-19740314.

Miles, Barry. *Ginsberg: A Biography*. London: Viking, 1989.

No Direction Home. Directed by Martin Scorsese. 2005. Hollywood, CA: Paramount, 2005. DVD.

Noland, Carrie Jaurès. *Poetry at Stake: Lyric Aesthetics and the Challenge of Technology*. Princeton, NJ: Princeton University Press, 1999.

———. "Rimbaud and Patti Smith: Style as Social Deviance." *Critical Inquiry* 21, no. 3 (1995): 581–610.

Renaldo and Clara. Directed by Bob Dylan. Los Angeles, CA: Circuit Films, 1978.

Ricks, Christopher. *Dylan's Visions of Sin*. London: Penguin, 2003.

Rotolo, Suze. *A Freewheelin' Time: A Memoir of Greenwich Village in the Sixties*. London: Aurum Press, 2008.

Schumacher, Michael. *Dharma Lion: A Biography of Allen Ginsberg*. New York: St Martin's, 1992.

Shelton, Robert. *No Direction Home: The Life and Music of Bob Dylan*. Cambridge, MA: Da Capo Press, 2003.

Sounes, Howard. *Down the Highway: The Life of Bob Dylan*. London: Doubleday, 2001.

Walker, Luke. "Allen Ginsberg's Blakean Albion." *Comparative American Studies* 11, no. 3 (2013): 227–242.

Warmuth, Scott. "A Tempest Commonplace." Pinterest, accessed March 4, 2014, http://www.pinterest.com/scottwarmuth/a-tempest-commonplace.

Wilentz, Sean. *Bob Dylan in America*. London: Bodley Head, 2010.

Yaffe, David. "Bob Dylan and the Anglo-American Tradition." In *The Cambridge Companion to Bob Dylan*, edited by Kevin J. H. Dettmar, 15–27. Cambridge: Cambridge University Press, 2009.

Chapter Two

Romanticism in the Park

Mick Jagger Reading Shelley

Janneke van der Leest

When Mick Jagger read a poem by the Romantic poet Percy Bysshe Shelley at the Rolling Stones's Hyde Park concert on July 5, 1969, it was not simply a coincidence. The entire rock and pop culture of the 1960s clearly express the legacy of the Romantic movement of the late eighteenth and early nineteenth centuries. This essay discusses what is at stake in both Shelley's poem and Jagger's act of reading. It explores the specific stanzas that Jagger read and shows in what ways he follows in the Romantics' footsteps. Finally, it discusses a link between rock and Romanticism revealed by a misinterpretation of Jagger's reading the day after the event in a newspaper.

The situation preceding the Rolling Stones's free Hyde Park concert, one that has gone down in rock history as a tribute to Brian Jones, is that this visionary rock artist drowned a few days earlier in the late evening of July 2, 1969, in his swimming pool at the age of twenty-seven. Several weeks before the concert, Jones was asked by the Stones to leave the band, and he seemed to have agreed with it. They had already found a new member to replace him: Mick Taylor. The Stones planned to introduce Taylor at the massive event at Hyde Park. But suddenly, the concert's initial intent was overshadowed by the death of Jones. About Jagger's reaction on hearing the news of Jones's death, Keith Altham states: "[He] got quite angry about [it] . . . almost as if Brian had committed hara-kiri on purpose, cos the Stones [were] planning their Hyde Park concert later that week."[1] Nevertheless, at the opening of the concert Jagger managed to hold a few hundred thousand people silent when he movingly read from Shelley's *Adonais*, a poem written on the death of John Keats.

SHELLEY ON KEATS

Although Keats and Shelley are often mentioned in the same breath, they met each other just a few times. It seemed as if the modest, middle-class Keats was not very eager to know the more elitist Shelley. Shelley overshadowed Keats as an acknowledged poet with a remarkable reputation marked by rebelliousness, radical idealism, and an eccentric lifestyle. Shelley once responded to Keats's poem *Endymion* both positively and negatively in a letter to him: he speaks of "the treasures of poetry it contains, though treasures poured forth with indistinct profusion."[2] In the same letter, Shelley invites Keats to stay with him in Italy in the winter because Keats was suffering from consumption, and the Italian climate would be good for his health. About his invitation, Shelley wrote to Marianne Hunt: "I am aware indeed in part [tha]t I am nourishing a rival who will far surpass [me] and this is an additional motive & will be an added pleasure."[3] The ill poet refused to stay with Shelley in Pisa and went to Rome instead.

Since the moment Shelley read Keats's *Hyperion* he recognized him as a "rival" and considered him to be a genius he had to advocate.[4] Nevertheless, Keats did not live long after Shelley's recognition. When he had died at the age of twenty-five, Shelley was convinced that such a genius deserved immortality; he was determined to offer it to him through the poem *Adonais*. Yet Shelley dedicated his poem more to the *poet* than to the *man* Keats, making the poem rather impersonal.[5] But Shelley was satisfied with his elegy—*Adonais; An Elegy on the Death of John Keats, Author of "Endymion," "Hyperion,"* etc. While working on it, he wrote to John and Maria Gisborne, "I have been engaged these last days in composing a poem on the death of Keats. . . . It is a highly wrought *piece of art*, perhaps better in point of composition than any thing I have written."[6] Three days later he wrote to Claire Clairmont that this poem "is better than any thing that I have yet written, & worthy both of him & of me."[7]

Adonais is a complex work of art. It is full of references to other works such as Goëthe's *Faust*, Shakespeare's *Romeo and Juliet*, *Henry V*, and *Hamlet*, Biblical passages, and to the works of Dante and Plato. The poem is inwrought with patterns of systematic allusions to Theocritus, Bion, Moschus, Horace, Vergil, Spenser, and Milton. Shelley also made Keats's work present in *Adonais*: "its brilliantly original approach is to weave the products of Keats's poetic imagination into the texture of his elegy."[8] Speculations on its title alone seem to be limitless. Does "Adonais" stand for the uplifting of Adonis (the vegetation figure of the Greek rebirth myth) to the monotheistic God, Adonai ("my Lord," the Hebrew acclamation for *Yahweh*)? Or is "Adonais" a reference to the sound of mourning, for in Greek "woe" is "*ai*"? Or should the name be read as a witty wordplay with the Greek word "nightingale," "*aedon*," that is associated both with poetry and with (and by) Keats?

These are just some elaborations on the title,[9] let alone what could be suggested concerning the rest of its intertextually rich verses. It is hard to unravel all *Adonais's* verbal and thematic interwoven echoes, its im- and explicit allusions, its complex imagery, its abstractions, its mythical and philosophical dimensions, or to lay bare its "organic unity."[10] It is even more difficult to answer the question whether it is a poem in honor of Keats or a self-portrait of Shelley. Yet, what could definitely be concluded from two centuries of literary criticism? That Shelley achieved his goal: Keats is remembered, in part, thanks to Shelley's work.

By the time of his death, it was not likely that Keats was to be forgotten soon. However, in the preface to *Adonais* Shelley sketched his purpose to offer Keats an established place among the great poets. He was convinced that Keats's work deserved to be remembered. But Shelley also influenced *the way* this young poet was going to be remembered. In the preface he portrayed Keats as an ill poet who suffered misfortune and who was physically and emotionally weak, "weaker than he ever was."[11] The intention to rescue Keats from oblivion is implied throughout the elegy, introducing this aim immediately in the first stanza: "Forget the Past, his fate and fame shall be / An echo and light unto eternity!"[12] And indeed, besides Keats's own work, it is also thanks to this elegy that we remember him today, through the mythologized image "Adonais": "weaned upon the tender emotions of 'true-lover tears' (49) and easily laid 'waste' (53) after 'a single painful event' . . . unable to endure suffering and tragedy."[13]

This elegy, however, also reminds us of Shelley. He is after all the author of the poem, who was visionary in drawing attention to the remembrance of Keats for the future. In this attempt, "Keats's poetic fate is inextricably bound up with Shelley's own, the presence in *Adonais* of Keats's voice will only secure its place in the tradition of English poetry if Shelley's elegy itself survives."[14] Although Shelley speaks directly to Keats in the poem only twice (footnote five), he does use the first person singular. And this is not without meaning: "The elegy pivots on the word 'I,' and Shelley's presence is crucial to the poem's effect. This elegy for Keats is less a self-elegy than an opportunity for the elegist to display his poetic power as he presides over and takes an increasingly central role in a 'highly wrought *piece of art.*'"[15] Note in this regard also the double interest of the poem that Shelley himself mentioned to Clairmont, cited above: the poem is "worthy both of him & of me."

Besides explaining his purpose to make Keats immortal, Shelley denounced in the preface the criticism from which Keats had suffered severely. According to Shelley, the Tory critic who was harsh on *Endymion* in the *The Quarterly Review* made Keats's illness progress unnecessarily quickly. This claim strongly influenced the myth of Keats as an unappreciated genius who died young and contributed to the Romantic sentiment in which the idea of artistic martyrdom took root.[16] To what extent Shelley fabricated this picture of an oversensitive Keats, and if there is an element of truth in it, is debatable.[17] But we may assume that he is exaggerating by sketching an image of Keats as being so upset by the criticism that it made him perish, and we may state that he took it as far as "a re-writing of mythology and an obscuring of biography."[18] As Sandy puts it, Shelley "erases actual events surrounding Keats's illness and death to evade history and time, thus securing Keats's name through the figure of Adonais."[19] Most likely, Shelley's comment on the literary critique was also a way to take revenge on his own behalf, because literary critics did not only harm Keats but also Shelley himself.[20]

Immortality is not just a theme in and an intention of the poem: this elegy as such is an embodiment of immortality. Keats's immortality is achieved by the remembrance through the poem, and Shelley obtains immortality because of the authorship of this "least imperfect of my compositions" as he calls it.[21] Every time Shelley's remembrance of Keats is repeated, for instance by citation in death notices, both poets are memorialized. Likewise, when Jagger read from *Adonais*, both Shelley and Keats were remembered through the way he honored Jones.

JAGGER AND JONES

Throughout the 1960s, Jagger started to overshadow Jones on stage as the band's frontman. The singer showed more and more talent as a songwriter and developed his management skills. Jones and Jagger were rivals within a rock band,[22] like Shelley and Keats were within the circle of Romantic writers.[23] In the act of citing Shelley's words for Keats, Jagger stands in the footsteps of Shelley's witty play. Both know how to kill two birds with one stone. But there is a difference: Shelley's double agenda seems to be profitable for both poets. Shelley does his best to make "the audibility of Keats's echoing voice"[24] to be heard. By this act he also made himself memorable. And *Adonais* indeed plays an important and ongoing role in the realization of the remembrance of Keats, mythologized by Shelley, as a Romantic idol. Jagger had a double agenda too: he combined the planned introduction of a new band member with the unforeseen honoring of a deceased one. But Jones's echoing voice seems to be wiped out of the Stones's history, especially by Jagger and Richards. The things that seem to be most momentous in the remembrance of Jones are the "myths" about his death instead of his artistic life.[25] Jagger's double agenda was profitable for Jagger in particular. He displayed his power as frontman at the impressive moment he commemorates the lost founder of the Stones. And at the same time it was the starting point of a manipulation of the band's biography, like Shelley did with Keats's. But what does that moment say about Romanticism's contribution to rock history?

JAGGER READS SHELLEY

In his composition of *Adonais* Shelley put himself in the tradition of the pastoral elegy. In the second century BCE the ancient Greek poet Bion wrote *Lament for Adonis*, lamenting the death of the mythological Adonis: hunter, shepherd, and lover. Another Greek poet, Moschus, in his *Lament for Bion*, adopted the form of Bion's elegy in order to lament the death of his friend poet Bion, whom he in his turn portrayed as shepherd.[26] Herewith Moschus initiated the tradition of one poet associating the death of another poet with the death of Adonis. Renaissance elegies in this tradition are Spenser's lament for Sir Philip Sidney, *Astrophel*, and Milton's *Lycidas* lamenting the death of Edward King.[27] Shelley both modeled his pastoral elegy on the Hellenistic poems and referred to English Renaissance poetry. By reciting *Adonais*, Jagger also puts himself in this tradition: he laments the death of his fellow band member and musician by citing from the pastoral tradition.

Adonais consists of fifty-five Spenserian stanzas. This verse form might be a way to honor Keats, who was an admirer of Edmund Spenser.[28] The poem starts with a mythical narrative. According to the ancient Greek fertility myth, Aphrodite mourns the loss of her adopted son and lover Adonis, who was killed by a boar. Zeus could no longer bear the grief of Aphrodite and made a deal with Hades, the god of the underworld, who would free Adonis every year in spring, while every autumn he would be killed and mourned again. Therefore Adonis is the symbol of death and rebirth in nature and eternal youth. Shelley's version, however, differs from the original myth. Urania[29] is now not the lover, but only the mother who mourns for the loss of her son Adonais/Keats. Living and dead English poets also mourn the death of Keats in the first part of the elegy. Shelley identifies Urania as the muse of the English poetic tradition. He imagines her as the widow of Milton, and as a consequence Keats as Milton's heir.

In stanza thirty-seven Shelley condemns the *Quarterly*'s reviewer who in Shelley's perception contributed to Keats's rapidly worsening health. This is the tragic finale of the first part of the poem which created a place for a mythology of Keats in the landscape of the English poetic tradition.[30] Stanza thirty-eight marks the point of transition away from a mythological to a philosophical mode. Shelley, as Silverman shows, ascends "a Platonic ladder to revelation" from the beginning to the end of the poem.[31] In the second part of the poem, Shelley "has transcended the mundane" and is "no longer dependent upon myth; he no longer perceives multiplicity and fragmentation, but unity; and thus the character of Urania merges with the One."[32] Jagger chooses two stanzas from this second part: the thirty-ninth and fifty-second. Before considering Jagger's first choice, one cannot skip the important preceding stanza.

> XXXVIII
> Nor let us weep that our delight is fled
> Far from these carrion kites that scream below;
> He wakes or sleeps with the enduring dead;
> Thou canst not soar where he is sitting now.—
> Dust to the dust! but the pure spirit shall flow
> Back to the burning fountain whence it came,
> A portion of the Eternal, which must glow
> Through time and change, unquenchably the same,
> Whilst thy cold embers choke the sordid hearth of shame.
>
> XXXIX
> Peace, peace! he is not dead, he doth not sleep—
> He hath awakened from the dream of life—
> 'Tis we, who lost in stormy visions, keep
> With phantoms an unprofitable strife,
> And in mad trance, strike with our spirit's knife
> Invulnerable nothings.—*We* decay
> Like corpses in a charnel; fear and grief
> Convulse us and consume us day by day,
> And cold hopes swarm like worms within our living clay.[33]

Although the poem is composed in order to make Keats immortal, "Shelley remains agnostic as to literal immortality."[34] This agnosticism becomes clear in stanza thirty-eight: "He wakes or sleeps with the enduring dead." The word "or" refers to Shelley's uncertainty about what happens after death. Nevertheless, he splits the materialistic dimension of death from the spiritual one. He makes a reference to Ecclesiastes—"Dust to the dust!"—pointing to the material dimension of death, and to the "cold embers" in the last line of the stanza. Regarding the spiritual dimension, he sketches, "the pure spirit shall flow / Back to the burning fountain whence it came . . . In the light of that fountain, the dead poet is neither dead nor asleep, but 'awakened from the dream of life' by having 'outsoared the shadow of our night.'"[35] This kind of fountain belongs to the image of heaven that Shelley doubts but which he pictures in his *Essay on Christianity*. "The unobscured irradiations from the fountain-fire of all goodness shall reveal all that is mysterious and unintelligible" appear to us in heaven, after "that mysterious change which we call death" takes place.[36]

In relation to this thematic fields of *afterlife* and *agnosticism* it is important to look at Shelley's *Essay on Christianity*, wherein he comes to speak of the image of heaven, as displayed by Jesus Christ. Shelley doubts this image: "even if it be not true! . . . even if it be no more than the imagination of some sublimest and most holy poet," he still appreciates it as a "delightful picture."[37] In this essay Shelley imagines Christian heaven through *the eyes of* Jesus. His doubt obstructs him from creating *his own* vision of afterlife. In the last stanza of *Adonais* Shelley writes about heaven, but "Shelley is surrendering to Heaven, though it is the heaven not of any orthodoxy but of his own agnostic will."[38] He puts heaven in his myth about Adonais/Keats, but he does not create a concrete picture of it. It seems that Shelley tends toward unbelief concerning Christian afterlife, while a certain kind of immortality is celebrated in *Adonais*.

In stanza thirty-nine Shelley writes about a specific state of being, one that is awakened from the dream of life.[39] In his essay, Shelley links this state to Jesus's prophecy of salvation after death.[40] In the elegy, Shelley links this state to the main character of a fertility myth, who returns and is celebrated every springtime. "He"/Adonais/Keats is not dead in the sense that he definitively and materially decays; he is neither dead in the sense that he remains spiritually in heaven; instead he will be remembered again and again in our minds. Those mythical deaths of Adonis, Jesus, and Adonais/Keats are intertwined with immortality, at least in the sense of remembrance. *He* will be remembered—no matter if there exists an afterlife or not, but *we*, the ones who honor and remember—will decay.

Jagger also speaks of afterlife and agnosticism in an interview in the documentary *The Stones in the Park*.[41] He says he is convinced that Brian will be there at the concert. He realizes that the idea of the presence of a deceased person depends on what you believe, but he does not agree with the materialist view that "he's just dead and that's it." Jagger says he does not believe in "Western bereavement," but adds that this is not a real comfort, because it is "still very upsetting" that "Brian is sent off from" our world. Jagger does not tend toward agnosticism in his ideas about afterlife; his attitude is more Romantic than Shelley's, for Romantic authors do fantasize about the existence of an afterlife. The German poet Novalis, for instance, said that he tried to follow his fiancée in death by crossing the borders of the living "I" and experienced an afterlife beyond this material world, comparing it with a kind of rebirth.[42] Furthermore, ghost stories and Gothic novels were very popular among the Romantics, which points toward certain fantasies about afterlife. *Weltschmerz* and deep disappointment in love, sometimes leading to suicide, were phenomena Romanticism dealt with since the success of Goëthe's *Die Leiden des jungen Werthers*.[43] Such strong reactions to the dissatisfaction with one's life are connected to a longing for the "afterlife." So, the afterlife and its unorthodox (not religiously bound) approach is a Romantic theme, and Jagger's open attitude is consistent with it.

In stanza thirty-nine, not only Shelley's doubt but also his distance from Keats are strongly felt: "he is not dead, he doth not sleep"—Shelley addresses Adonais/Keats in the third person singular. Jagger chooses these impersonal but deeply emotional lines. They fit with the not so warm friendship between Jones and Jagger. Jagger focuses on a stanza that pays attention to "*We*" which Shelley already emphasized by the use of italics. Not Jones, but "we," Jagger together with Richards, will take over the lead in the band that will go on in the material world. "*We*"—the ones who decay, Jagger, his colleagues, and audience—have to deal with the filthiness and cruelty of life on earth, while Jones "hath awakened from the dream of life":

> LII
> The One remains, the many change and pass;
> Heaven's light forever shines, Earth's shadows fly;
> Life, like a dome of many-coloured glass,
> Stains the white radiance of Eternity,
> Until Death tramples it to fragments.—Die,
> If thou wouldst be with that which thou dost seek!
> Follow where all is fled! [—Rome's azure sky,
> Flowers, ruins, statues, music, words are weak
> The glory they transfuse with fitting truth to speak.] [44]

Jagger does not read the last two and a half lines of this second recited stanza. Those lines are connected to four previous stanzas dedicated to Rome, the city that shows the destructive power of time, but at the same time reminds us of "the ravages of man and the immortality of genius." [45] It is the city where Keats died and is buried. At the end of the four stanzas about Rome (fifty-one), Shelley asks,

> From the world's bitter wind
> Seek shelter in the shadow of the tomb.
> What Adonais is, why fear we to become? [46]

Whereas stanza thirty-eight marks a transition in the complete poem, the movement from stanza fifty-one to fifty-two is an important moment of transition within its second part. It indicates the poem's "dialectical resolution as Shelley chooses the fate of Keats for himself." [47] We may speak of a certain death wish. It is still uncertain whether Shelley killed himself or died by accident when he drowned. And here, a year before his own death, he flirts with it. Sandy recognizes Shelley's "overriding desire" not to simply die, but to "undergo the same transformation as Adonais" and therewith Shelley "faces his own irreplaceable death in order to perpetuate his unique literary legacy. According to *Adonais's* argumentation it is more desirable to be at one with a 'white radiance of Eternity' (464) than to view its brilliance through a distorting lens of life's 'many-coloured glass' dome (463)." [48]

Some stanzas before, forty-five, Shelley mentions three poets who died young—

Chatterton (suicide), Sidney (war victim), and Lucan (forced suicide)— and continues in the next stanza: "And many more, whose names on Earth are dark / But whose transmitted effluence cannot die."[49] They left their imprints, despite their early legendary deaths. Both the Romantic desire to die young and the flirt with death—or at least the wish not to become old—are common themes in rock culture. The Who expressed it in 1965 in "My Generation": "Hope I die before I get old."[50] This attitude, found in rock and roll sub-cultures of the 1960s, has to do with the wish not to become bourgeois.[51] The same is true of the Romantic revolutionary young spirits who rebelled against the older generation: their parents and their artistic, philosophic, and political predecessors. Shelley, for example, rebelled against his aristocratic father—a Member of Parliament—and against conservative Oxford, against inequality (slavery, gender-related issues, injustice to animals), against oppression of people and religions, etc. Nevertheless, most Romantics who did grow old eventually became more or less bourgeois, or at least more conventional. The ones who died young are still being remembered for their refreshing, sometimes naïve, and typically rebellious attitude.

The flirtation with death in Romanticism as well as in rock culture could be a sign of depression, but also of bored self-destructiveness. Coleridge was a drug addict; Byron went to war; Shelley—who could not swim—went sailing while it was known that dangerous weather was soon to come. Jones is a good example of rock culture's self-destructiveness,[52] whether it is motivated by boredom, hopelessness for the future, or rebellion against conventionalism. Nevertheless, being unafraid of death makes a cool impression. And Jagger—usually preferring a tougher image—uses these gentle Romantic words in order to refer to a flirtation with death. In this second cited stanza—the most famous lines of the elegy—Shelley focuses on both death *and* life. Life stains the white radiance of eternity, and so life penetrates indirectly and colorfully the eternal from within its safe dome, and vice versa: the eternal white light indirectly penetrates life. The world we live in sustains the illusion of unity in life. But eventually death destroys the dome and tramples it to fragments—like "dust" or "cold embers," the lifeless materials of stanza thirty-eight. In stanza fifty-two Shelley commands to "Die," stated as an imperative. If we want to be with what we seek, we have to die. Shelley puts an exclamation mark at the end of the sentence that emphasizes that everyone before us has died.

Everest signals that the idea of this stanza is in line with the ideas about the prophetic identity of the poet that Shelley expounds in *Defence of Poetry*: "a poet participates in the eternal, the infinite and the one."[53] Shelley opens this fifty-second stanza with "The One," and "According to Shelley, then, all poets participate in the One Spirit; they are 'mirrors of / The fire for which all thirst,'"[54] of which he speaks two stanzas later. With this reference to the fire, the inspiring burning fountain of stanza thirty-eight is back in mind again. "The One remains," so the One is immortal; therewith we meet the neoplatonic and mystical dimension of the poem, a dimension that gives shelter to Keats who participated during his life in the One—like all great poets, according to the *Defence*. In that way he abided even then in the domain of immortality, the domain of the eternal world. But by honoring Keats with this poem, Shelley takes care that in our mortal world the deceased Keats and his work will not be forgotten; he creates for Keats a lasting link to eternity, to make him really immortal.

The abstract concepts life, eternity, and death "end up entangled in one another; Life's staining is enrichment as well as disfigurement; Death's resolving of the tension between color and 'white radiance' is also a form of wanton, fragmentary destructiveness."[55] So, life has a positive and negative side coming together in death that is wanton and destructive, as did Brian Jones. His mysterious death might be a result of his characteristic drive, which was both wanton and destructive. Although he almost literally represented the white radiance with his fair hair, figuratively he personified the many-colored dome; he explored many challenges in music (many genres and many instruments), in drug use, and in relationships. This almost restless "colorfulness" was enriching as well as disfiguring his life and the course of his band.

The many-colored dome counts probably more for a poet than for any other being. Shelley calls the identity of a poet "camaeleonic" in his letter of the July 13, 1821, to John and Maria Gisborne with which he includes a copy of *Adonais*: "Poets, the best of them—are a very camaeleonic race: they take the colour not only of what they feed on, but of the very leaves under which they pass."[56] This idea of a chameleonic poet is in accordance with Keats's words three years earlier in his letter to Richard Woodhouse:

> What shocks the virtuous philosop[h]er, delights the camelion poet. It does no harm from its relish of the dark side of things any more than from its taste for the bright one; because they both end in speculation. A poet is the most unpoetical of anything in existence; because he has no Identity—he is continually in for–and filling, some other Body–The Sun, the Moon, the Sea and Men and Women. . . When I am in a room with People . . . the identity of every one in the room begins so to [for so] press upon me that, I am in a very little time an[ni]hilated.[57]

This Romantic idea of a poet seems to be applicable to Brian Jones: an artist who has no identity, is variable, and is not self-confident. Keats felt like an outsider in the circle of elite poets, which made him unsure about himself. Jones became an outsider in the Rolling Stones when Jagger, Richards, and manager Andrew Oldham stood more and more unified against him. Literary critique and the detective force had the same destabilizing effect on respectively Keats and Jones. This is a reason why both Shelley and rock and roll artists and fans denounced those oppressive forces, those representatives of the establishment. Nevertheless, the free spirits Jones and Keats were both in search for inspiration, open to the world, greedy for new experiences. Their identity, or rather "non-identity," as poet and musician made them unreliable in the sense that they were very dynamic and volatile—chameleons.

REVOLUTION AFTER THE READING

The next day there appeared a misunderstanding in a British newspaper. This anecdote is worthy of discussion here because it refers to a connection between late 1960s' rock engagement and Romanticism. Jagger had introduced the recital with the words: "I'm just going to say something that was written by Shelley." A reporter understood instead of "Shelley" "Che" from "Che Guevara," the most famous Cuban rebel of the 1960s.[58] Strange that those words of a nineteenth-century English poet were understood as the words of a contemporary Marxist revolutionary hero. What conclusions about the profile of Romanticism in the 1960s could be drawn from this confusion?

The Marxist revolutionary Guevara does certainly owe something to the Romantics. For, inspired by the French Revolution and triggered by the wrongs of the Industrial Revolution, many of them foreshadowed socialist and Marxist ideas. A pacifist support of the oppressed and a call for freedom and equality are characteristic of Shelley. He had an anti-dogmatic religious attitude and was follower and friend of philosopher William Godwin, who promoted philosophical anarchism. At the age of nineteen Shelley went to Ireland to support the religious and political freedom of the Catholic Irish. His political opinions get close to future Marxism and socialism, and many authors credit him with a socialist spirit.[59]

Although it seems farfetched to connect Guevara's Marxism to Shelley, the revolt against capitalism and the anti-bourgeois critique—also observed in rock culture—do certainly have Romantic roots, a point Löwy and Sayre elaborate throughout their book *Romanticism Against the Tide of Modernity* (2001). Some Romantics, such as Coleridge and Southey, developed the idea of a utopian communism that abolished private property.[60] And Lord Byron made, in the House of Lords, a stand for the condemned victims of the Industrial Revolution, who protested against the unemployment caused by machines taking over the production process. Some socially critical late Romantics directly influenced and inspired Marx and Engels. Löwy and Sayre even claim, "In reality, Romanticism is one of Marx's and Engels's neglected sources."[61] Thus, the reporter's misunderstanding reveals a common thread through history from the Romantic movement to twentieth-century politics. In the 1960s, politics played an important role in rock music and at music festivals at which the Vietnam war was severely condemned by audiences and artists, and where, soon after his death, Guevara could be spotted on t-shirts and flags as an anti-US icon. He became idolized in ways similar to Romantic poets and rock stars.

CONCLUSION

One can trace a tradition of revolution from Shelley to Guevara, and Jagger indirectly underlines it with his reading thanks to its misapprehension. In the Romantic era, revolutionary spirits wrote sophisticated texts, while in the 1960s, artists and crowds shouted louder. Nevertheless, concerning Romantic content not much changed—we see the same themes and attitudes a hundred and fifty years later. From a political and social level to a more personal level this essay discussed the following Romantic features returning in rock culture: radical political opinions related to socialist or Marxist views, anti-establishment and anti-bourgeois mentality, doubts about religious dogma, rebelliousness, flirtation with death, the glorification of young, deceased poets, self-destructiveness, mythologizing the artist, chameleonic character of artists, and an artistic companionship characterized by both rivalry and collegiality. These shared characteristics lead us to believe that a focus on rock music and its youth culture offers a way to study Romanticism and Romantic literature. At the same time, it reveals how Romanticism lives on, and how rock culture can be put in a historical perspective that goes all the way back to Romanticism.

Adonais's Romantic theme, "immortality," returns in Jagger's presentation, but perhaps the Romantics made themselves immortal. They criticized the old abusive and oppressive forms of government and religious systems and were the first generation to explore new, Romantic ways to deal with political and existential issues. The Romantic revolutionary spirit lives on among moderns, as proved by Jagger and the late 1960s' generation for whom the interpretation of Romantic issues still proved to be essential.

NOTES

1. Paul Trynka, *Brian Jones: The Making of the Rolling Stones* (New York: Viking, 2014), 314; Trynka goes on: "the chilling fact remains that the man who has often accused Brian Jones—the founder of the Rolling Stones, who gave Mick a job that would last for half a century—of being a self-centred, jealous type was upset because Brian's death threatened to overshadow his big media event."

2. Percy Bysshe Shelley, *The Letters of Percy Bysshe Shelley*, ed. Frederick L. Jones (Oxford: Clarendon, 1964), 2:221.

3. Shelley, *Letters*, 2:240.

4. In the preface to *Adonais*, Shelley praises *Hyperion* as follows: "I consider the fragment of 'Hyperion,' as second to nothing that was ever produced by a writer of the same years." Percy Bysshe Shelley, *The Works of P.B. Shelley* (Hertfordshire: Wordsworth Editions, 1994), 420.

5. Harold Bloom, *The Visionary Company. A Reading of English Romantic Poetry* (Ithaca, NY: Cornell University Press, 1971), 343. Not only Keats, but also Byron, Thomas Moore, Leigh Hunt, and Shelley himself are present in the poem, and "Once again, Shelley deliberately ignores the poets as men, and emphasizes only their symbolic aspects" (Bloom, *Visionary Company*, 345). O'Neill notes that Shelley addresses Adonais / Keats only twice in direct speech and points to the effects of the poor use of it: Shelley speaks to and about Keats as if it is a form of high courtesy, and it prepares "the reader for the transformation of the dead 'he' into the majestically alive 'he' in the final third of the poem." Michael O'Neill, "Shelley's Pronouns: Lyrics, Hellas, Adonais and The Triumph of Life," in *The Oxford Handbook of Percy Bysshe Shelley*, ed. Michael O'Neill, Anthony Howe, and Madeleine Callaghan (Oxford: Oxford University Press Online publication 2013), 5. Shelley himself remarks concerning *Adonais*, "The poet & the man are two different natures: though they exist together they may be unconscious of each other, & incapable of deciding on each other's power & efforts by any reflex act" (Shelley, *Letters*, 2:310).

6. Shelley, *Letters*, 2:293–294. Italics by Shelley.

7. Shelley, *Letters*, 2:296.

8. Kelvin Everest, "Shelley's *Adonais* and John Keats," *Essays in Criticism* 57, no. 3 (2007): 243.

9. Resp. by Earl R. Wasserman, *Shelley: a Critical Reading* (Baltimore: John Hopkins UP, 1971), 464–465; H.J. Jackson, "The 'Ai' in 'Adonais,'" *The Review of English Studies, New Series* 62, no. 257 (2011), 777–784; and Everest, "Shelley's *Adonais* and John Keats," 258.

10. Edwin B. Silverman, *Poetic Synthesis in Shelley's* Adonais (The Hague, Paris: Mouton, 1972). This book summarizes and criticizes *Adonais* research up to 1972 concerning model, structure, imagery, and the background of the poem's figures Urania and Adonais. It also defends its "organic unity."

11. Mark Sandy, *Poetics of Self and Form in Keats and Shelley. Nietzschean Subjectivity and Genre* (Aldershot: Ashgate, 2005), 94.

12. Shelley, *Works*, 421.

13. Sandy, *Poetics of Self and Form in Keats and Shelley*, 98.

14. Everest, "Shelley's *Adonais* and John Keats," 249. A few pages earlier (239) Everest put it differently: Shelley is convinced Keats deserved a place in the canon of English poetry, and his "permanent presence within that tradition is partly dependent on the success of Shelley's own poem in establishing his subject's claim to be so regarded, and that success in turn offers a guarantee of Shelley's own status."

15. O'Neill, "Shelley's Pronouns," 4.

16. Andrew Bennett, *Romantic Poets and the Culture of Posterity* (Cambridge: Cambridge University Press, 2004), 249.

17. Bennett, *Romantic Poets and the Culture of Posterity*, 152, 153, and 249.

18. Sandy, *Poetics of Self and Form in Keats and Shelley*, 98.

19. Ibid., 96.

20. Arnold Heumakers, "Nawoord," in *Keats en Shelley. Gedichten 1820*, vertaling en aantekeningen Jan Kuijper (Amsterdam: Athenaeum, Polak & Van Gennep, 2014), 259.

21. Shelley, *Letters*, 2:355; in a letter of September, 25th, 1821, to his publisher.

22. Trynka, *Brian Jones*, 89 and 176.

23. See the above-mentioned letter to Marianne Hunt in which Shelley calls Keats a "rival."

24. Everest, "Shelley's *Adonais* and John Keats," 249.

25. Although the official verdict sounds: "Death by misadventure," there are many scenarios of possible murder, see, for example, Trynka, *Brian Jones*, from page 323 (*Coda*).

26. Silverman, *Poetic Synthesis in Shelley's* Adonais, 15–16; Everest, "Shelley's *Adonais* and John Keats," 237–239; Theocritus et al., *Theocritus. Moschus. Bion*, ed. and trans. Neil Hopkinson (Cambridge, Massachusetts/London: Harvard University Press, 2015), 504–517 and 467–481.

27. Ibid., 26–45 and 94–95. For the poems see resp.: Edmund Spenser, *Complete Works of Edmund Spenser*, ed. Richard Morris (London: Macmillan, 1886) 559–561; John Milton, *The Complete Poems of John Milton*, ed. Charles W. Eliot (New York: Collier, 1909), 74–79.

28. English poet, 1552–1599, invented the Spenserian stanza: a stanzaic form used in his *The Faerie Queene*. In England "for the Romantics, Spencer was the poet's poet, a poet of dreams, beauty and sensuous appeal." Ian Ousby ed., *The Wordsworth Companion to Literature in English* (Hertfordshire: Wordsworth Editions Ltd, 1994), 880–881.

29. In a Platonist view Aphrodite Urania symbolizes heavenly love, while Aphrodite Pandemia symbolizes earthly love. In Plato's *Symposium* Uranian love is related to music and poetry, virtuosity, and inspiration. Therefore Urania is the perfect image for Shelley to link Greek mythology to his own created myth about the English poetic tradition in the first part of *Adonais*, while in the second part this muse can become the personification of a more abstract image of human creativity, and through its creations, of immortality.

30. With the underlying idea, *"Adonais* transforms one specific historical occurrence [Keats's death] into a universal mythology to empower a deceased Keats at the expense of Shelley's own poetic powers" (Sandy, *Poetics of Self and Form in Keats and Shelley*, 107).

31. Silverman, *Poetic Synthesis in Shelley's* Adonais, 47: "To begin with, the ascension of the poet speaker in *Adonais* may be illuminated by the stages of cognition in *The Republic*, the related Platonic ladder of love in the *Symposium*, and the Neoplatonic modification as it appears in Spencer's *Fowre Hymnes*, as well as by Shelley's *Prometheus Unbound*."

32. Silverman, *Poetic Synthesis in Shelley's* Adonais, 48.

33. Shelley, *Works*, 427–428.

34. Bloom, *Visionary Company*, 346.

35. Ibid.

36. Percy Bysshe Shelley, "Essay on Christianity," in *The Necessity of Atheism and Other Essays* (New York: Prometheus Books, 1993), 10.

37. Shelley, "Essay on Christianity," 11.

38. Bloom, *Visionary Company*, 349.

39. Which finds its reference in the literary tradition in Shakespeare's *Hamlet*; see Stuart Peterfreund, "The Color Violaceous, or, Chemistry and the Romance of Dematerialization: The Subliming of Iodine and Shelley's *Adonais*," *Studies in Romanticism* 42, no. 1 (2003): 52. According to Sandy it is even a *central claim* in the elegy that Adonais "hath awakened from the dream of life." He recognizes that Shelley's "metaphysical speculations about an afterlife has led him into his own rhetorical trap. Shelley is compelled, through his own symbolic argumentation, to deny life in favour of a transcendental haven for Adonais" (Sandy, *Poetics of Self and Form in Keats and Shelley*, 104, 105).

40. Shelley, "Essay on Christianity," 10: "awaken from the sleep of life."

41. *The Stones in the Park*, dir. Leslie Woodhead and Jo Durden-Smith, 56 min., Granada Ventures, 2006, DVD. Quotes from Jagger are from this documentary.

42. In the third hymn of *Hymnen and die Nacht* he describes it poetically; see Novalis, *Werke, Tagebücher und Briefe Friedrich von Hardenbergs*, hrsg. Hans-Joachim Mähl und Richard Samuel (München/Wien: Carl Hanser Verlag, 1978), 1:153–155.

43. For Romantic longing for life after death, see, for example, Ted Underwood, "Romantic Historicism and the Afterlife," *PMLA* 117, no. 2 (March, 2002): 237–251.

44. Shelley, *Works*, 430.

45. Silverman, *Poetic Synthesis in Shelley's* Adonais, 62.

46. Shelley, *Works*, 430.

47. Bloom, *Visionary Company*, 348.

48. Sandy, *Poetics of Self and Form in Keats and Shelley*, 106.

49. Shelley, *Works*, 429.

50. Townshend, Peter. "My Generation," in *My Generation*, Brunswick LAT 8616, 1965, 33 1/3.

51. Peter Wicke, *Rock Music: Culture, Aesthetics and Sociology* (Cambridge: Cambridge University Press, 1990), 85: die young "was the one possibility of escaping from the clutch of bourgeois ideology."

52. Jones is the first "member" of the 27 Club: artists who died at the age of 27, many of them by self-destructive behavior. The first one is (retrospectively) Robert Johnson (1911–1938), the blues guitarist who was Jones's most important source of inspiration. See, for example, Howard Sounes, *27: A History of the 27 Club Through the Lives of Brian Jones, Jimi*

Hendrix, Janis Joplin, Jim Morrison, Kurt Cobain, and Amy Winehouse (Boston, MA: Da Capo Press, 2013).
53. Everest, "Shelley's *Adonais* and John Keats," 257.
54. Silverman, *Poetic Synthesis in Shelley's* Adonais, 63.
55. O'Neill, "Shelley's Pronouns," 7.
56. Shelley, *Letters*, 2:308.
57. John Keats, *Letters of John Keats*, ed. Robert Gittings (Oxford: Oxford University Press, 1987), 157, 158.
58. Richard Holmes, "'He Doth Not Sleep,'" *The New York Review of Books* 39, no. 15 (September 1992): 19.
59. Paul Foot, *Red Shelley*, (London: Sidgwick & Jackson, 1980); Michael Löwy and Robert Sayre, *Romanticism Against the Tide of Modernity* (Durham/London: Duke University Press, 2001), 76: Edward and Eleanor Marx Aveling represented Shelley in 1888 as a socialist in the brochure *Shelley's Socialism*.
60. Löwy and Sayre, *Romanticism Against the Tide of Modernity*, 117, 118.
61. Ibid., 90.

BIBLIOGRAPHY

Aveling, Edward and Eleanor Marx Aveling. *Shelley's Socialism*, New Edition. Newburyport, MA: The Journeyman Press, 1975.
Bennett, Andrew. *Romantic Poets and the Culture of Posterity*. Cambridge: Cambridge University Press, 2004.
Bloom, Harold. *The Visionary Company. A Reading of English Romantic Poetry*. Ithaca, NY: Cornell University Press, 1971.
Everest, Kelvin. "Shelley's *Adonais* and John Keats." *Essays in Criticism* 57, no. 3 (2007): 237–264.
Foot, Paul. *Red Shelley*. London: Sidgwick & Jackson, 1980.
Gittings, Robert. *John Keats*. London: Penguin Books, 2001.
Heumakers, Arnold. "Nawoord." In *Keats en Shelley. Gedichten 1820*, vertaling en aantekeningen Jan Kuijper, 255–259. Amsterdam: Athenaeu–Polak & Van Gennep, 2014.
Holmes, Richard. "'He Doth Not Sleep.'" *The New York Review of Books* 39, no. 15 (September 1992): 19–24.
Jackson, H.J. "The 'Ai' in 'Adonais.'" *The Review of English Studies, New Series 62*, no. 257 (2011): 777–784.
Keats, John. *Letters of John Keats*. Edited by Robert Gittings. Oxford: Oxford University Press, 1987.
Löwy, Michael, and Robert Sayre. *Romanticism Against the Tide of Modernity*. Durham/London: Duke University Press, 2001.
"Mick Jagger Pays Poetic Tribute to Brian Jones." *The Observer Archive*, July, 6, 1969. http://www.theguardian.com/news/2014/jul/06/mick-jagger-brian-jones-hyde-park-observer-archive.
Milton, John. *The Complete Poems of John Milton*. Edited by Charles W. Eliot. New York: Collier, 1909.
Novalis. *Werke, Tagebücher und Briefe Friedrich von Hardenbergs*. Vol. 1 Herausgegeben von Hans-Joachim Mähl und Richard Samuel. München/Wien: Carl Hanser Verlag, 1978.
O'Neill, Michael. "Shelley's Pronouns: Lyrics, Hellas, Adonais and The Triumph of Life." In *The Oxford Handbook of Percy Bysshe Shelley*, edited by Michael O'Neill, Anthony Howe, and Madeleine Callaghan, 1–13. Oxford: Oxford University Press Online publication, 2013.
Ousby, Ian, ed. *The Wordsworth Companion to Literature in English*. Hertfordshire, UK: Wordsworth Editions Ltd, 1994.
Peterfreund, Stuart. "The Color Violaceous, or, Chemistry and the Romance of Dematerialization: The Subliming of Iodine and Shelley's *Adonais*." *Studies in Romanticism* 42, no. 1 (2003): 45–54.

Sandy, Mark. *Poetics of Self and Form in Keats and Shelley. Nietzschean Subjectivity and Genre*. Aldershot: Ashgate, 2005.

Shelley, Percy Bysshe. *The Letters of Percy Bysshe Shelley*. Vol. 2. Edited by Frederick L. Jones. Oxford: Clarendon, 1964.

———. "Essay on Christianity." In *The Necessity of Atheism and Other Essays*, 1–30. New York: Prometheus Books, 1993.

———. *The Works of P.B. Shelley*. Hertfordshire, UK: Wordsworth Editions, 1994.

Silverman, Edwin B. *Poetic Synthesis in Shelley's Adonais*. The Hague, Paris: Mouton, 1972.

Sounes, Howard. *27: A History of the 27 Club through the Lives of Brian Jones, Jimi Hendrix, Janis Joplin, Jim Morrison, Kurt Cobain, and Amy Winehouse*. Boston, MA: Da Capo Press, 2013.

Spenser, Edmund. *Complete Works of Edmund Spenser*. Edited by Richard Morris. London: Macmillan, 1886.

Stones in the Park, The. 1969. Directed by Leslie Woodhead and Jo Durden-Smith. 56 min. Granada Ventures, 2006. DVD.

Theocritus et al. *Theocritus. Moschus. Bion*. Edited and translated by Neil Hopkinson. Cambridge, Massachusetts/London: Harvard University Press, 2015.

Townshend, Peter. "My Generation." In *My Generation*, Brunswick LAT 8616, 1965, 33 1/3.

Trynka, Paul. *Brian Jones: The Making of the Rolling Stones*. New York: Viking, 2014.

Underwood, Ted. "Romantic Historicism and the Afterlife. "*PMLA* 117, no. 2 (March, 2002): 237–251.

Wasserman Earl R. *Shelley: A Critical Reading*. Baltimore: John Hopkins UP, 1971.

Wicke, Peter. *Rock Music: Culture, Aesthetics and Sociology*. Cambridge: Cambridge University Press, 1990.

Wordsworth, William, and Samuel Taylor Coleridge. *Lyrical Ballads*. Edited by R.L. Brett and A.R. Jones. London: Routledge, 1996.

Chapter Three

William Blake

The Romantic Alternative

Douglas T. Root

In 1798, the same year that the watershed Romantic work *Lyrical Ballads* was penned, renowned artist Joshua Reynolds's *Works* were published. William Blake owned a copy and annotated the work, as was his habit, confuting Reynolds at one point by noting: "To Generalize is to be an Idiot. To Particularize is the Alone Distinction of Merit. General Knowledges are those Knowledges that Idiots possess."[1] Clearly, Blake believed that *anyone* was capable of putting simple thoughts down in writing, and in *Milton* (1804) Blake cautions readers about the "idiot reasoner [who] laughs at the man of imagination."[2] Indeed, many poets of his day, specifically Wordsworth, Coleridge, and Lamb, "found Blake maddening and called him mad [and] doubted whether his language, however like theirs, was the same as theirs,"[3] implying what they believed to be some degree of linguistic inferiority or distance. Blake was uncompromising in his "madness" and refused to change his style or attitude to accommodate popular sentiment.

The inherent difficulty in labeling Blake may have been an intentional construct on his part, for

> The Blake who reveals himself in his more personal writings is an obstinate, even pig-headed individual who is not afraid to reject traditional concepts if he can find no validity in them, or to distort themes of the perennial philosophy if that is the only way of bringing them into line with his own vision.[4]

In fact, just a year after *Lyrical Ballads* was published, Blake declared, "that which can be made explicit to the idiot is not worth my care."[5] One might surmise, then, that Blake's (what I call) *macabre Romanticism* was never

35

intended to attract a mass audience, but a progressive one that could appreciate how rapidly the world around them was disintegrating.[6] To Blake, the true idiots were those who simply bore the shackles of tradition because it was easier than thinking for themselves. Saree Makdisi contends that to truly understand Blake's work would involve "unlearning" whatever it is that supposedly makes one "learned."[7]

In what may seem an odd comparison, post-punk/grunge rockers of the late 1980s and early 1990s possessed a similar recalcitrance in the face of what was popular or had simply come to be accepted by the mainstream. For instance, Jane's Addiction front-man Perry Farrell's pseudonym (*peri-pheral*) evidences the feeling that many "alternative" artists had about the position they occupied on the fringe of the musical spectrum. In a 1989 interview, Farrell referred to his lyrics in a way that echoes how Blake's contemporaries saw his odd verse, admitting: "I don't feel a part of everything. I feel like I'm speaking a foreign language."[8] Music aficionado Chris Norris believes Nirvana's music "*feels* very strange,"[9] and for many post-punk era musicians, this was a common reaction. It was not just their mode of expression that made them feel alienated; their frustration with the excessive nature of rock music as it had been historically positioned only fueled their resentment of being viewed as "rockers."

Steve Albini, the lead singer of Chicago punk band Big Black, succinctly explains the bohemian, yet ironically fundamentalist ideology of the alternative movement by comparing its more austere view of showmanship with that of its "traditional" rock predecessors:

> I was looking forward to playing with Green River because I was into a cassette of theirs I'd gotten. But they were acting like fucking rock stars. They were kind of petulant . . . everyone I had grown up admiring in the punk scene thought of all that rock-star behavior as stupid and offensive. I don't know how to describe it, except maybe like going to a vegetarian restaurant and seeing them slaughtering hogs in the lobby.[10]

Grunge rockers were, like Blake, proactively dissociating themselves from many established artists of the past.[11] As far as style is concerned, the unpretentious and gritty trademark features of prototypical grunge music and its accompanying lifestyle are in some ways reminiscent of how we might imagine Blake sounding (and living), for Blake's voice and aura was described as "low and musical, his manners gentle and unassuming," adding that, "he had never tasted the luxury of that independence which comes from personal profit."[12] While never widely read during his own lifetime, and far from a commercial success with his engravings, Blake was a copious letter-writer; however, from 1809 to 1815 there are no recorded epistles from his pen. Apparently depressed and downtrodden over his diminishing career prospects and accompanying penury, he intentionally distanced himself from friends and acquaintances.[13] As early as 1800, though, Blake indicates in a letter to his friend George Cumberland that he has not been of sound mind for quite some time and cannot explain his lapses (or relapses) into despair: "I begin to emerge from a deep pit of melancholy, melancholy without any real reason for it, a disease which God keep you from & all good men."[14]

Even a cursory reading of any Blake biography reveals a man who, while probably not quite a misanthrope, was certainly prone to brooding—the "artistic temperament" as some may call it. Nirvana lead singer Kurt Cobain had a similarly acerbic air, though perhaps in a bit more bipolar sense, for his "ability to switch at lightning speed from hopefulness to cynicism was one of the quirks of his artistic personality."[15] In his own suicide note, Cobain—like Blake—invokes God in his rationale, confessing:

> The worst crime I can think of would be to rip people off by faking it and pretending as if I'm having 100% fun. Sometimes I feel as if I should have a punch-in time clock before I walk out on stage. I've tried everything within my power to appreciate it (and I do, God, believe me I do, but it's not enough).[16]

I believe that Max Byrd articulates an intricate, internalized conflict that Blake may have experienced simply by being a poet in England at the time, for modern readers "tend to class [Blake] with a later generation of Romantic poets and to neglect his inevitable affinities with the midcentury world, the Age of Johnson, in which he was reared. But the affinities are clear and firm and unmistakable."[17] Quite literally, then, it seems as if Blake was stuck in the middle: on one side, the Age of Ideas; on the other, a burgeoning movement that would become known as Romanticism. Blake certainly was not foolishly clinging to the past, but it also seems evident that he did not view Romanticism as the wave of the future, either. David Simpson (2003) believes that, in as far as the Romantic movement was concerned, "the relative marginality of Blake to the 'official' critical establishment was part of his appeal to the counterculture" and that this could "simply be one more instance of criticism's demonstration of the prickly relationship between Blake and its constructions of romanticism."[18]

"WHICH CAME FIRST—THE MUSIC OR THE MISERY?"[19]

Simpson's idea reiterates the influential theory forwarded by Raymond Williams (1977) known as the "structure of feeling." Williams notes that often an artistic movement is not acknowledged as such while it is actually occurring because both participants *and* observers are unable to objectively distance themselves far enough from it to classify it.[20] Romanticism, as a genre, was likely not given that designation in England until over two decades after its watershed work, *Lyrical Ballads*, was published. Thomas

Pfau, addressing the historicist critique of Romanticism, similarly observes that "the period's subtle, figural idioms were fundamentally aimed at *aestheticizing* the period's political, gendered, and economic antagonisms, thereby effectively preempting any possible consciousness *of* these antagonisms."[21] I would argue that Blake's philosophy does not coincide with such ideology; he would not have believed that these "antagonisms" were obfuscated, but that people were too steeped in tradition to see them *or* they were simply too *idiotic* to do so.

Dave Laing, specifically referencing members of the punk subculture, believes that they would likewise have viewed an idiot as a dilettante with no esoteric knowledge of a particular art or the subculture that reveres it:

> While the subculture (or more precisely its interpreters) may pride itself on its ability to subvert dominant or established meanings, a listener to a manifestly punk song may be able to miss the point, and avoid reacting either as a punk initiate or as a shocked adherent of dominant social values. (1985: 56)[22]

However, record companies viewed such "idiots" as a perfect customer-base, as the poetaster is likely to have much lower standards about what constitutes "crossing over" or "selling-out." Laing continues:

> Those individuals with high cultural capital are likely to be well educated and to share tastes in classical art, while those with low cultural capital are mostly uneducated consumers of popular culture. By the same measure, individuals possess different levels of economic capital but there is no certain correspondence between their material wealth and their wealth of cultural resources.[23]

Although possessing little by way of economic capital, it seems indisputable that Blake maintained a wealth of cultural capital. As a result, he may well have believed that many poets of the era were simply employing bombast in their depictions of the rural and pastoral, perhaps even to the point of pandering to idiots who had no appreciation for, or concept of, true art. On more than one occasion Blake reproached Wordsworth for his idolatry of nature, suggesting that it was akin to atheism.[24] Thus, if we are to consider Blake and Wordsworth both "card-carrying members" of the Romantic movement, then it becomes obvious that issues of legitimacy and consistency have likely always been embedded in all artistic genres. The same can be said about grunge music when it became mainstream, because the

> ideological opposition between art and commerce that alternative culture inherited from bohemia, *romanticism*, and modernism collapsed in this new age of capitalism where markets absorb new trends faster than ever before and the consumer culture thrives on expressions of difference, novelty, and authenticity.[25]

During one of his more profitable periods, Blake concluded that he could mass-produce "illuminated manuscripts" instead of customizing them for individual buyers, though, as G. E. Bentley, Jr. notes, Blake's "mass" print-run for an illuminated manuscript was typically less than a dozen.[26] Jane Stabler furthers the idea that mass-production in our modern world has all but eliminated the sort of free-thinking that someone like Blake championed, for "free from the coercive pressures of McDonald's, Microsoft and the Murdoch empire the intellectual climate of the 1790s in England was extraordinarily diverse."[27]

Much like Blake's rather underwhelming printing endeavor, the first major label that really pushed the post-punk/alternative/grunge sound, Sub Pop Records (founded in Seattle in 1986), started out rather inauspiciously. Co-founder Bruce Pavitt conceived a number of ways to truly prostitute the working class, not only as potential consumers, but as his very own clients. One of Pavitt's earliest strategies was to fly in a British music journalist to watch several Seattle-based bands; when the journalist subsequently returned to England he raved about the bands.

> In ways that played on British stereotypes about working-class American "rednecks," . . . Sub Pop's fabrication of backwoods authenticity was also applied to their dealings with Nirvana, as Pavitt once explained that he saw them as "the whole real genuine work class—I hate to use the phrase "white trash"— something not contrived that had a more grassroots or populist feel.[28]

Essentially equalizing the working-class to "white trash" (or, as described earlier, those with limited cultural *or* economic capital)—the very people who in all likelihood would be purchasing albums by groups on a label like Sub Pop—hardly seems like a shrewd business model. However, Craig Schuftan attests to its effectiveness: "Nirvana, to some extent, revived the UK music press's hopes of finding rock's noble savage in the forests of the American Northwest."[29] Though antedating the Romantics by several decades, Jean-Jacques Rousseau influenced many of them heavily, and he would almost certainly aver that there was nothing more Romantic than the concept of the noble savage which Sub Pop sought to engender by shrewdly marketing groups like Nirvana and TAD as "everymen." The label actually went so far as to dub TAD's lead singer as "The Butcher from Idaho," posing him in a promotional picture with a chainsaw. In actuality he was a music student at the University of Idaho who had never used a chainsaw in his life.[30] Like TAD, who viewed themselves as charlatans for impersonating woodsmen in order to uphold their status as grunge rockers, Blake had little regard for the noble savage or the cult of natural man—beliefs commonly embraced by the Romantics. In fact, Blake would have further distanced himself from many of the Romantics by attacking Rousseau in *Jerusalem*,[31] branding him a hypocrite who claimed to believe in the goodness of natural man, yet he did not have a single friend.

The cultural values of grunge, then, were clearly steeped in a blue-collar ethic. Possibly more surprising, however, is that Romanticism's mores were also closely entwined with the organized movement of the working class.[32] Perhaps no poem better exemplifies this relationship than Wordsworth's "Simon Lee, The Old Huntsman" (1798). The narrator describes an old man unsuccessfully hacking away at a tree root. While to many, Lee's stubborn perseverance might be pathetic or futile, the eyewitness (presumably Wordsworth himself) nevertheless finds beauty in his simplicity and meekness. Before finally taking the ax from the old man and splitting the root for him, the narrator essentially tells readers that the greatness of Simon Lee's story is that it is not actually much of a story at all; it is, instead, the omnipresent cycle of life, and anyone who is willing to look around can see it for himself (lines 73–76). It is intriguing, though, that Simon Lee actually becomes less a passive object and instead becomes one whose failed attempts at self-reliance are romanticized. While there is a certain understated beauty or dignity to the old man's fruitless toil, there is also the narrator's somewhat paradoxical self-satisfaction in completing the task *for* the elderly man.

Comparatively speaking, post-punk's way of infiltrating popular culture was exceedingly Romantic (not just Blakean), as musicians uninterested in achieving commercial success were sometimes called *slackers.* While the term normally carries a negative connotation, it took on an element of pride within the punk community: "Slacking is a way of life that developed out of DIY [Do-It-Yourself] punk's refusal of wage labor and careerism, not for the sake of laziness but in favor of cultural production and control over creative work."[33] I think we can envision the narrator of "Simon Lee" as a Rousseauian man in the midst of a reverie. He is likely not a man of any particular occupation or with any rigid schedule which would preclude him from stopping to help an octogenarian in a bind; regardless, the DIY exploits of both the aged huntsman and the narrator are ultimately exalted. Of course, Blake occupied a slightly different position in the sense that his endeavors were artistic in nature as opposed to physically rigorous, but 200 years later his aforementioned recalcitrance may well have earned him the *respectable* title of "slacker" as members of the punk subculture—*not idiots*—would have used the term.

Blake was, on a firsthand level, involved in *creating* both his poetry and his engravings in the sense that they were his own unique intellectual property; but moreover, he possessed the ability to *produce* (and *reproduce*) that property without requiring the assistance of outside publishers or printers, at least later in his career. At one point, Blake actually lamented that he had not simply dedicated his energies to printing all along, as he believed it would have afforded him more financial security[34] —once again evidence that separating artistic (re)production from capitalist/consumer culture is a Herculean task. However, his oft-intriguing duality shows that there was still at least a part of Blake that viewed mechanical reproduction as beneficial, not because he profited from it monetarily, but because it gave his works a sense of permanency: "Reengraved Time after Time [,] / Ever in their Youthful prime / My Designs unchanged remain."[35] He was gratified that his engravings, for better or worse, would maintain his legacy, and Frye adds that "it is pathetic [to see] how wistful is the feeling that he must depend on posterity for appreciation."[36]

Therefore, while his motivations seem to have been far from grandiose in financial scope, Blake's ability to "cut out the middle man" must have, at the bare minimum, given the contentious poet and engraver an element of smug self-satisfaction. After all, many readers probably do not put much thought into the literal production of the tangible product they hold in their hands in either economic or epistemological terms. Blake, however, aimed to elaborate upon the metaphor in an engraving that featured

> A Printing house in Hell . . . to show the way that knowledge is transmitted from generation to generation . . . one purpose of the description is to contrast the common idea of making a book (the mental labour, the intricate technical processes) with the inward process involved. The true end of printing is that infinite energy shall be transferred from the artist to the apprehension of his fellow human beings, who otherwise lie imprisoned in the cavern of their five senses.[37]

It seems as if Blake viewed his own work in much the same light that the great lexicographer Samuel Johnson viewed his own: that of drudgery, regardless of the exacting detail such employments demanded.[38] Moreover, Stabler contends that having been steeped in the engraving/copying trade since age fifteen only exacerbated Blake's contempt for the industry, and that his experiences "must have fueled his hatred of servitude and sharpened his desire to make things anew" as opposed to doing mere copy-work.[39] Walter Benjamin, writing from a Marxist position, describes a fundamental problem with the mass reproduction of art:

> The technique of reproduction detaches the reproduced object from the domain of tradition. By making many reproductions it substitutes a plurality of copies for a unique existence. And in permitting the reproduction to meet the beholder or listener in his own particular situation, it reactivates the object reproduced.[40]

More than one grunge performer took umbrage with the idea of being made to reproduce his or her creative work ad nauseum at the behest of record labels and fans alike. Consumers, justifiably, expect to hear their favorite songs recapitulated *exactly* as they have heard them on the radio or on the CD they purchased. In the digital age, record companies more than ever before expected *and demanded* that their property (clients) be able to reproduce nearly flawless renditions of their songs on command. As a result, many artists felt that their creativity was being stifled in favor of commercialism. "This wasn't the non-service industry anymore. It wasn't even the we'll-serve-you-when-we-feel-like-it industry of indie-rock" in which so many up-and-coming grunge bands had been steeped; instead, this was "the actual service industry, where markets had to be serviced, and the goods delivered exactly as advertised."[41] The music had become so homogenized that it was like buying a Big Mac, for when people buy Big Macs, they expect two all-beef patties, special sauce, pickles, and onions on a sesame-seed bun *every* time.

"DRIVE YOUR CART AND PLOUGH OVER THE BONES OF THE DEAD": BREAKING WITH TRADITION

We might conclude that even in the late twentieth-century United States there was a similar aesthetic appeal to the Protestant work ethic of a bygone era, for "the hardcore kids' scene was founded upon a 'do-it-yourself-or-have-nothing' cultural practice ethic. The movement took root in bleak, decaying suburbs and urban sectors where disaffected kids resisted boredom by dissenting with purpose."[42] A "bleak and decaying" environment spurned by an Industrial Revolution left much of England in a similar state, and it seems, evoked a similar response from the avant-garde that sought to capitalize on emphasizing the beauty of nature in a world that was placing an increased value on anything but—or in Blake's case, decry the urban blight that induced child labor and elevated pollution to never before seen levels. Blake's individuality was readily apparent in a world where many Englishmen believed that industrialism actually *added* something to England's rural landscape.[43] Even though the Thames River depicted by Blake in "London" is the same one that is "celebrated" by Defoe and so many other English authors, Blake defiles it, making it feel odious and even tawdry.[44]

In this light Blake may be seen *not* so much as a nascent "tree-hugger" but more of a whistle-blower, drawing attention to problems that many would have been content to ignore or to which they had simply become desensitized; simultaneously he depicted those disenfranchised members of society who had no voice. And, by the time he reached the last decade of his life, Blake's public outcries had actually earned him a cult of personality—almost as if he were a primordial rock star. In 1818, he inherited "a tiny but expanding circle of young admirers who called themselves, in mockery of their extreme youth, 'The Ancients'. . . they found in Blake a serenity and an inspiration which transformed their lives."[45] I think one can easily envision a humorously parallel scene as painted by Roger Beebe, who asserts that mourners of Kurt Cobain "will be represented as an image of a group of friends on their thrift-store couch across from an illuminated cathode-ray tube momentarily breaking off conversation and cranking up the volume when the video for 'Smells Like Teen Spirit' comes on."[46]

Ultimately, then, grunge rockers of the late 1980s and early 1990s, I believe, can (like Blake) be viewed as criticizing the existing social reality from a progressive perspective.[47] "Progressive" in this circumstance may not necessarily mean socially liberating or politically correct; instead, many artists accepted a completely new role of representing the downtrodden. Kurt Cobain and Eddie Vedder of Pearl Jam were two such artists who reluctantly symbolized the "twentynothing" generation, embodying "alienation, cynicism, and [a] prevailing sense that things aren't what they seem."[48] Indeed, Pearl Jam's "Jeremy" is a morose track about a neglected teenage boy who seemingly anticipates the frustrations of many adolescent males, particularly those who perpetrated events like Columbine or the Virginia Tech Massacre. Vedder's trademark deep baritone voice describes the young man, Jeremy, drawing pictures where "the dead lay in pools of maroon." The verse culminates with the most important aspect of his change in behavior, however, as the regularly muted Jeremy "spoke in class today."[49] Seung-Hui Cho, the Virginia Tech gunman, refused to speak in class when called upon, and wrote violent plays, including one where a high school student wishes she could watch her teacher "bleed the way he made us kids bleed."[50] Cho's refusal to speak, in addition to his violent artistic expression, echoes Jeremy's conduct, thereby demonstrating a fundamental *need* to express oneself despite lacking the ability to do it publicly, only adding to the shock when he "spoke in class today." The young man was described by one of his teachers as "extraordinarily lonely—the loneliest person I have ever met in my life."[51] Northrop Frye describes Blake facing a similar quandary, albeit in an entirely different time, for Blake's "spiritual loneliness" was more a byproduct of "his age" than him as an individual.[52] It seems quite likely that there are numerous parallels between the alienation created by Blake's rapidly industrializing world and the dissociative effect that our technologically overwhelming and oversaturated society has engendered in us.

Forms of written and verbal expression are no different; times and nuances admittedly change, but the changes are not necessarily drastic in nature, either. Raymond Williams contends that "in spite of the substantial and at some levels decisive continuities in grammar and vocabulary, no generation speaks quite the same language as its predecessors."[53] Lamb, Wordsworth, and Coleridge may have viewed Blake as a bizarre, curmudgeonly predecessor when expressing frustration with his "language." As previously noted, Blake was in a sense revolutionary—a rebel-poet who sought to separate himself from the Age of Reason; simultaneously, though, he seems to have realized that his sensibilities did not really mesh with the major poetic movement of his lifetime, Romanticism. Nevertheless, I believe that both the Romantic (*with* or *without* Blake) and grunge movements were fueled by a desire to break away from the popular works that preceded them, even if as Ecclesiastes says, "There is no new thing under the sun."[54]

The following Cobain journal entry exhibits angst, dark humor, and a general frustration with the music (and by extension, the attitude) that was popular among Baby Boomers. In referring to Nirvana drummer's Chris Novolesic's album collection, the deceased Nirvana front man opines:

> I searched thru [sic] the rest of the row and found Eagles, Carpenters, Yes, Joni Mitchell and said with frustration, "What in the FUCK do you own these for?" And so throughout the night we busted about 250 shitty Chris Novoselic records. Not only did we clear more space in the living room but Chris declared that he feels cleansed and revitalized.[55]

Through physical destruction, in this instance, apparently comes catharsis.

Though much less humorous in his appraisal of past writers than Cobain, Blake takes issue with the rational and scientific approach of many of England's past "great" writers, noting that their logic did not coincide with his creative tendencies, and in fact, being made to read them nearly quashed his imaginative vision:

> I read [Edmund] Burkes Treatise when very young [;] at the same time I read Locke on Human Understanding and Bacons Advance[*ment*] of Learning [;] on every one of thse books I wrote my opinions . . . [*of*] contempt & abhorrence. . . They mock Inspiration & Vision[.] Inspiration & Vision was then & now is & I hope will always remain my element [,] my eternal dwelling place.[56]

It is hard to imagine that Blake, a publisher in his own right, would enjoy destroying books in the same fashion that Cobain and Novoselic did records. Blake was, however, notorious for annotating (in a sense, a primitive form of musicians making liner notes) the books he owned; so, in a manner of speaking, he did participate in defacing mass-produced goods.

Among his many occupations, Blake also spent time as a teacher and was even offered the opportunity to teach drawing to the Royal Family. He declined the invitation, believing that to do so would run counter to the simplicity of both his works and his life.[57] Walt Whitman, an American Romantic of the mid-1800s, ironically wrote, "He most honors my style who learns under it to destroy the teacher."[58] In one of his journal entries, Cobain writes, sounding ever so Whitman-like:

I like to complain and do nothing to make things better. I like to blame my parents' generation for coming so close to social change then giving up after a few successful efforts . . . I like to infiltrate the mechanics of a system by posing as one of them then slowly start the rot from the inside of the empire.[59]

Blake chose to circumvent the system altogether while Cobain describes destroying it from within. Regardless of this difference in philosophy, the similarity in attitudes between Blake and Cobain in distancing themselves from "history" is evident. Cobain's attitude seems to encapsulate punk ideology perfectly, for as Ryan Moore forwards, "The emergence of punk has been seen as a response to the demise of rock and the failure of Sixties utopianism."[60] Meanwhile, one of Blake's crown jewels, *Jerusalem* (1804), is widely considered Blake's scathing response to what the traditional view of a nineteenth-century utopian England would have been.[61] Pfau argues that Blakean prophecy "seems intent on recovering an as yet unrealized, imaginative past from the one that had usurped its place and that had gradually reproduced itself through the oppressive psycho-political institutions of memory, morality, and state-sponsored art."[62] Perhaps Blake was a Marxist before Marx himself.

Blake's "fundamental revision of history"[63] anticipates that of a disillusioned Kurt Cobain, whose own writing reveals a somewhat vicious, albeit ironic, cycle: he has convinced himself that the failures of the previous generation provide him carte-blanche not only to criticize *them*, but also to complain about contemporary issues plaguing his *own generation* as a result. After all, if the socially conscious protesters of the 1960s accomplished nothing, surely no one would expect the apathetic Generation X to make an impression of any import on the world (Cobain included). "Heart-Shaped Box" can be construed as a direct response to those targeted in his journal, as Cobain drones, "Hate! Haight! / I've got a new complaint / Forever in debt to your priceless advice!"[64] Blake had a similar response for his predecessors—specifically Sir Joshua Reynolds and other members of the Royal Academy, whom he believed hamstrung him in his early efforts to make a living as a creator—regretting that he had "spent the vigour of my youth & Genius under the Opression of Sir Joshua & his gang of cunning hired knaves without employment & as much as could possibly be without bread."[65] The "mind forg'd manacles" of which Blake wrote in his poem "London" (1794) are an allusion not only to slavery in a literal sense, but to the importance of breaking established, yet stagnant, modes of thought.

CONCLUSION

Industries *and* traditions are responsible for shaping genres. *Rolling Stone* journalist Kim Neely noted that by 1991 alternative music became popular and accepted by mass culture largely because of the distinction between the way major record labels and independent record labels go about signing new artists. "Historically, indie labels have signed *bands*," she argues, "but major labels tend to sign by *genre*."[66] When Sub Pop sold Nirvana's contract to DGC Records,[67] they went on to become the progenitors of a *genre*, thereby ceasing to be just another "rock band." They were, instead, *the* alternative band; and ironically, at the peak of their "alternativeness," they were never more ubiquitous. Heavy rotation on radio, MTV, and even appearing on *Saturday Night Live* no doubt damaged their credibility with the punk sub-culture, but they never would have achieved such feats toiling in Seattle's underground scene, either.

Similarly, in literature critics and scholars develop canons, which in turn, create categories and place value judgments on authors. In principle, it seems that Blake would have been aghast at the thought of his work being codified in such a way. Stabler, in fact, refers to "the Blakean artist" as an archetype who is a "prophet-figure inevitably at odds with systems of imaginative restriction, and these systems always threaten to overwhelm free thought and free expression."[68] One of Cobain's journal entries, I believe, shows him as "the Blakean artist," for Cobain writes, "I like to have strong opinions with nothing to back them up but my PRIMAL sincerity."[69] So, it seems as if Blake and Cobain were certainly cut from the same earnest piece of cloth (one might suspect flannel); but, was either man truly able to separate himself from his predecessors?

Williams suggests that in the moment, we are constantly "defining a social experience which is still in process, often indeed not yet recognized as social but taken to be private, idiosyncratic, and even isolating."[70] Romanticism and grunge, for example—which seemingly are tantamount to subcultures as they are occurring—have their own "hierarchies," even though such categorizations and ranks are "often more recognizable at a later stage, when they have been formalized, classified, and in many cases built into institutions and formations."[71] Chris Norris addresses similar concerns with regard to the use of terminology that may actually be more appropriately called buzzwords:

> *The New York Times* bestowed on Kurt Cobain the absurd title "Hesitant Poet of Grunge Rock." Sociologically, the term "grunge" echoes "punk"—another vague, contested, commercialized catchall applied by various segments of society to a huge array of ideas, sounds, styles, and personalities. It's ridiculously imprecise and inadequate.[72]

Cobain came to be the face of an entire genre that has no rigidly identifiable traits; on the other hand, Blake has just sort of been absorbed, or slowly admitted, into a genre that has fairly consistent criteria (Romanticism).

Whether or not he actually meets those requirements is still up for debate. Neither William Blake nor Kurt Cobain (specifically in this instance) probably cared enough about what others thought to feel liberated—or confined—by being labeled with terms as seemingly arbitrary and indeterminate as "Romantic poet" or "hesitant poet of grunge rock." Then again, the sometimes irascible Blake—despite being resigned to the fact that he, and his work, would likely only be understood or appreciated upon his death—may have been just as easily inclined to "cast off the idiot Questioner who is always questioning / But never capable of answering."[73]

NOTES

1. G. E. Bentley, Jr., *The Stranger from Paradise: A Biography of William Blake* (New Haven: Yale University Press, 2003), 52–53.
2. Max Byrd, *London Transformed* (New Haven: Yale University Press, 1978), 159.
3. Jacob Bronowski, *William Blake and the Age of Revolution* (London: Routledge and K. Paul, 1972), 35.
4. John Beer, *Blake's Humanism* (New York: Barnes & Noble, 1968), 11.
5. William Blake, "Letter to Dr. Trusler," in *The Letters of William Blake Together with a Life*, vol. 1, ed. Archibald G. B. Russell, (London: Meuthen and Company, 1906), 61.
6. Byrd, *London*, 159.
7. Saree Makdisi, "The Political Aesthetic of Blake's Images," in *The Cambridge Companion to William Blake*, ed. Morris Eaves (Cambridge: Cambridge University Press, 2003), 111.
8. Craig Schuftan, *Entertain Us!* (Sydney: HarperCollins Publishers, 2012), 55.
9. Chris Norris, "The Ghost of Saint Kurt: Nirvana," in *Spin: 20 Years of Alternative Music*, ed. Will Hermes (New York: Three Rivers Press, 2005), 160.
10. Steve Albini quoted in Yarm, 84.
11. See chapter 7 of Leon Guilhamet, *The Sincere Ideal* (London: McGill-Queen's University Press, 1974), which addresses Blake's sincerity and how it distanced him from earlier writers, many of whom he read. Among those named are Shakespeare, Wordsworth, Bacon, Gray, Godwin, Richardson, Rousseau, and Voltaire.
12. Allan Cunningham quoted in Patricia Hodgart, ed., *Romantic Perspectives* (New York: Barnes and Noble, 1964), 129.
13. Russell, introduction to *The Letters of William Blake*, xl.
14. Blake, *Letters*, 17.
15. Schuftan, *Entertain*, 67.
16. Kurt Cobain, "Kurt Cobain's Suicide Note," *Kurt Cobain's Suicide Note*, accessed October 5, 2015, http://kurtcobainssuicidenote.com/kurt_cobains_suicide_note.html.
17. Byrd, *London*, 157–158. Further, Northrop Frye's seminal work, *Fearful Symmetry: A Study of William Blake* (1947), theorizes that Blake's poems and even his ideology often have much more in common with Renaissance writing and thinking than it did with his own era.
18. David Simpson, "Blake and Romanticism," in *The Cambridge Companion to William Blake*, ed. Morris Eaves, (Cambridge: Cambridge University Press, 2003), 177–178.
19. Nick Hornby, *High Fidelity* (New York: Riverhead Books, 1995), 24.
20. Raymond Williams, *Marxism and Literature* (Oxford: Oxford University Press, 1977), 128–135.
21. Thomas Pfau and Robert F. Gleckner, *Lessons of Romanticism* (Durham: Duke University Press, 1998), 3.
22. Dave Laing quoted in *Music and Youth Culture*, ed. Dan Laughey (Edinburgh: Edinburgh University Press), 35.
23. Laing quoted in Laughey, 38.
24. Henry Crabb Robinson quoted in Hodgart, 137.

25. Ryan Moore, *Smells Like Teen Spirit: Music, Youth Culture, and Social Crisis* (New York: New York University Press), 11 (my emphasis).
26. Bentley, *Stranger*, 149.
27. Jane Stabler, *Burke to Byron, Barbauld to Baillie, 1790–1830* (London: Palgrave, 2002), 43.
28. Moore, *Smells*, 125
29. Schuftan, *Entertain*, 62.
30. Moore, *Smells*, 125.
31. Northrop Frye, *Fearful Symmetry: A Study of William Blake* (Princeton: Princeton University Press, 1969), 36.
32. Robert Sayre and Michael Löwy, "Figures of Romantic Anti-Capitalism," *New German Critique* 32 (Spring/Summer 1984), 50.
33. Moore, 134
34. Blake quoted in Hodgart, *Romantic*, 147.
35. Blake quoted in Bentley, *Stranger*, 37.
36. Frye, *Fearful*, 4.
37. Beer, 55.
38. In an 1803 letter Blake wrote to his brother: "Profits arising from publications are immense, & I now have it in my power to commence publication with many very formidable works, which I have finish'd & ready. A book price half a guinea may be got out at the expense of ten pounds & it is almost certain profits are 500 G. I am only sorry that I did not know the methods of publishing years ago & this is one of the numerous benefits I have obtain'd by coming here, for I should never have known the nature of Publication. . . it now would be folly not to venture publishing" (*Letters* 51).
39. Stabler, *Burke*, 30–31.
40. Walter Benjamin, "The Work of Art in the Age of Mechanical Reproduction," in *The Norton Anthology of Theory and Criticism*, ed. Vincent B. Leich (New York: W.W. Norton & Co., 2001), 1169.
41. Schuftan, *Entertain* 104.
42. Donna Gaines, "The Local Economy of Suburban Scenes," in *Adolescents and their Music: If It's Too Loud, You're Too Old*, ed. Jonathon S. Epstein (New York: Garland Publishing, 1994), 53.
43. Peter Quennell, *Romantic England: Writing and Painting 1717–1851* (London: Weidenfeld and Nicolson, 1970), 254.
44. Byrd, *London*, 159.
45. Bentley, *Stranger*, 363.
46. Roger Beebe, "Mourning Becomes . . . ? Kurt Cobain, Tupac Shakur, and the 'Waning of Effect,'" in *Rock Over the Edge: Transformations in Popular Culture*, eds. Roger Beebe, Denise Fulbrook, and Ben Saunders (Durham: Duke University Press, 2002), 316.
47. Sayre and Löwy, *Figures*, 49.
48. Jim DeRogatis, *Milk It! Collected Musings on the Alternative Music Explosion of the 90's* (Boston: Da Capo Press, 2003), 57.
49. Eddie Vedder, "Jeremy," in *Ten*, by Pearl Jam, Epic Associated ZK 47857, 1991, compact disc.
50. Cho Seung Hui, "Mr. Brownstone," *Cho Seung-Hui's Plays (AOL News)*, April 17, 2007, accessed December 20, 2016, http://www.yellodyno.com/virginia_tech/cho_seungs_plays.pdf.
51. Professor Lucinda Roy, quoted in Ned Potter, David Schoetz, Richard Esposito, and Pierre Thomas, "Killer's Note: 'You Caused me to do this,'" *abcnews.com*, April 17, 2007, accessed December 20, 2016.
52. Frye, *Fearful*, 5.
53. Williams, *Marxism and Literature*, 131.
54. Ecclesiastes 1:9, *The King James Version*. *The Bible Gateway*, accessed July 27, 2017, https://www.biblegateway.com/passage/?search=Ecclesiastes+1%3A9&version=KJV.
55. Kurt Cobain, "Journal Entry," *Brainpickings*, accessed September 25, 2015, https://www.brainpickings.org/wp-content/uploads/2013/02/kurtcobainjournals3.jpg.

56. Blake quoted in Bentley, *Stranger*, 26.
57. Ibid., 185.
58. Walt Whitman, "Song of Myself," *Leaves of Grass* (New York: Modern Library, 1891), 70.
59. Cobain, "Journal Entry."
60. Moore, *Smells*, 8.
61. Quennell, *Romantic*, 240.
62. Pfau and Gleckner, *Lessons*, 12.
63. Stabler, *Burke*, 38.
64. DeRogatis, *Milk*, 7.
65. Blake quoted in Bentley, *Stranger*, 52.
66. Kim Neely quoted in Steve Waskman, ed., *This Ain't the Summer of Love* (Berkeley: The University of California Press, 2009), 254.
67. Sub Pop originally signed Nirvana for a mere $600; they sold Nirvana's contract to DGC Records in April 1991 for $75,000. Accessed 28 October 2015, http://www.nirvanaclub.com/info/articles/02.14.97.html.
68. Stabler, *Burke*, 32–33.
69. Cobain, "Journal Entry."
70. Williams, *Marxism and Literature*, 132.
71. Ibid.
72. Norris, *Ghost*, 160.
73. William Blake, *Milton, The Complete Poetry and Prose of William Blake*, Newly Revised Edition, ed. David V. Erdman (Berkeley, CA: University of California Press, 1982), 95–143.

BIBLIOGRAPHY

Beebe, Roger. "Mourning Becomes . . .? Kurt Cobain, Tupac Shakur, and the 'Waning of Effect.'" In *Rock Over the Edge: Transformations in Popular Culture*, edited by Roger Beebe, Denise Fulbrook, and Ben Saunders, 311–334. Durham: Duke University Press, 2002.

Beer, John. *Blake's Humanism*. New York: Barnes & Noble, 1968.

Benjamin, Walter. "The Work of Art in the Age of Mechanical Reproduction." In *The Norton Anthology of Theory and Criticism*, edited by Vincent B. Leich, 1163–1189. New York: W.W. Norton & Co., 2001.

Bentley, Jr., G. E. *The Stranger from Paradise: A Biography of William Blake*. New Haven: Yale University Press, 2003.

Blake, William. "Letter to Dr. Trusler." In *The Letters of William Blake Together with a Life*, volume 1, edited by Archibald G.B. Russell, 61. London: Meuthen and Company, 1906.

———. *Milton. The Complete Poetry and Prose of William Blake*, Newly Revised Edition, edited by David V. Erdman, 95–143. Berkeley, CA: University of California Press, 1982.

Bronowski, Jacob. *William Blake and the Age of Revolution*. London: Routledge and K. Paul, 1972.

Byrd, Max. *London Transformed: Image of the City in the Eighteenth Century*. New Haven: Yale University Press, 1978.

Cobain, Kurt. "Journal Entry." *Brainpickings*, accessed September 25, 2015, https://www.brainpickings.org/wp-content/uploads/2013/02/kurtcobainjournals3.jpg.

———. "Kurt Cobain's Suicide Note." *Kurt Cobain's Suicide Note*, accessed 5 October 2015, http://kurtcobainssuicidenote.com/kurt_cobains_suicide_note.html.

DeRogatis, Jim. *Milk It! Collected Musings on the Alternative Music Explosion of the 90's*. Boston: Da Capo Press, 2003.

Ecclesiastes. *The King James Version. The Bible Gateway*, accessed July 27, 2017, https://www.biblegateway.com/passage/?search=Ecclesiastes+1%3A9&version=KJV.

Frye, Northrop. *Fearful Symmetry: A Study of William Blake*. Princeton: Princeton University Press, 1969.

Gaines, Donna. "The Local Economy of Suburban Scenes." In *Adolescents and their Music: If It's Too Loud, You're Too Old*, edited by Jonathon S. Epstein, 47–66. New York: Garland Publishing, 1994.

Guilhamet, Leon. *The Sincere Ideal*. London: McGill-Queen's University Press, 1974.

Hodgart, Patricia. *Romantic Perspectives*. New York: Barnes and Noble, 1964.

Hornby, Nick. *High Fidelity*. New York: Riverhead Books, 1995.

Hui, Cho Seung. "Mr. Brownstone." *Cho Seung-Hui's Plays (AOL News)*, April 17, 2007, accessed December 20, 2016, http://www.yellodyno.com/virginia_tech/cho_seungs_plays.pdf.

Laughey, Dan, ed. *Music and Youth Culture*. Edinburgh: Edinburgh University Press, 2006.

Makdisi, Saree. "The Political Aesthetic of Blake's Images." In *The Cambridge Companion to William Blake*, edited by Morris Eaves, 110–132. Cambridge: Cambridge University Press, 2003.

Moore, Ryan. *Smells Like Teen Spirit: Music, Youth Culture, and Social Crisis*. New York: New York University Press, 2009.

Norris, Chris. "The Ghost of Saint Kurt: Nirvana." In *Spin: 20 Years of Alternative Music*, edited by Will Hermes, 156–162. New York: Three Rivers Press, 2005.

Pfau, Thomas, and Robert F. Gleckner. *Lessons of Romanticism*. Durham: Duke University Press, 1998.

Potter, Ned, David Schoetz, Richard Esposito, and Pierre Thomas. "Killer's Note: 'You Caused me to do this.'" *abcnews.com*, April 17, 2007, accessed December 20, 2016.

Quennell, Peter. *Romantic England: Writing and Painting 1717–1851*. London: Weidenfeld and Nicolson, 1970.

Sayre, Robert, and Michael Löwy. "Figures of Romantic Anti-Capitalism." *New German Critique* 32 (Spring/Summer 1984): 42–92.

Shuftan, Craig. *Entertain Us!* Sydney: HarperCollins Publishers, 2012.

Simpson, David. "Blake and Romanticism." In *The Cambridge Companion to William Blake*, edited by Morris Eaves, 169–187. Cambridge: Cambridge University Press, 2003.

Stabler, Jane. *Burke to Byron, Barbauld to Baillie, 1790–1830*. London: Palgrave, 2002.

Vedder, Eddie. "Jeremy." In *Ten*, by Pearl Jam, Epic Associated ZK 47857, 1991, compact disc.

Waskman, Steve, ed. *This Ain't the Summer of Love*. Berkeley: The University of California Press, 2009.

Whitman, Walt. "Song of Myself." *Leaves of Grass*. New York: Modern Library, 1891.

Williams, Raymond. *Marxism and Literature*. Oxford: Oxford University Press, 1977.

Yarm, Mark, ed. *Everybody Loves our Town: An Oral History of Grunge*. New York: Three Rivers Press, 2011.

Chapter Four

Digging at the Roots

Martha Redbone's The Garden of Love: Songs of William Blake

Nicole Lobdell

Martha Redbone's album *The Garden of Love: Songs of William Blake* (2012) reimagines the songs of William Blake through the sounds, rhythms, and melodies of Appalachian folk music, blues, and American southern gospel. She prominently features Native Cherokee and Choctaw chants and uses traditional instruments, including rattles, shakers, fiddles, banjos, steel guitars, and autoharps to blend the music of her heritage with Blake's poetry. Described by one reviewer as a "Brooklyn-born, Kentucky-raised troubadour," Martha Redbone is a descendent of the Choctaw / Shawnee / Cherokee / Blackfeet tribes on her mother's side; her father is African American.[1] She draws musical inspiration from these cultures and sets those sounds against the coal mining country of Appalachia and the Kentucky Black Mountains. *The New Yorker* described the album as "a brilliant collision of cultures . . . In it, the mystical, humanistic words of the eighteenth-century English poet are fused with the melodies, drones, and rhythms of the Appalachian string-band music that Redbone absorbed as a child."[2] The album offers up a complex personal narrative, infusing Blake's poetry with new sounds, but studies of the origins of Appalachian music have uncovered links between both Appalachian and traditional English lyrical ballads, suggesting that the Appalachian ballad is an adaptation of the older form.[3] Is it so surprising, therefore, that Redbone can effortlessly reimagine Blake's poetry in the sounds of Native Appalachia? In many ways, *The Garden of Love* showcases a collective lyrical history that joins, across centuries and continents, Blake's Romantic England with Redbone's modern America.

In discussing her initial work on the album, Redbone expressed her desire to honor the traditional mountain music of the Black Mountain region: "My grandmother passed away. We lost a lot of elders in our community. I wanted to sing the songs that I sang in school and that I know my mom sang in school and my grandparents sang and so on and so forth. That was the idea back then."[4] Between the 1960s and 1990s, there was a great migration out of Appalachia as industries changed and shifted away from the harvesting of natural resources, such as coal and timber, and turned to more technology-based enterprises. Whole communities relocated to urban settings, leaving parts of the region economically and culturally depressed. Redbone's project memorializes not only her family but also her community—it is in essence an archive of sound.

Blogger Zach Hudson describes the thematic links between Redbone's music and Blake's poetry as "love, suffering, salvation, journeys, and music itself. There is a certain mystic weirdness, often involving metaphor, that American folk music inherited from the English ballad . . . and Blake shares this mystical quality."[5] The links between Redbone and Blake demonstrate the universality of the poetry and the timelessness of the Romantic ideals that the music embodies. In an interview with Nicole S. Colson, Redbone describes Blake's poems as being "about mercy, peace, love, nature, [and] colonialism. They reminded me of Appalachia."[6] Several musical genres and styles inspired her, from "Choctaw dance song, an Appalachian mountain song, [and] African field song," and Redbone insists that "these forms of music are the foundation of our country . . . It feels natural. That's why I like melody. That's where it all begins."[7] Describing her own sound as "native soul" and "native storytelling,"[8] Redbone interprets Blake's poetry through memory, eulogizing what has been lost to time and progress, and celebrating, through lyric and melody, what remains. The result is what I have termed Appalachian Romanticism, a moving and powerful sound revealing to listeners that Redbone's music and Blake's poetry are two pieces of the same puzzle originating from a common inspirational source.

The album is also a collective effort symbolic of both the community and the communal memory that inspire the sounds. The ensemble of musicians and musical craftsmen Redbone assembles around her add their own touches of rhythm, melody, and tone to the raw materials of Blake's language. Studies of Romanticism demonstrate many collaborative partnerships and artistic friendships that produced great works, such as Wordsworth's and Coleridge's *Lyrical Ballads*. In many ways, Redbone's *Garden of Love* is a similar imaginative partnership. Appalachian Romanticism captures both the sound of Appalachia and the intrinsic values of Romanticism. It is independent, self-sufficient, close to nature, but also communal, collaborative, and spiritual.[9] The connection to nature and art inherent in the ideals of Romanticism is mirrored by Appalachia's relationship to the landscape and use of natural resources to create art, such as the mountain holler, which is a musical form that reflects the geographic feature of the same name. The geographical region takes its name from the Appalachian mountain range, named after the Native American tribe, the Apalachee, who once occupied the Florida panhandle. Appalachia refers also to a cultural region that runs along the Appalachian mountain range and stretches from southern New York to Mississippi, moving through portions of Pennsylvania, Ohio, Maryland, West Virginia, Virginia, Kentucky, Tennessee, North Carolina, South Carolina, Georgia, and Alabama.[10] In colonial America, the mountain range served as a geographical barrier, hindering the initial western movement of colonial settlements. In the nineteenth century, as mobility technologies improved and profitable natural resources, such as coal, were discovered, towns and villages formed in the valleys and hollows between the peaks of the Appalachian Mountains. In the nineteenth and twentieth centuries, the mountain range isolated its communities, preserving many of the original traditions and unique cultural inheritances, such as the music, arts and crafts, and language of the immigrant communities who settled the region. The people of Appalachia value hard work, economy, and independence, and, due to the geographic isolation of the region, they can be overly suspicious of outsiders and governmental agencies, preferring autonomous self-rule.[11] These values and ideals were not foreign to the writers and artists of the Romantic period.

As a description, Appalachian Romanticism fits aptly with Redbone's adaptation. She reimagines Blake's poetry spanning the physical and cultural divide between America and England, the temporal divide between childhood and adulthood, and the spiritual divide between life and death. The overlapping ideals of Appalachia and Romanticism—organic imagination, self-reliance, and a spiritual connection to nature—influence Redbone's sound, and Blake harmonizes well with Appalachia, in part, because of their shared treatment by outsiders. Scorned by the public and living in obscurity, Blake turned inward, looking to his own vision of the world as a renewing spring of inspiration. His original voice and personal aesthetic were unlike anything else found in eighteenth-century London, and his disregard for public opinion was just one of the features that drew Redbone to his work: "I think he was very very brave. He took chances. He was a maverick. He didn't really care what other people thought. He really spoke his mind . . . People kind of wrote him off as a madman but when you look at his writings, he was absolutely brilliant."[12] Like Blake, Appalachia possesses its own voice and style derived from its appreciation of the land and the resiliency of its people. Yet the derisive labels associated with Appalachia persist, trading in stereotypes of ignorance, grossness, and artlessness. Facing ridicule, the peoples of Appalachia, like Blake, turn inward, relying on their own resources for inspiration.

So, what does it mean for the study of Romanticism to have the canonical poetry of Blake reimagined in the sounds of American Appalachian, or blues, or American Southern gospel? What does it mean for a woman of both Native American and African-American heritage to set Blake's poetry to the music of Appalachia? How might these songs contribute to current definitions of Romanticism, and how are the boundaries of Romanticism tested when musicians set Romantic poetry to the sounds of indigenous America?

ROMANTIC ORIGINS

The origin story of *The Garden of Love: Songs of William Blake* has several Romantic elements, and it begins with a moment of intuition—spontaneous, Romantic genius. At home, Redbone says, "Aaron [her husband] found the anthology of William Blake. It opened to 'A Poison Tree,' where the spine is bent . . . He brought that to me and I immediately heard a melody . . . We started flipping through the work and we saw another piece . . . 'I Heard an Angel Singing.'"[13] In another version of the origin story, Redbone describes the book as "dropp[ing] open" to Blake's "A Poison Tree"; "I picked it up and read it and right away the words read to me like an old bluegrass tune."[14] The language with which Redbone describes the scene—the book falling open to a specific poem, the melody presenting itself to her—has all the characteristics of a Romantic narrative. The melody came to her as if pulled by an ethereal force from some internal, personal reserve. "Every time I looked at something that spoke to me," she says, "the melody just came out. I ran to the studio and threw myself in front of a mic . . . It all came naturally: I had all the melodies."[15] As an origin story, it's not unlike those associated with Romanticism; the auspicious origins suggest a spiritual involvement that recalls Blake's own claims of supernatural intervention. As an origin story, it's equal parts inspiration, spontaneity, and genius.

The terms—inspiration, spontaneity, and genius—I've used deliberately with their Romantic definitions in mind. In 1759, Edward Young described the relationship between originality and genius: "An Original may be said to be of a vegetable nature; it rises spontaneously from the vital root of genius."[16] Concurrent Romantic era definitions of genius emphasize it as "a private source of art in the individual" with "an origin beyond the reach of consciousness or conscious thought."[17] These concepts, which have their roots in organic imagery, inform Redbone's work and link it with Romanticism and William Blake in surprising ways.

In a letter dated 25 April 1803, Blake writes about his composition of *The Four Zoas*: "I have written this Poem from immediate Dictation, twelve or sometimes twenty or thirty lines at a time, without Premeditation & even against my Will . . . an immense Poem Exists which seems to be the Labour of a long Life, all produc'd without Labour or Study."[18] Blake worked on *The Four Zoas* for more than a decade; the product was a meandering poem on the Creation of Man ending with a scene of judgment. His comment on the process of composition, however, resonates with Redbone's own comments on writing the album. The idea of spontaneous, natural creation is a Romantic one; it is not creation through sheer will but creation against the will, a creation out of necessity. In Redbone's Romanticism, although she never uses the term genius—the divine spark of brilliance that resides within individuals—or Genius—the overarching philosophical concept that informs Romanticism—they are as intrinsically significant to her creative process as they were to Blake's.

We might be tempted to read the opening to "The Poison Tree" as symbolic of the project's origins and purpose. That Redbone calls her traveling band Roots Project is also suggestive of her own search into her familial and musical lineages, and that the first poem she claims to consider as part of this work is "The Poison Tree" suggests that the tree is a symbolic representation of those origins. In Blake's poem, the tree symbolizes relationships poisoned by pride and conflict, an image that resonates with the fraught landscape and the diverse groups of people that inhabit the American Appalachian range. The tree may represent origins, but they are origins rooted in pain, struggle, and grief.

An undercurrent of prophecy and destiny also runs through the origin story, informing Redbone's selection of poems. The work Redbone does on this album, which is an album ultimately about redemption, is a musical cleansing—one prophesied by Blake himself. In an interview, Redbone discusses her grandmother and Blake's poem "Why Should I Care for the Men of Thames":

> The reason we chose that poem was because Blake talks about his disgust for slave-trading . . . He says, "Tho his waters bathed my infant limbs, / The Ohio shall wash his stains from me. / I was born a slave but I go to be free." It's amazing because the Ohio River is on Shawnee land. My grandmother is Cherokee and Shawnee. Blake didn't say the Mississippi. He didn't say the Gulf. He said the *Ohio* shall wash the stain from me. That's where my family first began and where my ancestors came from, who were English as well.[19]

As if the words have been waiting for her, Redbone finds her relationship to the poetry beyond coincidental: it is a natural alignment, mystical and prophetic. Her interpretation of "Why Should I Care for the Men of Thames," however, is unlike anything else on the album. Redbone's chanting of a traditional Shawnee chant underlines the spoken recitation of the poem by English singer songwriter Jonathan Spottiswoode, one of Redbone's guest artists, who recites the poem rather than singing it. Above all the others, this song stands out not only for its use of spoken word and Native chanting but because Spottiswoode is the opposite of Blake's enslaved speaker. The tension created by his recitation highlights the musical and cultural differences between the Native chant and the poetic text; their collaborative use, however, transcends those differences to promote a new understanding of both Blake's poetry and Redbone's music.

"NATIVE STORYTELLING"

The Garden of Love: Songs of William Blake is an orchestration of sound and word; it is a diverse, multiethnic, collective project that mixes musical elements to create a new interpretation that transcends temporal and geographic boundaries. The organic, diverse language of sound pushes against definitions of Romanticism by reimagining Blake's canonical poetry in a feminine voice set against the musical backdrop of Appalachia. Redbone and her fellow musicians are not, however, merely overlaying chords and melodies on top of Blake's language. If anything, the players construct a musical structure that intertwines with Blake's poetry, enacting a kind of mutually dependent relationship between the two elements, wherein both the music and the lyrics grow together.

Redbone's combinations of musical styles and musical arrangements accord well with the themes and ideals of Romanticism. The minor chords of songs such as "The Garden of Love" and "On Another's Sorrow" express themes of frustration, unfulfilled desires, and despair associated with Romantic elegy, and the improvisational style of Appalachian and blues music fits with the spontaneity of emotion of the Romantic imagination. The sorrow and frustration of "The Garden of Love" is erased in the next song, "Hear the Voice of the Bard," whose major chord emphasizes the triumph of the bard's individual spirit over obstacles and hardships. Similarly, bringing her American South upbringing to bear, Redbone reimagines "I Rose Up at the Dawn of the Day" as a Southern gospel hymn. Complete with choir that sings and claps the refrain, "Get thee away get thee away" (2),[20] the singers enact a battle of temptation and resistance with Blake's devil.[21]

Another characteristic element of Redbone's style is her incorporation of Native instruments and chanting in her music. Her use of traditional instruments such as rattles, shakers, fiddles, banjos, steel guitars, and autoharps along with traditional techniques that include picking and plucking and Native chanting blend effortlessly with the aural effects of Blake's poetry. Most prominent on "A Dream," the Native chanting reinforces the legacy that Redbone is exploring and brings the discussion of Native legacy upon more traditional forms of European-inspired music. The organic instruments of the Native rattles, flutes, and shakers contrast with the sharper sounds of instruments made from man-made materials, including the steel guitars and auto-harps present in Redbone's music.

Appalachian folk and Native music is inspired by and formed from the natural environment. They create what I would call shaping sounds, or sounds that are dependent on the structure of space. These include the mountain holler and the organic instruments—rattles, shakers, and wooden flutes—which are crafted from the environment. Appalachian music is a regional music derived from European and African influences, including the English ballad tradition. The mountain holler refers both to a musical technique and a geographical feature referring to the small valleys formed between the mountains of the Appalachian range. Used most prominently in "The Ecchoing Green," the mountain holler merges sound and landscape. The use of mountain holler in combination with a cappella singing on "The Ecchoing Green" highlights the loneliness of the individual and the smallness of man within a vast empty space. At the same time, the voice of the individual stands out from the collective.

Blues music shares connections with the mountain holler; blues music derives, in part, from the field songs and field hollers of slaves in the American Deep South. The use of the holler in both Appalachian music and blues music emphasizes the emotional tolls and pains of the individual. On Redbone's album, these two genres are combined with elements of soul music, which emphasizes emotional, vocal improvisations. Lastly, the inclusion of spoken word, namely on "The Men of Thames," highlights the experimental poetry and sound of the album as a whole. From the materials with which the instruments are built to the terrestrial imagery of Blake's poetry, it seems Redbone's album was destined to reimagine Blake's poetry in the image of indigenous America.

THE GARDEN OF LOVE: SONGS OF WILLIAM BLAKE

Redbone's selection and arrangement of Blake's poems, which include three from *Songs of Innocence*, four from *Songs of Experience*, four from *Songs and Ballads*, and one from Blake's miscellaneous poems, charts a loose narrative of fall and redemption alongside one about the individual's search for community and home. On one level, the album is Redbone's navigation among communities that seem at odds with one another, such as New York and Kentucky. Of her selection process, Redbone says, "I looked at his [Blake's] imagery and the messages about religion and poverty and they were so relevant to today, and out of 150 poems I picked out a bunch that reminded me of Appalachia."[22] The narratives she creates through her lyrical arrangements are interdependent on one another and teach relevant valuable morals for a contemporary audience. Morris Eaves describes some of the poems in *Songs of Experience*, such as "A Poison Tree," as "psychological fables . . . components in an evolving narrative framework of fall and redemption . . . in a system constructed to deliver simultaneously the fall and redemption of a single human life *and* of humankind *and* of a single work of art *and* of Art, etc."[23] In Redbone's album, we not only hear this enacted through Blake's language but also through the layers of folk, Native, and blues music, which refocus a listener's attention away from eighteenth-century England to contemporary rural America.

The opening song, "The Garden of Love," weaves together the sounds of different musical genres, establishing at the outset the album's multi-genre and multi-form style. Clacking and jingling together in the background, shakers, rattles, and bells are joined by the first notes and slide of a steel guitar; and then, we hear Redbone's wailing mountain holler: "I laid me down upon a bank / Where love lay sleeping / I heard the rushes dank / Weeping Weeping" (1–4).[24] As a musical form, mountain holler is somewhere between spoken word and song; the voice lilts upward on the last word of a line, projecting the notes upward and outward, a vocal action that colonializes silence and creates presence. This interweaving of words and sounds in the opening stanza identifies the work as a collaboration between styles, genres, and cultures.

There is little editing or altering of Blake's poems, the most noticeable exception being the opening song. Redbone transposes two stanzas from Blake's notebooks *Songs and Ballads* and affixes them to "The Garden of Love," which Blake published originally in *Songs of Experience*. Her choice of stanzas includes such organic images as "a bank" (1), "rushes" (3), "heath & the wild" (5), and "thistles & thorns" (6) and accords well with Blake's own use of organic imagery in his original poem.[25] Redbone's "The Garden of Love" ends with the image of Priests "binding with briars, my joys & desires" (20).[26] The result is a song framed by nature that is at odds with human institutions.

Aileen Ward notes "the numerous images of Jesus in the *Songs of Innocence* (1789) are supplanted in the *Songs of Experience* (1794) by naturalistic imagery and anti-clerical protests. After 1790 . . . [Blake] never attended any church but followed the path of his own religious explorations."[27] "The Garden of Love" demonstrates distrust of institutionalized religion, and a turn toward the natural innocence, the garden of love, remembered from the singer's youth—only to discover the garden has been built over with churches and graveyards. Kevin Hutchings argues that the poem is "about a fall marking the end of prelapsarian innocence . . . not to any personal sin of disobedience . . . but to the intervention in a child's paradise of an institutionalized religious order . . . functioning to constrain the speaker's childish exuberance."[28] The speaker returns to the green space of his or her childhood. It's easy to imagine Redbone returning to her geographic roots and finding the countryside altered. Or to find that those institutions and possibilities open to one as a child are now closed to one as an adult.

The second stanza opens with "And the gates of this Chapel were shut, / and Thou shalt not. writ over the door; / So I turn'd to the Garden of Love" (5–7).[29] Sung in a strong, major chord, the stanza takes on new meaning. "this Chapel" represents not only conventional religious institutions but all institutions, including the traditional Romantic literary canon, that would ignore the presence of minority and feminine voices. Redbone's mountain holler combined with the major chord cannot be ignored. If we read "The Garden of Love" with this in mind, the narrative that orders the songs on the album unfolds and becomes clear. Sung as a bold declaration, "Hear the voice of the bard" features as the second song on Redbone's album.[30] "Hear the voice of the bard" functions as both a command and a call, proclaiming the presence, which was hinted at in the previous song, of a new bard—a female, ethnic minority bard. The singer calls for a return—"O Earth O Earth return!"—and a new beginning: "And the morn / Rises from the slumberous mass" (11, 14–15).[31] She demands listeners "Turn away no more" (16).[32] A new contemporary bard emerges.

"A DREAM"

Within the larger narrative of fall and redemption, there are subnarratives arranged within sets of songs. One such set is the trio of songs "A Dream," "I Heard an Angel Singing," and "I Rose Up at the Dawn of Day." The narrative is one of struggle and resolve. Opening with "A Dream," the narrative begins at night, representative of personal struggle, and gives way to the dawn, a moment of realization, faith, and strength. In "A Dream," the speaker enters a dreamscape and finds herself transformed into a small creature, one the size of an insect. The upright bass pulses a quick tempo, emphasizing the dreamscape's movement. In her dream, the singer encounters insects, including an ant, "Troubled wilderd and fo[r]lorn," and a glow-worm, the "watchman of the night" (5, 16).[33] The anthropomorphism of the ant makes the song seem more whimsical and endearing. With Redbone's treatment, however, the lyrics take on a more somber tone. The addition of Native chanting is particularly strong in the refrain: "Oh my children! do they cry / Do they hear their father sigh. / Now they look abroad to see, / Now return and weep for me" (9–12).[34] In Redbone's voice, the lyrics have new resonance and a powerful vulnerability. By singing the lines, Redbone reimagines the rhythm. Zach Hudson writes, "Whereas we read a line of Blake's like this: [']Oh my children! do they cry['] . . . Redbone can reimagine it as this: [']Oh my child- (beat, beat)—ren! do they cry (beat, beat, beat)[']."[35] The Native chanting and wailing mountain holler weave haunting reminders of an American past; it draws together Redbone's familial past with the present. In Redbone's voice, the song becomes a generational search for home, and the refrain, "Now return and weep for me," a tenuous musical thread stretching across the temporal divide (12).[36]

"I Heard an Angel Singing" meditates on the balance between good and evil; for there to be good, there must be evil: "Mercy could be no more / If there was nobody poor" (11–12).[37] "I Rose Up at the Dawn of Day" is a triumphant rejection of temptation and the Devil and a joyful joining with God. The speaker is tempted by monetary and material wealth, but she rejects them: "So as I dont value such things as these / You must do Mr Devil just as God please" (27–28).[38] Blake provides the joyful refrain, although in his original poem "Get thee away get thee away" only appears once at the beginning of the poem (2).[39] Redbone reimagines the poem as a Southern gospel song featuring a choir that claps and sings the refrain, which echoes throughout the song after every couple of lines. It bolsters the poem and serves as shield for the singer against temptation with each incantation, or refrain, serving to reinforce its power. The song recounts the speaker's temptation to pray at the throne of Mammon, to confuse the throne of Mammon for the throne of God. The speaker refuses to pray for wealth: "If I pray it must be for other People" (24).[40] The speaker prays for the spiritual and physical wellness of others, and Mammon loses his power.

"I Heard an Angel Singing" and "I Rose Up at the Dawn of Day" are the musical and emotional centerpieces of Redbone's album. They enact natural and supernatural struggles, the depth of human suffering, and the height of human triumph. In "I Heard an Angel Singing," the singer is alone, but in "I Rose Up at the Dawn of Day," a community, the chorus, backs the singer. Community and the search for home are undercurrents that shape the narrative of the album as a whole, and they reflect Redbone's commitment to Native communities and her work with outreach programs that focus on Native heritage, traditions, and music. Through her unique blend of sounds and singers, Redbone demonstrates the strength of community.

"THE FLY"

Yet, for all the strength demonstrated in songs such as "I Rose Up at the Dawn of Day," there is a musical and thematic vulnerability expressed at the end of the album in the interpretations of "The Ecchoing Green" and "The Fly." As a pair, they comment on the innate innocence and the fragility of human life. On "The Ecchoing Green," Redbone sings a cappella, incorporating mountain holler sounds that emphasize the vastness of the space and the "ecchoing" effect suggested by the poem's title. Again, Redbone feels a connection between Blake and herself: "I wanted to do a straight-up mountain holler. We discovered that poem after the bulk of songs we did . . . I wanted to do a real a cappella mountain holler with no music. I liked the idea of the word 'echo,' which is great for a holler. Sure enough, staring in front of me was another sign. William Blake knew that I was going to do this song."[41] The poem's structure follows the course of a day, with the sun rising at the poem's opening and setting at its close. Children play in the sunshine and elders sit under oak trees, carefully observing and reflecting on the past. The two images are echoes of one another; as time moves on, the children will replace the elders.

"The Fly," a poem about the brevity of life, is made more fragile by the choice of instrument that leads the musical accompaniment. The autoharp, a singular instrument with a familial link to the Romantic Aeolian harp, is an appropriate musical metaphor for Romanticism. It is simultaneously organic and mechanical, delicate and steely, sharp and smooth. Traditional techniques include picking and plucking the strings individually, but they can also be strummed together. To play, one must embrace the instrument, supporting it with the player's body, melding player and instrument together. In this way, the autoharp represents the Appalachian Romanticism of Redbone's album; it embodies best those dichotomies of Romanticism and Appalachia that Redbone confronts and engages through music.

In "The Fly," the delicate sounds of the autoharp are joined by the giggles and laughter of children audible in the background, and it is with the image of children that Redbone closes her album. The final song, "Sleep Sleep Beauty Bright," is a lullaby sung a cappella by Redbone.[42] As a final song, it functions on several levels. It closes the album by stripping away the musical accompaniment in order to focus solely on the individual voice. We can easily imagine the speaker singing softly to a child, so that the album, which began in the garden of love destroyed by man's institutions, returns to the organic image of vulnerable, new life with the final line: "infant wiles & infant smiles / Heaven & Earth of peace beguiles" (19–20).[43]

The Garden of Love: Songs of William Blake traces narrative pathways that begin in a communal, organic, and sacred space that is ruined by human institutions. The loss of these spaces causes the singer to roam, searching for a replacement. The middle songs of the album demonstrate a spiritual confrontation and then awakening, leading to moments of redemption and the revelation that, although physically gone, the sacred space exists still within the self. The final songs on the album, including "The Fly" and "Sleep Sleep Beauty Bright," are tributes to that realization; the singer finds the communal space again not in the physical landscape but in individuals whose lives the speaker learns to cherish for their brevity.

Redbone's interpretation of Blake's poetry demonstrates a flexibility and applicability that is unprecedented. Many artists have offered musical interpretations of Blake's poetry, and Redbone is not the first bluegrass and folk musician to reimagine his poetry in the sounds of Appalachia. There are none, however, who combine ancestral and musical heritages like Martha Redbone and demonstrate the universal and contemporary appeal of Blake's poetry. Redbone's reimaging expands the reach of Romanticism from Blake's cityscape and Wordsworth's English countryside to include the untenured lands and wilds of America. It tests boundaries by associating canonical poetry with bodies, voices, and musical styles not included in the canon. "The poems are so special," Redbone writes, "and I think the meanings are so relevant to things that are happening today. We're all judging each other for our religion and our religious beliefs. We're all still fighting wars and fighting for equal rights and all of these things that are in these poems."[44] In many ways, Redbone's musical adaptations free the poetry from the page and from the masculine, Anglo-Saxon voice, allowing a more diverse, contemporary audience access to Blake, demonstrating his continued relevancy. Redbone's adaptation transplants author and text to a new land with a new set of sounds and voices for a new audience.

NOTES

1. Christian John Wikane, "Tales from Black Mountain: A Conversation with Martha Redbone," *Popmatters.com*, January 17, 2014.
2. "Martha Redbone," Night Life, *The New Yorker*, December 1, 2012, http://www.newyorker.com/goings-on-about-town/night-life/martha-redbone.
3. Debby McClatchy, "Appalachian Traditional Music: A Short History," *Musical Traditions*, June 6, 2000, https://www.namb.net/send-relief/arm/appalachian-culture.
4. Wikane, "Tales from Black Mountain: Conversation with Martha Redbone."
5. Zach Hudson, "Martha Redbone's Journey to William Blake," *No Depression*, November 1, 2012, http://nodepression.com/article/martha-redbones-journey-william-blake.
6. Nicole S. Colson, "Choctaw, Cherokee and African-American descent have shaped Martha Redbone," *Sentinel Source*, March 21, 2013, http://www.sentinelsource.com.
7. Ibid.
8. Tom Pearson, "Interview with Martha Redbone," *Native Theater Festival Interview Series*, Hemispheric Institute, 2008, http://hemisphericinstitute.org/hemi/hidvl/hidvl-int-native-theater/item/1356–ntfest-mredbone.
9. "Appalachian Culture," *North American Mission Board*, https://www.namb.net/send-relief/arm/appalachian-culture.
10. "What is Appalachia?" *The Alliance for Appalachia*, http://theallianceforappalachia.org/background/.
11. Sarah Baird, "Stereotypes of Appalachia Obscure A Diverse Picture," *Code Switch*, April 6, 2014, http://www.npr.org/sections/codeswitch/2014/04/03/298892382/stereotypes-of-appalachia-obscure-a-diverse-picture.
12. Wikane, "Tales from Black Mountain: Conversation with Martha Redbone."
13. Ibid.
14. Jim Bessman, "Singer-songwriter Martha Redbone merges Native American roots with William Blake," *The Examiner*, October 30, 2012, http://www.examiner.com/article/singer-songwriter-martha-redbone-merges-native-american-roots-with-william-blake.
15. Ibid.
16. "Genius," in *An Oxford Companion to the Romantic Age: British Culture 1776–1832*, ed. Iain McCalman (Oxford: Oxford University Press, 1999), 519.
17. Ibid., 519.

18. William Blake, "Letter to Mr. Butts, Great Marlborough Street," in *The Complete Poetry and Prose of William Blake*, ed. David Erdman (Berkeley: U of California P, 1982), 728.
19. Wikane, "Tales from Black Mountain: Conversation with Martha Redbone."
20. William Blake, "I rose up at the dawn of the day . . . ," in *The Complete Poetry and Prose of William Blake*, ed. David Erdman (Berkeley: U of California P, 1982), 481.
21. All quotations from Blake's poetry are from David Erdman's edition of *The Complete Poetry and Prose of William Blake* (1982). I have included Blake's punctuation and capitalization, but it should be noted that Redbone's punctuation and capitalization appear differently in the album's accompanying booklet. There are some slight variations (missing apostrophes in contractions, for example) in Redbone's songs as printed in the booklet. It's unclear if these are purposeful edits or editorial errors.
22. Bessman, "Singer-songwriter Martha Redbone."
23. Morris Eaves, "Introduction: to Paradise the Hard Way," in *The Cambridge Companion to William Blake*, ed. Morris Eaves (Cambridge: Cambridge University Press, 2003), 4.
24. William Blake, "I laid me down upon a bank . . . ," in *The Complete Poetry and Prose of William Blake*, ed. David Erdman (Berkeley: U of California P, 1982), 468.
25. Ibid.
26. Blake, "The Garden of Love," 26.
27. Aileen Ward, "William Blake and His Circle," in *The Cambridge Companion to William Blake*, ed. Morris Eaves (Cambridge: Cambridge University Press, 2003), 24.
28. Kevin Hutchings, "Nature, Ideology, and the Prohibition of Pleasure in Blake's 'Garden of Love,'" in *Romanticism and Pleasure*, ed. Thomas M. Schmid and Michelle Faubert (New York: Palgrave, 2010), 191.
29. Blake, "The Garden of Love," 26.
30. Redbone titles this song "Hear the Voice of the Bard," but Blake's original poem is titled as "Introduction" and is the opening poem in *Songs of Experience*.
31. William Blake, "Introduction to the *Songs of Experience*," in *The Complete Poetry and Prose of William Blake*, ed. David Erdman (Berkeley: U of California P, 1982), 18. Redbone renames the song on album as "Hear the Voice of the Bard."
32. Ibid.
33. William Blake, "A Dream," in *The Complete Poetry and Prose of William Blake*, ed. David Erdman (Berkeley: U of California P, 1982), 16.
34. Ibid.
35. Hudson, "Martha Redbone's Journey."
36. Blake, "A Dream," 16.
37. William Blake, "I Heard an Angel Singing . . . ," in *The Complete Poetry and Prose of William Blake*, ed. David Erdman (Berkeley: U of California P, 1982), 470.
38. Blake, "I rose up at the dawn of the day . . . ," 481.
39. Ibid.
40. Ibid.
41. Wikane, "Tales from Black Mountain: Conversation with Martha Redbone."
42. Redbone retitles this song "Sleep Sleep Beauty Bright" but Blake's original poem is titled "A Cradle Song" and appears in *Songs and Ballads*.
43. William Blake, "A Cradle Song," in *The Complete Poetry and Prose of William Blake*, ed. David Erdman (Berkeley: U of California P, 1982), 468.
44. Wikane, "Tales from Black Mountain: Conversation with Martha Redbone."

BIBLIOGRAPHY

"Appalachian Culture," *North American Mission Board*, https://www.namb.net/send-relief/arm/appalachian-culture.
Baird, Sarah. "Stereotypes of Appalachia Obscure A Diverse Picture." *Code Switch*, April 6, 2014. http://www.npr.org/sections/codeswitch/2014/04/03/298892382/stereotypes-of-appalachia-obscure-a-diverse-picture.

Bessman, Jim. "Singer-songwriter Martha Redbone merges Native American roots with William Blake." *The Examiner*, October 30, 2012. http://www.examiner.com/article/singer-songwriter-martha-redbone-merges-native-american-roots-with-william-blake.

Blake, William. "A Cradle Song." In *The Complete Poetry and Prose of William Blake*, edited by David Erdman, 468. Berkeley: University of California Press, 1982.

———. "A Dream." In *The Complete Poetry and Prose of William Blake*, edited by David Erdman, 16. Berkeley: University of California Press, 1982.

———. "I Heard An Angel Singing . . ." In *The Complete Poetry and Prose of William Blake*, edited by David Erdman, 470. Berkeley: University of California Press, 1982.

———. "I laid me down upon a bank . . ." In *The Complete Poetry and Prose of William Blake*, edited by David Erdman, 468. Berkeley: University of California Press, 1982.

———. "I rose up at the dawn of the day . . ." In *The Complete Poetry and Prose of William Blake*, edited by David Erdman, 481. Berkeley: University of California Press, 1982.

———. "Introduction to the *Songs of Experience*." In *The Complete Poetry and Prose of William Blake*, edited by David Erdman, 18. Berkeley: University of California Press, 1982.

———. "Letter to Mr. Butts, Great Marlborough Street." In *The Complete Poetry and Prose of William Blake*, edited by David Erdman, 728. Berkeley: University of California Press, 1982.

———. "The Garden of Love." In *The Complete Poetry and Prose of William Blake*, edited by David Erdman, 26. Berkeley: University of California Press, 1982.

Colson, Nicole S. "Choctaw, Cherokee and African-American descent have shaped Martha Redbone." *Sentinel Source*, March 21, 2013. http://www.sentinelsource.com.

Eaves, Morris "Introduction: to Paradise the Hard Way." In *The Cambridge Companion to William Blake*, edited by Morris Eaves, 1–18. Cambridge: Cambridge University Press, 2003.

"Genius." In *An Oxford Companion to the Romantic Age: British Culture 1776–1832*, edited by Iain McCalman, 518–19. Oxford: Oxford University Press, 1999.

Hudson, Zach. "Martha Redbone's Journey to William Blake." *No Depression*, November 1, 2012. http://nodepression.com/article/martha-redbones-journey-william-blake.

Hutchings, Kevin. "Nature, Ideology, and the Prohibition of Pleasure in Blake's 'Garden of Love.'" In *Romanticism and Pleasure*, edited by Thomas M. Schmid and Michelle Faubert, 187–207. New York: Palgrave, 2010.

"Martha Redbone." Night Life, *The New Yorker*, December 1, 2012. http://www.newyorker.com/goings-on-about-town/night-life/martha-redbone.

McClatchy, Debby. "Appalachian Traditional Music: A Short History." *Musical Traditions*, June 6, 2000. https://www.namb.net/send-relief/arm/appalachian-culture.

Pearson, Tom. "Interview with Martha Redbone." *Native Theater Festival Interview Series*, Hemispheric Institute, 2008. http://hemisphericinstitute.org/hemi/hidvl/hidvl-int-native-theater/item/1356–ntfest-mredbone.

Redbone, Martha. *The Garden of Love: Songs of William Blake*. Blackfeet Productions / CD Baby 5637916988, 2012, compact disc.

Ward, Aileen. "William Blake and His Circle." In *The Cambridge Companion to William Blake*, edited by Morris Eaves, 19–36. Cambridge: Cambridge University Press, 2003.

"What is Appalachia?" *The Alliance for Appalachia*. http://theallianceforappalachia.org/background/.

Wikane, Christian John. "Tales from Black Mountain: A Conversation with Martha Redbone." *Popmatters.com*, January 17, 2014.

Chapter Five

"Tangle of Matter and Ghost"

U2, Leonard Cohen, and Blakean Romanticism

Lisa Crafton

The title of U2's 2014 release, *Songs of Innocence*, makes apparent the band's dialogue with poet William Blake, whose presence throughout the U2 oeuvre is an influence both conscious at times but more often palimpsestic, as it were. Thematic attention to spirituality (and the exposure of false gods made fashionable by orthodox religious institutions), individualism, social (in)justice, and the "states" of innocence and experience that humans pass in and out of at various times in their lives, as well as shared use of poetic narrative techniques, link the Romantic poet and the contemporary Irish band in significant ways. All of these similarities, however, resonate more deeply when we consider another artistic presence, that of Leonard Cohen. In a commencement address to Harvard, Bono asserts that rock music is rebel music, but not just against the external world:

> If I am honest I'm rebelling against my own indifference. I am rebelling against the idea that the world is the way it is and there's not a damned thing I can do about it. So I'm trying to do some damned thing.[1]

Bono's juxtaposition between frustration about conflicts in our world and the commitment to never give in to indifference speaks to a belief in a visionary element in rock music that channels energy. Leonard Cohen, in a nod to his most famous song "Hallelujah," similarly expresses the power of music as a kind of catharsis to cultural anxiety:

The only moment that you can live here comfortably in these absolutely irrec-
oncilable conflicts is in this moment when you embrace it all, and you say
"Look, I don't understand a fucking thing at all—Hallelujah!"[2]

The explicit dialogue between the works of Leonard Cohen and U2 reveals
the extent to which rock music serves as a vessel of Blakean Romanticism,
and my study traces this artistic triangle shared by Blake, Cohen, and U2. In
the Toronto date of U2's 2017 concert tour celebrating the thirtieth anniversary of *The Joshua Tree*, Bono paid tribute to Cohen (who died November 7,
2016) by singing lyrics from "Suzanne" and avowing that "[Leonard Cohen]
is an addiction I'm not ready to give up"; Bono's avowal that Leonard Cohen
"has you" at all stages of your life could just as well be a reading of Blake's
lifelong commitment to representing psychological states.[3]

The intertextual relationships that I explore here are strengthened by overt
acknowledgments of influence. U2's invocation of Blake's 1789 poetic volume in their latest album is certainly not their first. During their 1980s' work
on *The Joshua Tree*, U2 recorded "Beautiful Ghost/Introduction to Songs of
Experience," a haunting, sonorous, Brian Eno-inspired, experimental version
of Blake's very atmospheric poem, "Introduction" to *Songs of Experience*,
led by Bono's chanting of Blake's lyrics. As for the influence of Cohen,
Bono recalls a formative high school teacher reading aloud Cohen's lyrics in
English class. Bono's tributes to Cohen include a version of Cohen's "Hallelujah" on the tribute album *The Tower of Song: Songs of Leonard Cohen*,
and, most significantly, critical commentary in the documentary *Leonard
Cohen: I'm Your Man*. In this film Bono avows the power of Cohen's artistry
as well as his imaginative power to express the range of human experience
and emotion.[4] Additionally, all three artists have created and published visual art which integrates with their written word. Thus, the essay situates this
triangle of artists in terms of acknowledged debts to their precursors, but,
more importantly, the profound metaphorical and thematic connections that
brand both Cohen and U2 as Romantic.

Forging a link between Romanticism as an artistic movement and rock
music is no new endeavor, as any student of the cultural history of the 1960s
knows. In general, such analogies stem from genre as well as political/cultu-
ral resonances. Robert Pattison's 1987 *The Triumph of Vulgarity: Rock Music in the Mirror of Romanticism*, for example, contends that rock unites
Romantic mythology and American ideals through the form of vulgar
counterparts of their originals. In an opinionated, highly selective analysis,
Pattison asserts that vulgarity is the quintessence of Romanticism: vulgarity
is "common, noisy, and gross, but above all, vulgarity is untranscendent."[5]
Theodore Gracyk's 1993 "Romanticizing Rock Music" links Romantic art
and popular folk music. Both of these critics attend to a genre-oriented mode
of comparison, while Camille Paglia emphasizes theme in an uncompromis-

ing romanticizing of rock. Just as Paglia celebrates rock's vital rhythms sung by "freaks, dreamers, and malcontents," she also decries rock's falling victim to capitalism.[6] Yet, she does not consider the power of art as social change to be a defining element as she subscribes to the subset of "dark" Romanticism, calling the Rolling Stones the "heirs of stormy Coleridge."[7] Conversely, Shultze uses the same laundry list of Romantic tenets as Paglia to denounce rock music as the "last gasp of Romanticism" in his Calvinist-inspired analysis of MTV.[8] All these critical models share a tendency toward circularity. Anything that does not reflect one critic's definition of the movement is written off; the selection of the example drives the argument without admitting that fact.

On the other hand, Sayre and Lowy's "Figures of Romantic Anti-Capitalism" employs their interest in the neo-romantic dimension of German art to assert that "Romanticism is an essential component of modern culture."[9] These critics provide a corrective to those who strip Romanticism from its political dimensions but invoke a definition of Romanticism as an enigma of opposites "at the same time (or alternately) revolutionary and counter-revolutionary . . . mystical and sensual."[10] These authors maintain an essential belief that Romanticism in Europe is opposition to capitalism, yet they do not simplify this as the sole premise of Romantic art, which also usually reveals something more akin to a mystical yearning. While it is impossible to persuade any cynics who would argue that uber-wealthy and successful figures like Bono cannot be seen as anti-capitalist because of their own riches, it is equally impossible to deny that from Live-Aid to Amnesty International to the One campaign (which Bono has labeled the "NRA for the world's poor"), Bono has consistently maintained that his rock band's idealism is at the heart of their identity, that committing to life in a band came with the clear conviction by all of U2 that "the world can be kissed or kicked into shape."[11] While this quest may become nostalgic or escapist (thus the pejorative label "romanticized"), at its best it offers an impetus for cultural renewal, as is certainly the case as Blakean Romanticism is manifested in the works of U2 and Leonard Cohen.[12]

One theoretical note: while I acknowledge statements of "influence" (overt or covert), my argument echoes Clark, Connolly, and Whittaker, in *Blake 2.0: William Blake in Twentieth-Century Art, Music, and Culture*, in that what "happens in the Blakean afterlife is detached from writer-on-writer models of influence and residually patrilineal concepts of inheritance and transmission . . . [alternative models] are less defined and confined by various forms of affiliation or resistance."[13] My study touches broadly on these areas of intersection: social and cultural protest, the conflation of erotic/spiritual love, and the representation of the rupture of that symbiosis, especially in the poetic treatment of Judas, Yahweh, and Jesus (Cohen, whose "Suzanne" conflates the bodies/minds of Suzanne/Jesus, says, as a Jew, that "the figure of Jesus is extremely attractive. It's difficult not to fall in love with that person"). These intersections dramatize the primary Blakean argument: opening the doors of perception implies a concomitant need to open real doors for liberation from oppression of all kinds.

While some of Blake's more esoteric mythical poems may not have been useful fodder for political activism, his radical political espousal of sexual, racial, and economic equality and his blistering repudiation of all forms of tyranny (government, church, culture) pervade even the *Songs* with the psychologically informed subtitle "Shewing the Two Contrary States of the Human Soul." *Songs of Innocence and of Experience* indicts slavery, racism, hypocritical institutional and prudish restrictions on sexuality, sectarian bigotry, and the powerful State/Church apparatus that maintains these divisive beliefs to secure control of its citizenry. Blake's condemnations of his culture's crimes against individual liberty provide the first link to the political critique of many contemporary rock artists.

Both U2 and Cohen are known for radical protests against war in their representations of, respectively, Irish and Israeli-Palestinian conflict. For U2, the anthemic "Sunday Bloody Sunday" is, at once, always about the Irish troubles and that conflict's continued effects and a commentary on contemporary battles, but even more significantly, "Bullet the Blue Sky" has been an evolving cornerstone of the U2 concert oeuvre. The fourth track from the 1987 *The Joshua Tree*, the song uses civil war in El Salvador with indictment of U.S. forces involved in a bombing of a small village. While the song invokes Biblical imagery (Jacob wrestling an angel, a demon seed, driving nails into the souls on the sea of pain), it abruptly ends with America, where under a rainy sky "ripped open" woman and children in El Salvador run "into the arms of America."

In subsequent concert performances, Bono used a flashlight/spotlight to sweep the faces of the crowds, implicating all in the complicity of American intervention. By the 2001 Elevation tour, the context broadened as video monitors simultaneously showed images of military units, the devastation of war, and the graphic "USA, UK, France, China, Russia . . . The Five Biggest Arms Traders in the World." During the Paris concert, Bono turned the spotlight on himself with the graphic "IRA, British army." In the third leg of the same tour, U2 scrolled the names of the victims of 9/11 in American venues during the song.[14] Transcending its origin, "Bullet the Blue Sky" maintains its dual-pronged attack on both the outside, the political machinations, and the inside, our own complicity, the Blakean "mind-forg'd manacles" we battle in war-torn times.

A similar duality characterizes Cohen's political activism, which, in terms of war, has centered on Israeli/Palestinian peace movements. Performing in front of 47,000 in the soccer stadium of the suburb Ramat Gan in "A Concert for Reconciliation, Tolerance and Peace," Cohen gave the profits of about

$1.5 million to a new charity he had created of the same name for groups focused on coexistence.[15] Two songs introduce listeners to the psychological states of awareness of those who breed war and terrorism. "Story Of Isaac" from *Songs from a Room* (1969) and the better known "First We Take Manhattan" from *I'm Your Man* (1988) demonstrate how Cohen's social protest songs work like dramatic monologues, favoring representations of psyche over political propaganda. "Story of Isaac" recounts the journey of Abraham toward the sacrificial altar but addresses contemporary sacrificial agents of war as well. Isaac stresses the visionary authority of his father Abraham, who is acting under orders, and as the father puts his hand upon Isaac's, the young boy of nine sees either an eagle or vulture, emphasizing his inability to understand the act of his father. Then an omniscient Isaac addresses a contemporary listener: "You who build these altars now to sacrifice these children / you must not do it anymore." In an interview in 1974, Cohen says, "It has fathers and sons in it and sacrifice and slaughter . . . The antiwar movement claims the song as its own and that's fine."[16] But in 1988, Cohen conflates its social protest with a broader register of meaning:

> I was careful in that song to try and put it beyond the . . . simple, anti-war protest, that it also is . . . In other words it isn't necessarily for war that we're willing to sacrifice each other . . . human beings being what they are we're always going to set up people to die for some absurd situation that we define as important.[17]

Perhaps most significantly, the song does not end with a stirring call to action but is more unsettling in its implication that we will turn on each other as we have to. Like U2's evolving performances of "Bullet the Blue Sky" ensuring different targets of critique, Cohen's narrator avoids self-righteousness, confessing "I will kill you if I must." Cohen's adamant claim about the true power of the song is instructive: "Outside all of those cultural attachments, which the song has gathered to itself as it moved through society in its limping way, I just know that as an experience it is authentic psychically. It doesn't betray itself."[18]

The social and political references in "First We Take Manhattan" are matched with a terrifying speaker. Notoriously noncommittal about this song, Cohen, in an interview a month after the terrorist attacks in America, stresses its manipulation of point of view: "Every succeeding moment changes what has happened the moment before . . . 'First We Take Manhattan' might be understood as an examination of the mind of the extremist. In a way it's a better song now than it was before."[19] The song offers the voice of one frustrated from years of political activism: "They sentenced me to twenty years of boredom."[20] But the speaker quickly turns from that "they/me" binary to an "I/we" in what Siemerling calls "ironically militant words that delineate, as so often in Cohen's work, a vague map with their pronouns."[21] By repeatedly saying "First, we take Manhattan," the speaker certainly addresses us, but how are we to take his offer of terroristic adventure? Are we his subjects or his adversaries? The song is Blakean in its intense representation of rage, its manipulative use of point of view, but also its sarcastic disavowal of postures of polite generosity as in the enigmatic last stanza where the speaker thanks a sender for the gifts of "the monkey and the plywood violin." [22] The line indicts the greedy part of ourselves that silences a commitment to action. The sender of the monkey and the violin, props for an organ grinder, would be, according to Cohen, "that part of ourselves that diminished that voice that. . . was demanding a spiritual aspect to our lives . . . We gave that part of us a monkey and a plywood violin, so that it would screech away and amuse us with its antics."[23]

While social protest is a defining characteristic of all three artists, the energy behind the critiques stems from a conflation of erotic/divine love. It is commonplace in Blake criticism, of course, as most of his poetry relies on the mantra that "Everything that lives is holy,"[24] a phrase made famous in Van Morrison's recitative version of a Blakean monologue, "Let the Slave." The synthesis of erotic/divine impels lyric poems like "The Garden of Love" as well as the extravagant mythical claim from *The Marriage of Heaven and Hell* that the apocalypse of psychic renewal will "come to pass through an improvement in sensual enjoyment"[25] and defines the work of both U2 and Cohen.

The U2 oeuvre is dominated by Christian iconography serving to valorize erotic love as divine and to humanize divine love. In the final song on *All That You Can't Leave Behind*, "Grace" reminds us that Grace is "the name of a girl" but also "a thought that changed the world"; Bono wrote the song about "Grace interrupting Karma," in his words.[26] More specifically, "I Still Haven't Found What I'm Looking For" and "With or Without You" remain the watershed U2 statements on erotic/divine. In the trademark love anthem "I Still Haven't Found What I'm Looking For," a lover's yearning for another—"I have kissed honey lips"—merges with the cosmic—"I have spoke with the tongues of angels / I have held the hand of the devil"[27] —and ends with a turn to Jesus and a belief that one day these separate realms can be integrated. Conversely, in "With or Without You," the song opens with a yearning that is replete with Christian images, a thorn in the side, but moves from this spiritual pain to erotic, a "bed of nails" on which "she makes [him] wait."[28] The ambiguous crossing of the pronouns "she" and "you" implicate the lover again in this overlay of erotic/spiritual yearning where he waits "with or without you."[29]

A similar nexus of erotic/divine love appears throughout Cohen's work, although when Cohen employs Christian characters, he does so as a Jew, or as an observer. The most powerful evocation of the link, "Sisters of Mercy," invokes the Catholic order founded in Dublin in 1831 as lay services for poor women and children. The allusion is vital to the layers of meaning in the song: the binary of cloistered/non-cloistered (institutional/secular) is exactly what the song dissolves in its erotic/divine continuum. The story behind the song has had an interestingly similar controversy since its 1967 appearance on *Songs of Leonard Cohen*. In early interviews Cohen explains the origin: "I met in a Cafe two young girls . . . they showed me through the snowstorm in Edmonton . . . and we slept together in the evening the three of us. And during the night, although the sleep was gentle, I woke up and I wrote this song very, very quickly."[30]

While many critics seize on this story as example of Cohen's free love as it implies a *ménage à trois* (the song compares the girls to religious sisters in a bold alliance of erotic/spiritual female love), in interviews in 1974 and 1993, Cohen narrates an encounter where strangers become a part of one another, with sexual desire but no sexual act:

> [So] we found ourselves in my little Hotel room . . . Of course I had all kinds of erotic fantasies of what the evening might bring . . . [but] it became clear that it wasn't the purpose of the evening at all. And at one point, in the night . . . I wrote that poem by the ice-reflected moonlight while these women were sleeping and it was one of the few songs that I ever wrote from top to bottom without a line of revision.[31]

Cohen's song opens with finding the sisters of mercy waiting for him, as he says, "when I thought that I just can't go on."[32] He then quickly turns to listeners, hoping that "you" too will find them, and the rest of the song invokes a very distinct audience: "Yes, you who must leave everything that you cannot control."[33] The person who tries to control even matters of the soul is also the one most troubled, the most "pinned," and who listens to a voice that condemns sin ("Your loneliness says that you've sinned").[34] Interweaving the erotic/divine, the persona recounts that as he laid down next to them he also made confession and touched their hems. Not leaving that ambiguity as closure, the persona turns back to the "you" earlier addressed and hopes for an encounter for him/her, willing to share a lover, offering a lover to "sweeten your night,"[35] leaving the next action on the part of the "you," who must decide about his own denial of joy.[36]

More specifically analogous to U2's nexus of erotic/divine, Cohen's "Suzanne" relies on a triangulated relationship among speaker, female lover figure, and Christ. Comments by both the Edge and Bono in *Leonard Cohen: I'm Your Man* emphasize this symbiosis. The Edge links the talent of Cohen to early Christian mysticism, but Bono, who also sees an otherness in the music, stresses instead the "sensuous overload," a confirmation that the world is "tactile, sensual, and brightly colored."[37] Bono responds to the figure of Jesus as an Irish Catholic, Cohen as a fellow, anguished Jew. A portrait of yearning no less strident than U2's speaker "on a bed of nails,"[38] and a manipulation of pronouns Blakean to the core, Cohen's narrator works in a tripartite poetic structure, moving from Suzanne to Jesus to Suzanne. Introduced as a sensual Other ("half-crazy"), Suzanne is also an exotic (who "feeds you tea and oranges that come all the way from China"), and a transcendent being who magically "gets you on her wavelength" and is associated with Nature in the form of the river.[39] The initial iteration of the chorus ("And you want to travel with her") asserts the first phenomenological premise: "And you know that she will trust you / For you've touched *her* perfect body with *your* mind."[40] Trust is here predicated on "you" having touched her body with your mind. The second stanza moves to Christ—Jesus as a sailor—echoing Suzanne's association with the river. The focus on Jesus's walking on the water, a moment exhibiting the power of faith, both humanizes Christ and stresses his divinity. As O'Neill says, "Cohen dramatizes Christ's dual nature . . . during the crucifixion. 'Broken/Long before the sky would open,' the martyred god is 'Forsaken/almost human.'"[41] The second repetition of the chorus shifts the binary: rather than "you" having touched her body, now Christ has touched "*your* perfect body with *his* mind." After these stanzas of secular/divine love, the third stanza inaugurates the conflation as natural scenes of Suzanne's (and Cohen's) Montreal become origins of the divine. The singer finds evidence of divine care in Montreal, where the sun beams down on "our lady of the harbor" referring to the statue of the Virgin atop the mariners' church of Notre Dame de Bon Secours which, as O'Neill notes, "looks out to sea and, in imitation of Christ's gesture to Peter, extends an outstretched hand to bless the departing sailors."[42] Suzanne as an eccentric goddess then stands in for Christ, as she wears clothes from the Salvation Army and guides the speaker to "heroes in the seaweed," a kind of watery restatement of Blake's famous aphorism, "To see the world in a grain of sand / Infinity in a wildflower."[43] The final choral refrain manipulates the body/mind duality for a final closure, assuring the listener that she has touched your body with "*her* mind." Having moved from "you" as the one who touches, to "he" as the one who touches, and now to "she" as the toucher, the triangulation of speaker / Suzanne / Christ is complete.[44]

Finally, even more significant than the symbiotic relationship of erotic/ divine are the ways in which Blake, U2, and Cohen all represent the rupture of this connection. In the poem "Service," Bono's mentor Irish poet Brendan Kennelly asserts, "The best way to serve an age is to betray it"; like David in the Psalms, Kennelly "scratches out screwtape letters to a God who may or may not have abandoned him."[45] Blake is, again, foundational on this issue; for all his avowals of the divinity of erotic love, Blake wrestles with the idea of a God who presides over evil and with the human will to mispresent God as a tyrannical judge. While *America*, for example, mythologically chronicles freedom in the colonies, the hero of liberty, Orc, is linked to Jesus but misinterpreted by humans as Satan. The famously anthologized poem "The Tyger" presents God as audaciously framing a dreadful being, leaving the narrator to question, "Did he who made the Lamb make [the tiger]?" These complex questions are reinforced by intricate uses of point of view as Blake offers a multi-layering of voices, requiring the reader to parse out the meaning very carefully. Both U2 and Cohen similarly rely on this kind of poetic ambiguity of point of view and multiple speakers. Through their representations of Judas, Yahweh, and Satan, both artists arrest listeners with betrayals of divine love and human inability to accept the truth of the erotic/divine continuum.

As a dramatic monologue, "Until the End of the World" provides a triptych of narrative moments of Judas's experience with Jesus (the Last Supper, the Garden of Gethsemane, and the afterworld) and ultimately portrays a Jesus who promises to wait, even for those who betray him. Judas has always been part of Bono's thinking about Jesus. In his paean to Martin Luther King, Jr. in "Pride," Bono's repetition of the "one man" refrain ends as he compares King to "one man betrayed with a kiss."[46] Inspired by Kennelly's "Book of Judas," the song engages Judas as a force, a trace of something from which we can never quite dissociate. Bono reviewed Kennelly's work in the Irish newspaper *The Independent*, stressing that when we encounter Jesus, we "know that Judas is just 'round the corner, and *he* knows."[47] Bono begins "Until the End of the World" with a memory of a meeting between Jesus and Judas in "a low-lit room" where they were as close together as a bride and groom, suggesting a pair of lovers at a wedding. Then the imagery shifts to Eucharistic ritual ("We ate the food, we drank the wine") and to Judas's recalling that in the midst of the party, "you" (Jesus) were "talking about the end of the world."[48] The second stanza shifts to Judas's confessional narration of his betrayal, again in the context of them as a couple, but hardly a romantic one, as Judas confesses to taking the money and kissing Christ in the garden. Finally, Judas narrates self-deprecatingly about his guilt and moves from judging Jesus as a voice of doom to realizing in a surprising epiphany that Jesus does not reject him for his treachery but instead makes a promise: even after the betrayal he says he will "wait till the end of the world."[49]

Finally, U2, despite their anthemic legacies of love, characteristically question the nature of God, but their most Blakean song in terms of point of view remains "Wake Up, Dead Man." Jarring and discordant, the song opens with a plea for Jesus's help as the narrator finds himself alone in the world, and "a fucked up world it is too."[50] The narrator's genuine suffering as well as his bitter label for the world resolves into plaintive requests—"Tell me the story, the one about Eternity"—but ends with the command "Wake up dead man."[51] Both the syntax and the energy of the line suggest the narrator's striking out at a deaf God. Continuing the bifurcated position, he asserts a belief that God is looking out for us only to challenge it ("But maybe your hands aren't free").[52] Alluding to at least some of the cause of this cynical view of God as dead, the narrator sketchily mentions a "her" whose unnamed tragedy came with no warning from a God who seems absent. No matter the reasons, the narrator repeatedly, with a discordant, pounding guitar for emphasis, shouts again, "Wake up dead man." Trost says that some reviewers see the song "flirting with blasphemy"; the bridge, however, reverses the speaker's point of view. In an unannounced shift to another speaker, the narrator is silenced from his monologue with "Listen": "Listen to your words / They'll tell you what to do / Listen over the rhythm that's confusing you."[53] Admonishing the speaker into silence, this voice enjoins the speaker to listen "over" and "through" the things that block his awakening. Finally, the voice moves to abstractions, employing the same advice when it comes to the disjunction between "hope" and "peace," which are, nevertheless, at least "try[ing] to rhyme." Repeated three times to end the song, the refrain "Wake up dead man" now has collectively accumulated double meaning: both speakers urge the other to wake up, and the adjective-rich "dead man" is, of course, both. The song sounds like a cry to a God who may or may not be there; the real power of the song, though, is that God is right there seeing through doubt, quick to point out our own dead cores.

The manipulation of point of view here is similar to Cohen's use of it in his powerful, liturgically inspired song "Who by Fire." A prayer of the Jewish New Year, this liturgy for the Day of Atonement is the subject of a 2010 scholarly anthology (*Who by Fire, Who by Water—Un'taneh Tokef*). In fact, the editor Lawrence A. Hoffman quotes both Blake and Cohen, arguing for a Blakean reading of this prayer.[54] Cohen underscores the interrogative nature of the prayer, posing questions not only about how a person may die but also the circumstances that define a human life. The song offers a mixture of verbatim and modern rewording of the prayer. First appearing on Cohen's 1974 album *New Skin for the Old Ceremony* as a duet with Janis Ian, the first five lines of each stanza offer parallel, contrasting scenarios, beginning with "Who by" or "Who in." It is only in the sixth line, as Jacobus points out, that a verb appears in a line that is not in the synagogue prayer: "Who shall I say is calling?"[55] It's an interesting rhetorical device, seemingly disconnected from the verse roll calls, and yet in an interview Cohen explains that the song, while based on the prayer, changes the central idea of judgment:

Cohen: That song derives very directly from a Hebrew prayer . . . But, of course, the conclusion of the song as I write it is somewhat different. "Who shall I say is calling."

Interviewer: Who is calling?

Cohen: Well, that is, that is, that is what makes the song into a prayer. For me, in my terms, who is it, or what is it, that determines who will live and who will die.[56]

The song mimics the structure of the prayer itself—it is rhythmic, rhymed, and structured around pairs of opposites (sunshine/nighttime, high ordeal/common trial). Both the prayer and Cohen's song echo the dualistic pairs of Ecclesiastes—"To everything there is a season"—that affirm an "order in all of this disorder," as Bono writes in "Wake Up Dead Man." "And who shall I say is calling," Cohen formally asks, as if answering a phone call. The final line as Cohen delivers it is, as he says, what turns it into a prayer just for him, but I believe a Blakean point of view is called for here. The ambiguity of the speaker of the line is compelling. Like the manipulation of pronouns in "Suzanne," U2's manipulation of the referent of "dead man" or of the "you" in "With or Without You," the question must come from some speaker. If the voice of the "Who by" lines is God, a kind of intoning of Biblical assertions of supremacy, then is the final line spoken by the human singer? If so, does he really not know who is calling? Is he dumbfounded, instead of comforted, by the array of ends that human life can take, and resistant in his question in a kind of "Yes, but who are you" tone? Or, on the other hand, can we read this question as spoken *to* the human singer? After all, the human narrator has offered his own version of a contemporary roll call of possible deaths in the twentieth century ("who by barbiturate, who by powder?") in an interrogative of the mystery of life and death, as if more information would aid understanding. Given this narrator's obstinate interrogation, then might not a divine voice from somewhere else say "Who are you" to question? Like a butler answering a call for his master, "Who can I say is calling" remarks on the unimportance of the speaker's questioning of the mystery.[57] In this way the Other presence may, like the bridge voice in U2's "Wake Up Dead Man," suggest that the human singer look to his own reactions before casting blame on a power that may not ultimately have anything to do with man's own end.

Finally, a similar manipulation of point of view pervades Cohen's "Nevermind," used as the introductory song for the 2015 second season of *True Detective*. Found on the 2014 album *Popular Problems*, "Nevermind" began its life as a poem. Described as a "dirge" that is nonetheless "sparse, gravely, and altogether badass," "Nevermind" provided the show's opening credits the atmospheric eeriness it became known for in its first season, and Cohen's voice, which "booms like an Old Testament God played by John Wayne," offers an ominous sense to the multiple voices within the song.[58] Like the narrator in "Wake Up Dead Man," the speaker problematically ponders both "truth that lives" and "truth that dies,"[59] and seems at some point to give up the burden of questioning, so "nevermind." Interestingly, the theme song as used in *True Detective* changed each week, substituting lyrics, as coinciding or contrapuntal to the episode. T. Bone Burnett says of the song and its function in the television show: "To me, 'Nevermind' is the song of the century so far, coming from one of the wisest men in our culture . . . It feels very much like Los Angeles right now: beautiful, dark, brooding, dangerous, covert."[60]

The song begins with a dystopian, noir-esque setting, referencing a lost war and a speaker who was not caught but who crossed a line. The speaker may identify as criminal, not being caught, but the context of postwar makes that status ambiguous—what line did he cross? A moral line? Enemy lines? With the second stanza, the reader seemingly gets an answer, as the speaker admits that he lives among us "well disguised," a somewhat fearful assertion for the reader. Adding to the complexity are the lyrics added in the second episode's version of the song which indict the reader as the speaker scorns a "you" who tried to turn him in and "whom you despise."[61] Significantly, in subsequent variations of the lyrics, the identity of the speaker becomes less specific, less mortal and more cosmic, situating himself in "layers of time." By this point in the trajectory of the television show, ambiguity of motive, character, and plot is in full force, and the vocals of the theme song suggest listeners' and viewers' inability to understand. In his final assertion of "truth that lives" and "truth that dies," the narrator calls out the lies of those who live in the open, not disguised as he is, but who are perhaps more criminal for it: "You serve them well I'm not surprised / You're of their kin you're of their kind."[62]

Kurt Cobain wrote these lines in 1990: "Give me the Leonard Cohen afterward / So I can sigh eternally."[63] The song "Pennyroyal Tea," the ninth track on Nirvana's final studio album *In Utero* (1993), was set to be released in April 1994, but with the death of Cobain, was not released until twenty years later. Cobain's reference to the Cohen legacy of somberness (Cohen's labels include the Godfather of Gloom) was shared with Cohen who said in an interview, "I'm sorry I couldn't have spoken to the young man. I see a lot of people at the Zen Centre, who have gone through drugs and found a way out that is not just Sunday school. There are always alternatives, and I might have been able to lay something on him."[64] Bono would agree that Cohen always has the ability to "lay something on [us]," seeing beyond the soberness of Cohen's landscapes a visionary one, sensuous and inviting. Cohen himself has tried to dispel the constant association of his works with melancholy: "My voice just happens to be monotonous and I'm somewhat whiney, so they are called sad songs. But you could sing them joyfully too. It's a completely biological accident that my songs sound melancholy when I sing them."[65] Like Blake's contrary states, Cohen's songs are both reflective and joyous, just as his exclamations of "Hallelujah" and "Fuck" at the same time convey a "higher innocence," just as U2's latest album *Songs of Innocence* was released with the promise that a second dialogue album *Songs of Experi-*

ence is in the works.[66] As much as Blake chronicles his eighteenth-century London, Cohen a mid-twentieth-century Montreal, and U2 a late twentieth-century Dublin, the three artists are prophets of imagination, artists whose exploration of that "tangle of matter and ghost" that is human life will have a permanent, as Blake would say, "Eternal" Romantic function.

NOTES

1. Bono, "Class Day Address June 6, 2001," *Harvard Gazette*, accessed July 14, 2017, https://news.harvard.edu/gazette/story/2001/06/class-day-address-june-6th-2001–bono/.
2. See Alan Light, "How Leonard Cohen's 'Hallelujah' Brilliantly Mingled Sex, Religion," *Rolling Stone*, Dec. 3, 2012, accessed July 14, 2017, http://www.rollingstone.com/music/news/exclusive-book-excerpt-leonard-cohen-writes-hallelujah-in-the-holy-or-the-broken-20121203.
3. See Karen Bliss, "U2 Pays Tribute to Leonard Cohen in Toronto," *Billboard* June 24, 2017, accessed July 14, 2017, http://www.billboard.com/articles/news/concerts/7842101/u2–leonard-cohen-tribute-toronto-concert.
4. Bono's comment that Leonard Cohen "has you" at all stages of your life comes from Lian Lunson's documentary *Leonard Cohen: I'm Your Man*, Lionsgate Films, 2006.
5. Robert Pattison, *The Triumph of Vulgarity: Rock Music in the Mirror of Romanticism* (Oxford: Oxford University Press, 1987), 6.
6. Theodore A. Gracyk, "Romanticizing Rock Music," *Journal of Aesthetic Education* 27, no. 2 (1993): 43–57; Camille Paglia, *Sex, Art, and American Culture* (New York: Vintage Books, 1992), esp. 19–21
7. See Paglia, *Sexual Personae: Art and Decadence from Nefertiti to Emily Dickinson* (New Haven: Yale University Press, 1990), 387.
8. Quentin Schultze, *Dancing in the Dark: Youth, Popular Culture, and the Electronic Media* (Grand Rapids: William B. Eerdmans Publishing Company, 1990), 164.
9. Robert Sayre and Michael Löwy, "Figures of Romantic Anti-Capitalism," *New German Critique* 32 (1984): 43.
10. Ibid., 42.
11. See Lee Mannion, "Bono at the Skoll World Forum," *Pioneers Post*, April 6, 2017, accessed July 14, 2017, https://www.pioneerspost.com/news-views/20170406/bono-the-skoll-world-forum-we-are-the-nra-of-the-poor.
12. Within Romantic scholarship, the combination of mystical/spiritual with the political/cultural dimensions has defined Blake studies for years (cf. Northrop Frye's Blake to David Erdman's, an apostle of Jesus the Imagination compared to a political activist). I agree with Peter Otto that 1960s' counterculture brought these disparate Blakes together, creating the composite that is the figure appropriated by The Doors, Patti Smith, and, I argue, U2.
13. Clark et al., 3.
14. Steve Taylor, "'Bullet the Blue Sky' as Evolving Performance" in *Exploring U2: Is This Rock'n'Roll? Essays on the Music, Work, and Influence of U2*, ed. Scott Calhoun (Lanham, MD: Scarecrow Press, 2012): 84–97.
15. Ethan Bronner, "Leonard Cohen's Legacy for his Concert in Israel," *The New York Times*, September 23, 2009.
16. Robin Pike, "Interview with Leonard Cohen," in *Leonard Cohen on Leonard Cohen*, ed. Jeff Burger (Chicago: University of Chicago, 2014), 69.
17. John McKellan, "Interview with Leonard Cohen," trans. Martin Godwyn, RTE Ireland. May 9, 12, 1988, accessed Feb. 29, 2016. http://www.leonardcohenfiles.com/rte.html.
18. Pike, 69.
19. Leonard Cohen, "The Chat," accessed Feb. 29, 2016, http://www.leonardcohenforum.com/viewtopic.php?t=15220.

20. Quotation from Leonard Cohen, "First We Take Manhattan," in *I'm Your Man*, Columbia CK44191, 1988, compact disc.

21. Winfried Siemerling, "Interior Landscapes and the Public Realm: Contingent Mediations in a Speech and a Song by Leonard Cohen," *Canadian Poetry* 33 (1993), accessed Feb. 29, 2016, http://www.uwo.ca/english/canadianpoetry/cpjrn/vol33/siemerling.htm.

22. Leonard Cohen, "First We Take Manhattan."

23. This interview from 1990 is quoted in Siemerling.

24. William Blake, *The Four Zoas*, in *The Complete Poetry and Prose of William Blake*, Newly Revised Version, ed. David V. Erdman (Berkeley, CA: University of California Press, 1982), 324.

25. William Blake, *The Marriage of Heaven and Hell*, in *The Complete Poetry and Prose of William Blake*, Newly Revised Version, ed. David V. Erdman (Berkeley, CA: University of California Press, 1982), 39.

26. See Adam Sweeting, "Time to Get the Leathers Out," *The Guardian*, October 27, 2000, accessed Feb. 29, 2016, http://www.theguardian.com/friday_review/story/0,388228,00.html.

27. U2, "I Still Haven't Found What I'm Looking For," in *The Joshua Tree*, Limited Edition, Reissue, Island Records 1750948, 2007, compact disc.

28. U2, "With or Without You," in *The Joshua Tree*, Limited Edition, Reissue, Island Records 1750948, 2007, compact disc.

29. Ibid.

30. Many of Cohen's comments on this song are collected on a French Leonard Cohen website. See "Leonard Cohen in his own live words," accessed Feb. 29, 2016, http://www.leonardcohen-prologues.com/sisters_of_mercy.htm.

31. Ibid.

32. Leonard Cohen, "Sisters of Mercy," in *Songs of Leonard Cohen*, Columbia CS 9533, 1967, 33 1/3 r.p.m.

33. Ibid.

34. Ibid.

35. Ibid.

36. The subtle challenge to a conventional morality that would restrict such encounters echoes Blake's point throughout the "flower poems" of *Songs of Experience*, all of which critique a refusal of sexual love for the sake of abstract moral premises.

37. It would be hard to find a better echo of Blake's belief that the epiphany of the infinite will come by "an improvement in sensual enjoyment" in *The Marriage of Heaven and Hell*.

38. U2, "Bullet the Blue Sky," in *The Joshua Tree*, Limited Edition, Reissue, Island Records 1750948, 2007, compact disc.

39. Leonard Cohen, "Suzanne," in *Songs of Leonard Cohen*, Columbia CS 9533, 1967, 33 1/3 r.p.m.

40. The italics for emphasis are mine as I quote all three different iterations of this line in the song.

41. Anne O'Neill, "Leonard Cohen: Singer of the Bible," *Crosscurrents* 65, no. 1 (2015): 95.

42. Ibid.

43. The alliance of Suzanne with "rags and feathers" and her ability to see heroes in the seaweed is similar to the way U2 in "MOFO" speak of searching for "baby Jesus under the trash."

44. Cohen's method here is comparable to Blake's craftsmanship at the end of "The Lamb," where the shifting pronouns "I," "thou," and "He" make the equality of the lamb, human, and Christ evident.

45. See Daniel T. Kline, "Playing the Tart: Contexts and Intertexts for 'Until The End of the World,'" in *Exploring U2: Is This Rock 'n' Roll? Essays on the Music, Work and Influence of U2*, ed. Scott D. Calhoun (Lanham, MD: Scarecrow Press, 2011), 135 and 134.

46. U2, "Pride (In The Name of Love) (Live at Madison Square Garden 1987)," in *The Joshua Tree*, Limited Edition, Reissue, Island Records 1750948, 2007, compact disc.

47. Kline, 135. Kline offers a succinct overview of both the ways in which *The Gospel of Judas* depicts Judas as Jesus's lone faithful follower and the major critical interventions (e.g.,

Ehrmann and Pagels) over-interpretation of this gospel in light of Gnosticism. See esp. 132 and 148, note 11.

48. U2, "Until the End of the World," in *Achtung Baby*, Island Records 314–510 347–2, 1991, compact disc.

49. Ibid.

50. U2, "Wake Up, Dead Man," in *Pop*, Island Records CIDU210, 524 334–2, 1997, compact disc.

51. Ibid.

52. Ibid.

53. Quoted in Theodore Louis Trost, "Transgressive Theology: The Sacred and the Profane at U2's Popmart," *U2 Above, Across, and Beyond: Interdisciplinary Assessments* (Lanham, MD: Lexington Books, 2015), 94.

54. Hoffman quotes the famous lines from "The Tyger"—"Did he smile his work to see? / Did he who made the Lamb make thee?"—in asking for similarly complex and poetic examinations of the "Who by Fire" prayer, 7.

55. Helen Jacobus, "The Story of Leonard Cohen's 'Who By Fire,' a Prayer in the Cairo Genizah, Babylonian Astrology, and Related Rabbinical Texts," *Reception History and Biblical Studies: Theory and Practice*, eds. William John Lyons and Emma England (London: Bloomsbury, 2015): 201–217.

56. Harry Rasky, *The Song of Leonard Cohen* (Montreal: Mosaic Press, 2001), accessed Feb. 20, 2016, http://www.leonardcohenfiles.com/rasky-fcc.html.

57. This rhetorical power would make the voice similar to God's voice in the whirlwind as heard by Job: "Where wast thou when I laid the foundations of the earth? Declare, if thou hast understanding. / Who hath laid the measures thereof, if thou knowest? or who hath stretched the line upon it?" Job 38:4–5 (AV).

58. Lindsay Zoladz, "A History of *True Detective*'s New Theme Song, 'Nevermind.'" *Vulture.com*, accessed Feb. 29, 2016, http://www.vulture.com/2015/06/true-detectives-theme-song-leonard-cohen-nevermind.html.

59. Leonard Cohen, "Nevermind," in *Popular Problems*. Columbia, Sony Music 88875014292, 2014, compact disc.

60. Richard Bienstock, "T Bone Burnett Explains Leonard Cohen *True Detective* Opening," *Rolling Stone*, August 14, 2015, accessed Feb. 29, 2016, http://www.rollingstone.com/music/news/t-bone-burnett-explains-leonard-cohen-true-detective-opening-20150814.

61. Leonard Cohen, "Nevermind," in *Popular Problems*. Columbia, Sony Music 88875014292, 2014, compact disc.

62. Ibid.

63. Kurt Cobain, "Pennyroyal Tea," in Nirvana, *In Utero*. DGC/Sub Pop DGCD-24607, 1993, compact disc.

64. Tim de Lisle, "Who Held a Gun to Leonard Cohen's Head," *The Guardian* Sept. 16, 2004, accessed Feb. 29, 2016, http://www.theguardian.com/music/2004/sep/17/2.

65. Burger, *Leonard Cohen on Leonard Cohen*, 26.

66. Higher innocence, a common term among Blakean critics to convey an epiphanic perspective that transcends the binaries, may well be what the 2015 U2 concert tour sought to dramatize with its literal showering of pages of texts down upon concertgoers, its visual depiction of various settings in Bono's early life, and its separation of the show into two parts, Innocence + Experience.

BIBLIOGRAPHY

Bienstock, Richard. "T. Bone Burnett Explains Leonard Cohen *True Detective* Opening." *Rolling Stone*, August 14, 2015, accessed Feb. 29, 2016, http://www.rollingstone.com/music/news/t-bone-burnett-explains-leonard-cohen-true-detective-opening-20150814.

Blake, William. *The Four Zoas*. In *The Complete Poetry and Prose of William Blake*, Newly Revised Version, edited by David V. Erdman, 300–407. Berkeley, CA: University of California Press, 1982.

————. *The Marriage of Heaven and Hell*. In *The Complete Poetry and Prose of William Blake*, Newly Revised Version, edited by David V. Erdman, 33–45. Berkeley, CA: University of California Press, 1982.

Bliss, Karen. "U2 Pays Tribute to Leonard Cohen in Toronto." *Billboard*, June 24, 2017, accessed July 14, 2017, http://www.billboard.com/articles/news/concerts/7842101/u2–leonard-cohen-tribute-toronto-concert.

Bono. "Class Day Address June 6, 2001." *Harvard Gazette*, accessed July 14, 2017, https://news.harvard.edu/gazette/story/2001/06/class-day-address-june-6th-2001–bono/.

————. "Hallelujah," in *The Tower of Song: Songs of Leonard Cohen*. A&M Records C 108110, 1995, 33-1/3 r.p.m.

Bronner, Ethan. "Leonard Cohen's Legacy for his Concert in Israel." *The New York Times*, September 23, 2009.

Burger, Jeff, ed. *Leonard Cohen on Leonard Cohen: Interviews and Encounters*. Chicago: Chicago Review Press, 2014.

Calhoun, Scott D., ed. *Exploring U2: Is This Rock 'n' Roll? Essays on the Music, Work and Influence of U2*. Lanham, MD: Scarecrow Press, 2011.

————. *U2 Above, Across, and Beyond: Interdisciplinary Assessments*. Lanham, MD: Lexington Books, 2015.

Clark, Steve, Tristanne Connolly, and Jason Whittaker, eds. *Blake 2.0: William Blake in Twentieth-Century Art, Music, and Culture*. New York: Palgrave, 2012.

Cobain, Kurt. "Pennyroyal Tea," in Nirvana, *In Utero*. DGC/Sub Pop DGCD-24607, 1993, compact disc.

Cohen, Leonard. "The Chat." *Leonard Cohen Forum*, accessed Feb. 29, 2016, http://www.leonardcohenforum.com/viewtopic.php?t=15220.

————. "First We Take Manhattan," in *I'm Your Man*. Columbia CK44191, 1988, compact disc.

————. "Leonard Cohen in his own live words." *Leonard Cohen Site*, accessed Feb. 29, 2016, http://www.leonardcohen-prologues.com/sisters_of_mercy.htm.

————. "Nevermind," in *Popular Problems*. Columbia, Sony Music 88875014292, 2014, compact disc.

————. "Sisters of Mercy," in *Songs of Leonard Cohen*. Columbia CS 9533, 1967, 33-1/3 r.p.m.

————. "Story of Isaac," in *Songs from a Room*. Columbia CS 9767, 1969, 33-1/3 r.p.m.

————. "Suzanne," in *Songs of Leonard Cohen*. Columbia CS 9533, 1967, 33-1/3 r.p.m.

————. "Who by Fire," in *New Skin for the Old Ceremony*. Columbia C 33167, 1974, 33-1/3 r.p.m.

De Lisle, Tim. "Who Held a Gun to Leonard Cohen's Head." *The Guardian*, Sept. 16, 2004, accessed Feb. 29, 2016, http://www.theguardian.com/music/2004/sep/17/2.

Gracyk, Theodore A. "Romanticizing Rock Music." *Journal of Aesthetic Education* 29, no. 2 (1993): 43–57.

Hoffman, Lawrence A., ed. *Who by Fire, Who by Water Un'taneh Tokef.* Woodstock, VT: Jewish Lights Publishing, 2010.

Jacobus, Helen. "The Story of Leonard Cohen's 'Who by Fire,' a Prayer in the Cairo Genizah, Babylonian Astrology, and Related Rabbinical Texts." In *Reception History and Biblical Studies: Theory and Practice*, edited by William John Lyons and Emma England, 201–217. London: Bloomsbury, 2015.

Kline, Daniel T. "Playing the Tart: Contexts and Intertexts for 'Until the End of the World.'" In *Exploring U2: Is This Rock 'n' Roll? Essays on the Music, Work and Influence of U2*, edited by Scott D. Calhoun, 129–150. Lanham, MD: Scarecrow Press, 2011.

Leonard Cohen: I'm Your Man. Directed by Lian Lunson. Santa Monica, CA: Lionsgate Films, 2006. DVD.

Light, Alan. "How Leonard Cohen's 'Hallelujah' Brilliantly Mingled Sex, Religion." *Rolling Stone*. Dec. 3, 2012, accessed July 14, 2017, http://www.rollingstone.com/music/news/exclusive-book-excerpt-leonard-cohen-writes-hallelujah-in-the-holy-or-the-broken-20121203.

Lyons, William John, and Emma England, eds. *Reception History and Biblical Studies: Theory and Practice*. London: Bloomsbury, 2015.

Mannion, Lee. "Bono at the Skoll World Forum." *Pioneers Post*. April 6, 2017, accessed July 14, 2017, https://www.pioneerspost.com/news-views/20170406/bono-the-skoll-world-forum-we-are-the-nra-of-the-poor.

McKellan, John. "Interview with Leonard Cohen." Trans. Martin Godwyn. RTE Ireland. May 9, 1988, accessed Feb. 29, 2016, http://www.leonardcohenfiles.com/rte.html.

Morrison, Van. "Let the Slave," in *A Sense of Wonder*. Mercury 822 895–2, 1984, compact disc.

O'Neill, Anne. "Leonard Cohen: Singer of the Bible." *Crosscurrents* 65, no. 1 (2015): 91–99.

Otto, Peter. "'Rouze up O Young Men of the New Age!': William Blake, Theodore Roszak, and the Counter Culture of the 1960s-1970s." In *Blake 2.0: William Blake in Twentieth-Century Art, Music, and Culture*, edited by Steve Clark, Tristanne Connolly, and Jason Whittaker, 27–40. New York: Palgrave, 2012.

Paglia, Camille. *Sex, Art, and American Culture*. New York: Vintage Books, 1992.

———. *Sexual Personae: Art and Decadence from Nefertiti to Emily Dickinson*. New Haven: Yale University Press, 1990.

Pattison, Robert. *The Triumph of Vulgarity: Rock Music in the Mirror of Romanticism*. Oxford: Oxford University Press, 1987.

Pike, Robin. "Interview with Leonard Cohen." In *Leonard Cohen on Leonard Cohen: Interviews and Encounters*, edited by Jeff Burger, 57–73. Chicago: Chicago Review Press, 2014.

Rasky, Harry. *The Song of Leonard Cohen*. Montreal: Mosaic Press, 2001, accessed Feb. 20, 2016, http://www.leonardcohenfiles.com/rasky-fcc.html.

Sayre, Robert, and Michael Löwy. "Figures of Romantic Anti-Capitalism." *New German Critique* 32 (1984): 42–92.

Schultze, Quentin. *Dancing in the Dark: Youth, Popular Culture, and the Electronic Media*. Grand Rapids: William B. Eerdmans Publishing Company, 1990.

Siemerling, Winfried. "Interior Landscapes and the Public Realm: Contingent Mediations in a Speech and a Song by Leonard Cohen." *Canadian Poetry* 33 (1993): accessed Feb. 29, 2016, http://www.uwo.ca/english/canadianpoetry/cpjrn/vol33/siemerling.htm.

Sweeting, Adam. "Time to Get the Leathers Out." *The Guardian*. October 27, 2000, accessed Feb. 29, 2016, http://theguardian.com/Friday_review/story/0,388228,00.html.

Taylor, Steve. "'Bullet the Blue Sky' as Evolving Performance." In *Exploring U2: Is This Rock 'n' Roll? Essays on the Music, Work and Influence of U2*, edited by Scott D. Calhoun, 84–97. Lanham, MD: Scarecrow Press, 2011.

Trost, Theodore Louis. "Transgressive Theology: The Sacred and the Profane at U2's Pop-Mart." In *U2 Above, Across, and Beyond: Interdisciplinary Assessments*, edited by Scott D. Calhoun, 91–104. Lanham, MD: Lexington Books, 2015.

U2. "Beautiful Ghost/Introduction to Songs of Experience," in *The Joshua Tree*, Limited Edition, Reissue. Island Records 1750948, 2007, compact disc.

———. "Bullet the Blue Sky," in *The Joshua Tree*, Limited Edition, Reissue. Island Records 1750948, 2007, compact disc.

———. "Grace," in *All That You Can't Leave Behind*. Interscope Records 314–548 328–2, 2000, compact disc.

———. "I Still Haven't Found What I'm Looking For," in *The Joshua Tree*, Limited Edition, Reissue. Island Records 1750948, 2007, compact disc.

———. *The Joshua Tree*. Limited Edition, Reissue. Island Records 1750948, 2007, compact disc.

———. "MOFO," in *Pop*. Island Records CIDU210, 524 334–2, 1997, compact disc.

———. "Pride (In The Name of Love) (Live at Madison Square Garden 1987)," in *The Joshua Tree*, Limited Edition, Reissue. Island Records 1750948, 2007, compact disc.

———. *Songs of Innocence*. Island Records 4704888, 2014, compact disc.

———. "Sunday Bloody Sunday (Live at Madison Square Garden 1987)," in *The Joshua Tree*, Limited Edition, Reissue. Island Records 1750948, 2007, compact disc.

———. "Until the End of the World," in *Achtung Baby*. Island Records 314–510 347–2, 1991, compact disc.

———. "Wake Up, Dead Man," in *Pop*. Island Records CIDU210, 524 334–2, 1997, compact disc.

————. "With or Without You," in *The Joshua Tree*, Limited Edition, Reissue. Island Records 1750948, 2007, compact disc.

Zoladz, Lindsay. "A History of *True Detective*'s New Theme Song, 'Nevermind.'" *Vulture.com*, accessed Feb. 29, 2016, http://vulture.com/2015/06/true-detectives-theme-song-leonard-cohen-nevermind.html.

Chapter Six

The Inner Revolution(s) of Wordsworth and the Beatles

David Boocker

Wordsworth's disillusionment with the French Revolution led him to develop new theories of poetry and of the role of the poet that marked an epistemic shift away from the neoclassic sensibilities of the eighteenth century. Generally speaking, the English Romantic movement fostered political opinions that celebrated the role of the individual's right to determine his/her own conduct in all areas except those few that the government must control. Romantics were willing to break long established political, social, and literary rules in their yearning to challenge the status quo to reclaim human freedom in all aspects of life. Central to the movement was Wordsworth's conceptions of the poet and poetry as imaginative agents for social change. Generations later, the Beatles, disenchanted with their concert performances, influenced by their experimentation with LSD, and on the verge of breaking up, made deliberate efforts to shift artistic expression for their times by focusing on the issues of their generation "to change the way people think about the world in order to create a better, more just world."[1] The "spirit of 1967" instilled in the Beatles "the belief that limits to the imagination were culturally imposed and should therefore be challenged,"[2] leading to their call for what Ian MacDonald effectively termed "revolutions in the head."[3] The shifts of both nineteenth-century Romanticism and twentieth-century rock were marked by changes in perception that focused the poet's powers inward, toward a more subjective and creative performance that asserted "the preciousness of the common person"[4] and called for social reform through personal, inner transformation.

In their essay "Figures of Romantic Anti-Capitalism," Robert Sayre and Michael Löwy write that Romanticism consists of a set of elements designed "to include all of the diverse manifestations"[5] of Romanticism that span historical periods and geographical locations. The foundation of one kind, "Restitutionist Romanticism," is a "hostility towards present reality" that manifests itself in a "revolt" against the "historical present"[6] and results in the isolation or alienation of the individual in society. Restoring social harmony is achieved "through imagination" and *nostalgia*," a recovery of "what has been lost" from the past.[7] This Marxist position provides a relevant framework for my discussion of Wordsworth and the Beatles, especially in understanding how they framed social problems and solutions. But visions of both Wordsworth and the Beatles demanded an additional transformational element. While both use nostalgia to restore or recreate a past state in the present, the efforts of Wordsworth and the Beatles to restore social harmony required turning inward and a focus on personal change. Wordsworth turned to common life for subjects, as he explains in his "Preface," giving a poetic voice to England's social and political outcasts, while the Beatles gave a lyrical voice that liberated in song the Romantic ideals of their generation in ways that affirmed "the dignity and significance of individual experience."[8]

WORDSWORTH'S POETIC REVOLUTION

Wordsworth's poetic subjects in *Lyrical Ballads* were often common, rustic people who were powerless and dispossessed. In "The Old Cumberland Beggar," Wordsworth describes a beggar whom he identifies as a member of a class of people that he has known since childhood. The poet fears that beggars will "soon become extinct,"[9] but their importance to society is measured by how people treat them. The old beggar is an isolated figure, and because his kind is disappearing he is presented as a nostalgic figure. Readers are taught about the beggar's value to society when they witness how he is treated by nature as he communes with sparrows and how the villagers respect his presence. The poet chastises statesmen for wanting to "rid the world of nuisances"[10] that they consider vile and brutish. But the villagers' humane and charitable treatment of him illustrates their Christian grace and spirit. Chandler cites this poem as the best example of the political poetry that Wordsworth includes in *Lyrical Ballads* because of "its elevation of feeling over incident and its close attention to a character from common life."[11]

Thus, when readers witness the villagers' humane treatment of the beggar, their attitudes toward the beggar are transformed as Wordsworth describes nostalgically how this beggar must be recognized as an important member of modern society. Chandler explains that the "way Wordsworth represents the problems of the poor from the point of view of those who are not poor"[12] demonstrates how the attitudes of those who observe the beggar's presence, including readers of the poem, are improved because "he reminds the villagers of their kind offices toward him."[13] In Book IX of *The Prelude*, Wordsworth wrote that growing up in the English Lake District, "which yet / Retained more of ancient homeliness, / Manners erect, and frank simplicity, / Than any other nook of English Land," taught him an egalitarianism that prevents him from judging people "with attention or respect / Through claims of wealth or blood."[14] Wordsworth's democratizing poetic voice requires the reader to realize that the lives of all human beings should be valued and respected.

The "Old Cumberland Beggar" provides the paradigm for how readers should interpret other poems by understanding them as "experiments . . . written chiefly with a view to ascertain how far the language of conversation in the middle and lower classes of society is adapted to the purposes of poetic pleasure."[15] He writes in the "Preface" to the *Lyrical Ballads* that "the manner in which our feelings and ideas are associated in a state of excitement"[16] is illustrated "by tracing maternal passion" in "Idiot Boy" and "Mad Mother," by witnessing the "struggles of a human being at the approach of death" as in "Forsaken Indian," and by showing the "perplexity and obscurity which in childhood attend our notion of death, as in 'We Are Seven.'"[17] Each of these poems typifies Wordsworth's poetic theory, "that the feeling therein developed gives importance to the action and situation and not the action and situation to the feeling."[18] For Wordsworth, a poet is "a man speaking to men,"[19] who is willing "to follow the impulses and volitions that impel all of us to search for meaning of the 'goings-on of the Universe.'"[20] Nostalgia for the past is often present in Wordsworth's poetry. In "'Tintern Abbey' we learn that 'thoughts are . . . the representatives of all our past feelings,'"[21] while in other poems, children's voices cry out to be heard over the din of the adult world.

Wordsworth's goal was for the readers of his poems to be in touch with their feelings, but to do so in a way that served political ends. When Wordsworth lost faith in the ability of mankind to empirically transform society, he joined Coleridge to begin a poetic movement that served as a mechanism for coping with their world: "No longer identified with revolutionary action or progress, human regeneration [became] the prerogative of the individual mind in communion with nature and, introspectively, the self."[22] Sayer emphasizes how this goal reinforced his belief that social reform begins with "an inner revolution—a revolution in the way of thinking and feeling."[23] Liu explains that "what matters is not so much what the poet does inside a poem as what the reader does outside it."[24] Many of his poems call for social reform not through mere public relief or action; for meaningful external change to occur, a corresponding internal change is necessary. Wordsworth's poetic and epistemological revolution reaffirmed his support for the egalitarian ideals of the French Revolution in a way that would lead to a moral revolution.

THE BEATLES'S LYRICAL REVOLUTION

The Beatles produced no lengthy manifesto explaining their purpose. But as with Wordsworth, the Beatles strove to initiate social reform through a process of inner revolution, one that changed the way that people thought about the issues of the day. They signaled to their fans a significant shift in their musical direction that would require their fans to alter their previous conceptions about the kind of music the band wrote. Lennon said in a 1967 interview, just before the release of *Sgt. Pepper*, "The people who have bought our records in the past must realize that we couldn't go on making the same type forever. We must change and I believe those people know this."[25] Gone are the popular love songs and ballads that "prominently feature first and second person pronouns."[26] In their place are "increasingly introspective"[27] lyrics that tell stories which focus on Romantic ideas, perception, and the power of the imagination. Their populist music after 1966 is often drawn from the stories of working-class people found in newspapers and television as well as from their lives in Liverpool. This inner revolution required a democratization of the poetic voice, one that demonstrated to listeners how they could overcome alienation to make the world a better place.

In *Revolution in the Head: The Beatles' Records and the Sixties*, Ian MacDonald writes that the counterculture that emerged in the 1960s was "an echo of the 19th-century Romantics' [attempts] to release the imagination from the tiresome constraints of rationalism."[28] He describes how the 1960s' generation, emerging out of the smugness of the post WW II 1950s, with its Cold War frenzy, developed ideas and attitudes that were anti-materialistic and against the status quo. Rock music and other forms of pop culture were revolutionary forms of self-expression. MacDonald explains that the Beats were "American cousins of the Existentialists" who influenced the Beatles in Paris in 1961. In Kerouac's terms, they were "on the road," alienated from society and "less preoccupied with integrity of the self than with transcending personal limits."[29] They opposed "Moneytheism" in favor of imaginative self-expression, believing in "the authenticity of individual experience over dogma handed down from the past or the ruling class."[30]

William Northcutt draws on the work of Frederic Jameson to argue that the album "is as much about separation and alienation as it is about unity"[31] caused in part by the Beatles's retreat from the public, manifested in their decision in 1966 to stop doing live concerts: "Such tensions presented the group with a crisis of identity, which the Beatles tried to resolve on *Sgt. Pepper*—through new 'readings' of their musical influences, newly developed philosophical ideals, the developing drug culture, and the world they wanted to change."[32] Northcutt demonstrates that the Beatles turned to "themes of death, loss, and alienation" beginning in 1964, in songs such as

"Eleanor Rigby," "In My Life," and "Taxman," and that *Sgt. Pepper* represents the culmination of their efforts to explore these themes.[33]

Lennon's "A Day in the Life"[34] is a song about perception built around "dreamy news images before and after the rush of a routine to so many of us: getting out of bed and trying to get to school or work on time."[35] Lennon's inspiration came from reading two stories in the January 17, 1967, *Daily Mail*. MacDonald observes that it is a "song not of disillusionment with life itself but of disenchantment with the limits of mundane perception. 'A Day in the Life' depicts the 'real' world as an unenlightened construct that reduces, depresses, and ultimately destroys."[36] The song begins with the story Lennon read about a man who died in a car crash, but what bothers him is the "detached view of onlookers whose only interest was in the dead man's celebrity."[37] Next he mentions a film he watched, "The English Army had just won the war" and, again, he describes the attitude of the audience, "A crowd of people turned away."[38] Finally, he writes about the story about how many holes there are in the road at Blackburn, Lancashire: "There are 4,000 holes in the road in Blackburn, Lancashire, or one twenty-sixth of a hole per person, according to a council survey."[39] Lennon's focus is on alienating effects of the media and on people who fail to process the meaning of news events that "remain in a superficial state of leaping from event to event."[40]

The "disenchantment" described by Lennon in "A Day in the Life" is present in a number of songs. In "Good Morning, Good Morning," Lennon uses the slogan from a Kellogg's Corn Flakes television commercial to develop a satirical song about everyday suburban life. Davies writes, "Paul thought it was John reacting against his own boring life and empty marriage and having nothing to do."[41] Throughout the activities of the day—waking up, going to work when "Everyone you see is half asleep, walking by the old school, returning home 'for tea and meet the wife—he's got nothing to say, but it's OK.'" MacDonald describes the song as a "disgusted canter through the muck, mayhem, and mundanity of the human farmyard."[42] McCartney, in "She's Leaving Home,"[43] turned to a February 27, 1967, story in *The Daily Mail* to tell the story of a girl who leaves home, disenchanted with her middle-class home life with its promises of "life devoted to a boring job with a secure pension, or a marriage to someone their parents considered suitable."[44]

As noted by Sayre and Löwy, restoring social harmony is achieved through nostalgia. Just as Wordsworth turned to childhood and reflection on the past in poems such as "Anecdote for Fathers" and "Tintern Abbey" to "see beyond the superficial confusion of phenomena to the laws of order and of cause which governed the world,"[45] the opening song of the album begins by turning back "twenty years ago," as Lennon and McCartney turned to children and nostalgia of their youth in Liverpool at this critical moment in their musical development. Indeed, the entire album concept is based on their attempt to assume alter egos, which was intended to show their fans that the music appearing on the album was going to be different. The costumes were designed to present "an Edwardian-style brass band giving a concert; the kind of band they'd seen giving Sunday concerts in the local park during the fifties, when they were growing up."[46]

The first songs written for *Sgt. Pepper*, "Strawberry Fields" and "Penny Lane," were released as singles in February 1967, but they ultimately did not appear on an album until *Magical Mystery Tour* in November 1967. They were companion pieces, the first of their songs to be named after real places, recalling childhood memories of Lennon and McCartney. George Martin wrote that "the original idea [behind *Sgt. Pepper*] was to do an album about the boys' Liverpool childhood, a real nostalgia trip."[47] MacDonald writes that "the true subject of English psychedelia was neither love nor drugs, but nostalgia for the innocent vision of childhood."[48] The nostalgia is intended not just "to render the specific sights and sounds of these places" but also to "depict the striking ways in which the mind interacts with environment."[49]

"Strawberry Fields," written by Lennon while in Spain in September 1966, was about the Salvation Army girls' reform school near his home, where he used to play with his friends, climbing trees, "imagining he was in an *Alice in Wonderland* magic world."[50] MacDonald wrote that the song is, on the one hand, "a study in uncertain identity, tinged with the loneliness of the solitary rebel against all things institutional; on the other, an eerie longing for a wild childhood of hide-and-seek climbing: the visionary strawberry fields of his imagination."[51] The song reflects Lennon's self-doubt, disorientation, and constantly altering perceptions of reality: "his own habit of saying one thing, then the next moment the opposite, believing it each time."[52] The world of "Penny Lane," based on Paul's childhood memories, is a cheerful song about a "rather featureless" Liverpool neighborhood,[53] which Paul transforms into a mythical place filled with happy childhood memories that include a barber, banker, and fireman. "When I'm Sixty-Four," which Paul wrote about his father when he was fifteen, presents a parodic vision of the challenges of old age from the perspective of a teen. For Wordsworth, childhood and early youth were the "source of his moral rectitude" and the Beatles follow his belief "that one did not necessarily become wiser while growing older in life."[54]

Lennon's "Lucy in the Sky with Diamonds," based on four-year-old Julian's drawing of his friend Lucy O'Donnell, looks through Lewis Carroll's "Looking Glass" (and probably LSD) to transform nature into an amusing, childlike world where a girl has "kaleidoscope eyes," flowers are made of cellophane "yellow and green," "Where rocking horse people eat marshmallow pies," and where "Lucy [is] in the sky with diamonds."[55] But in the end, nostalgia is not an entirely sufficient antidote: alienation must lead to social reform. Just as Wordsworth viewed an internal change as the key to social change and moral reform, the Beatles believed altering the perceptions of their listeners was the key to changing the world. Harrison's "Within You, Without You"[56] is the song that captures most of a philosophy that includes advice about how people can overcome disenchantment to make the world a better place. He writes that most people hide themselves from a reality that prevents them from seeing the truth. The revolution comes about through inner change that turns away from materialism and other socially accepted constructs and toward the liberation of the imagination. By taking this inward journey, Harrison challenges his listeners to look beyond themselves to better the world: those "who gain the world and lose their soul— / they don't know—they can't see . . . / are you one of them?" Saving this world is possible, he writes, through love. For McCartney this enlightenment is not brought on by absolute, rational certainty: ". . . it really doesn't matter if I'm wrong or right / Where I belong I'm right / Where I belong." Those who disagree with his worldview are shut outside his door.[57] McCartney believed this inward journey toward finding out truth ultimately helps us save the world through love. And even Lennon, in his darkest moments, suggests that escape from reality is unnecessary to make life beautiful, ending "A Day in the Life" with the line, "I'd love to turn you on." For Lennon and McCartney, turning on is no escape from reality; people change their lives and dream of a more beautiful world by "turning on to the truth rather than on to pot."[58]

THE INNER REVOLUTION

George Martin writes that Sir William Deedes, British Minister of Information in the mid-1960s, recognized that the Beatles has tremendous impact on western culture: "They [the Beatles] herald a cultural movement among the young which may become part of the history of our times."[59] Martin followed with this assessment of their influence: "the psychedelia, the fashions, the vogue for Eastern mysticism, the spirit of adventure, the whole peace and love thing, the anti-war movement; it was all there and more."[60]

One of the additional elements that marked the Beatles's impact was their intellectual tie to English Romanticism, which taught them to believe in and initiate social reform that began with an inner revolution and changed the way people felt and thought about the social issues of their day:

That "the Beatles changed the world" is not show biz hyperbole. They *did* change the world—by absorbing, focusing, and then transmitting, with unmistakable authority, their formulations of and responses to the core existential problems of life in our era: the conflict between ambition and collective solidarity, the role played by childhood memory in forming adult consciousness, the challenge in discovering purpose in an apparently meaningless world, and the difficulty of finding personal fulfillment while striving for professional accomplishment.[61]

In the end, what ultimately links the English Romantic movement to the Beatles is that they both signal momentous transitions after which poetry and music were never the same again. Wordsworth and the Beatles strove to initiate social reform through an inner revolution that changed the way people felt and thought about the issues of their day. Lennon best stated this philosophy in 1968; after dismissing "destruction" as the proper course of revolution, he wrote that changing the world could not be achieved by changing "the constitution" or "the institution . . . You better change your mind instead."[62] For Lennon, as for Wordsworth, social change would occur not through major social reform but through poetry's power to change the way individual people look at the world. He "believed that the only worthwhile revolution would come about through inner change rather than revolutionary violence."[63] The acts of reading the poetry and listening to the music become progressive acts that move us toward restoring social order. The more progressive act of taking them seriously and making their complaints part of our social and political debate is truly revolutionary. This is what Shelley meant when he wrote, "Poets are the unacknowledged legislators of the world."[64] Like Lennon, he credits poets with having power, great power, to shape people's perceptions to help them "imagine" a better world, one without heaven, religion, possessions, or countries.[65]

NOTES

1. Steven Baur, "You Say You Want a Revolution: Marx and the Beatles," in *The Beatles and Philosophy: Nothing You Can Think That Can't Be Thunk*, eds. Michael Baur and Steven Baur (Chicago: Open Court, 2006), 87.

2. Steve Turner, *The Beatles A Hard Day's Write: The Stories Behind Every Song* (New York: MJF Books, 1994), 185.

3. Ian MacDonald, *Revolution in the Head: The Beatles' Records and the Sixties*, 3rd ed. (Chicago: Chicago Review Press, 2007), 27.

4. Matthew Schneider, *The Long and Winding Road from Blake to the Beatles* (New York: Palgrave Macmillan, 2008), 6.

5. Robert Sayre and Michael Löwy, "Figures of Romantic Anti-Capitalism," *New German Critique* 32 (Spring/Summer, 1984): 54.

6. Ibid., 54.

7. Ibid., 56.

8. Schneider, *The Long and Winding Road*, 16.

9. William Wordsworth, "The Old Cumberland Beggar, A Description," in *Wordsworth's Poetry and Prose*, ed. Nicholas Halmi (New York: W. W. Norton, 2014), headnote.

10. Wordsworth, "The Old Cumberland Beggar," l. 67.

11. James K. Chandler, *Wordsworth's Second Nature: A Study of the Poetry and Politics* (Chicago: University of Chicago Press, 1984), 84.

12. Ibid., 85.

13. Ibid., 86.

14. William Wordsworth, *The Prelude*, in *Wordsworth's Poetry and Prose*, ed. Nicholas Halmi (New York: W. W. Norton, 2014), Book IX, ll. 218–221, 225–226.

15. William Wordsworth, "Advertisement to *Lyrical Ballads* with a Few Other Poems," in *Wordsworth's Poetry and Prose*, ed. Nicholas Halmi (New York: W. W. Norton, 2014), 8.

16. William Wordsworth, "Preface to *Lyrical Ballads*," in *Wordsworth's Poetry and Prose*, ed. Nicholas Halmi (New York: W. W. Norton, 2014), 79.

17. Ibid., 80.

18. Ibid., 80.

19. Ibid., 85.

20. Schneider, *The Long and Winding Road*, 80.

21. Wordsworth, *Preface*, 79.

22. Nicholas Roe, *Wordsworth and Coleridge: The Radical Years* (Oxford: Clarendon Press, 1988), 273.

23. Kevin M. Saylor, "Wordsworth's Prudent Conservatism: Social Reform in the *Lyrical Ballads*," *First Principles* 43:2 (Spring 2001), http://www.firstprinciplesjournal.com/print.aspx?article=843.

24. Yu Liu, *Poetics and Politics: The Revolutions of Wordsworth* (New York: Peter Lang, 1999), 35.

25. Norrie Drummond, "Dinner with the Beatles," *New Musical Express*. May 27, 1967, http://www.beatlesinterviews.org/db1967.0519.beatles.html.

26. Schneider, *The Long and Winding Road*, 83.

27. Ibid., 83.

28. MacDonald, *Revolution*, 30.

29. Ibid., 6.

30. Ibid., 6–7.

31. William M. Northcutt, "The Spectacle of Alienation: Death, Loss, and the Crowd in *Sgt. Pepper's Lonely Hearts Club Band*, in *Reading the Beatles: Cultural Studies, Literary Criticism, and the Fab Four*, eds. Kenneth Womack and Todd F. Davis (New York: State University of New York Press, 2006), 131.

32. Ibid., 131.

33. Ibid., 132.

34. John Lennon and Paul McCartney, "A Day in the Life," in the Beatles, *Sgt. Pepper's Lonely Hearts Club Band*, Parlophone CDP 3 82419 2 8, 2009, compact disc. Originally released in 1967.

35. Erin Kealey, "Nothing's Gonna Change My World: The Beatles and the Struggle Against Authenticity," in *The Beatles and Philosophy: Nothing You Can Think That Can't Be Thunk*, eds. Baur and Baur (Chicago: Open Court, 2006), 112.

36. MacDonald, *Revolution*, 229.

37. Ibid., 229.

38. Lennon and McCartney, "A Day in the Life."

39. MacDonald, *Revolution*, 229.

40. Kealey, "Nothing's Gonna Change My World," 112.

41. Hunter Davies, *The Beatles Lyrics: The Stories Behind the Music, Including the Handwritten Drafts of More Than 100 Classic Beatles Songs* (New York: Little, Brown and Company, 2014), 225.

42. MacDonald, *Revolution*, 235.

43. John Lennon and Paul McCartney, "She's Leaving Home," in the Beatles, *Sgt. Pepper's Lonely Hearts Club Band*, Parlophone CDP 3 82419 2 8, 2009, compact disc. Originally released in 1967.

44. Davies, *The Beatles Lyrics*, 211.

45. Morse Peckham, *Beyond the Tragic Vision: The Quest for Identity in the Nineteenth Century* (New York: George Braziller, 1962), 113.

46. Davies, *The Beatles Lyrics*, 191.

47. George Martin, *With a Little Help from My Friends: The Making of Sgt. Pepper* (Boston: Little, Brown and Company, 1995), 64.

48. MacDonald, *Revolution*, 216.

49. Schneider, *The Long and Winding Road*, 82.
50. Davies, *The Beatles Lyrics*, 181.
51. MacDonald, *Revolution in the Head*, 216.
52. Davies, *The Beatles Lyrics*, 181.
53. Ibid., 184.
54. Liu, *Poetics and Politics*, 35.
55. John Lennon and Paul McCartney, "Lucy in the Sky with Diamonds," in the Beatles, *Sgt. Pepper's Lonely Hearts Club Band*, Parlophone CDP 3 82419 2 8, 2009, compact disc. Originally released in 1967.
56. George Harrison, "Within You, Without You," in the Beatles, *Sgt. Pepper's Lonely Hearts Club Band*, Parlophone CDP 3 82419 2 8, 2009, compact disc. Originally released in 1967.
57. John Lennon and Paul McCartney, "Fixing A Hole," in the Beatles, *Sgt. Pepper's Lonely Hearts Club Band*, Parlophone CDP 3 82419 2 8, 2009, compact disc. Originally released in 1967.
58. Turner, *A Hard Day's Write*, 213.
59. Martin, *With a Little Help*, 157.
60. Ibid.
61. Schneider, *The Long and Winding Road*, 3.
62. John Lennon and Paul McCartney, "Revolution 1," the Beatles, *The Beatles* [The White Album], Parlophone CDP 3 82466 2 6, 2009, compact disc. Originally released in 1968.
63. Turner, *A Hard Day's Write*, 276.
64. Percy Bysshe Shelley, "A Defence of Poetry; or, Remarks Suggested by an Essay Entitled 'The Four Ages of Poetry,'" in *Shelley's Poetry and* Prose, eds. Donald H. Reiman and Neil Freistat (New York: W. W. Norton, 2002), 1821.
65. John Lennon, "Imagine," in *Imagine*. Apple CDP 7 90803 2, 2000, compact disc. Originally released in 1971.

BIBLIOGRAPHY

Baur, Steven. "You Say You Want a Revolution: Marx and the Beatles." In *The Beatles and Philosophy: Nothing You Think That Can't Be Thunk*, edited by Michael Baur and Steven Baur, 87–105. Chicago: Open Court, 2006.

The Beatles. *Sgt. Pepper's Lonely Hearts Club Band*. Parlophone CDP 3 82419 2 8, 2009, compact disc. Originally released in 1967.

———. *The Beatles* [The White Album]. Parlophone CDP 3 82466 2 6, 2009, compact disc. Originally released in 1968.

Chandler, James K. *Wordsworth's Second Nature: A Study in the Poetry and Politics*. Chicago: University of Chicago Press, 1984.

Davies, Hunter. *The Beatles Lyrics: The Stories Behind the Music, Including the Handwritten Drafts of More Than 100 Classic Beatles Songs*. New York: Little Brown, 2014.

Drummond, Norrie. "Dinner with the Beatles." *New Musical Express.* May 27, 1967.

Kealey, Erin. "Nothing's Gonna Change My World: The Beatles and the Struggle Against Authenticity. In *The Beatles and Philosophy: Nothing You Think That Can't Be Thunk*, edited by Michael Baur and Steven Baur, 109–123. Chicago: Open Court, 2006.

Lennon, John. *Imagine*. Apple CDP 7 90803 2, 2000, compact disc. Originally released in 1971.

Liu, Yu, *Poetics and Politics: The Revolutions of Wordsworth*. New York: Peter Lang, 1999.

MacDonald, Ian. *Revolution in the Head: The Beatles' Records and the Sixties*, 3rd edition. Chicago: Chicago Review Press, 2007.

Martin, George. *With a Little Help From My Friends: The Making of Sgt. Pepper*. Boston: Little, Brown and Company, 1995.

Northcutt, William M. "The Spectacle of Alienation: Death, Loss, and the Crowd in *Sgt. Pepper's Lonely Hearts Club Band*." In *Reading the Beatles: Cultural Studies, Literary*

Criticism, and the Fab Four, edited by Kenneth Womack and Todd F. Davis, 129–148. Albany, NY: SUNY Press, 2012.

Peckham, Morse. *Beyond the Tragic Vision: The Quest for Identity in the Nineteenth Century.* New York: George Braziller, 1962.

Roe, Nicholas. *Wordsworth and Coleridge: The Radical Years.* Oxford: Clarendon Press, 1988.

Saylor, Kevin M. "Wordsworth's Prudent Conservatism: Social Reform in the *Lyrical Ballads.*" *First Principles* 43, no. 2 (Spring 2001).

Sayre, Robert and Michael Löwy. "Figures of Romantic Anti-Capitalism." *New German Critique* 32 (Spring/Summer 1984): 42–92.

Schneider, Matthew. *The Long and Winding Road from Blake to the Beatles.* New York: Palgrave Macmillan, 2008.

Shelley, Percy Bysshe. "A Defence of Poetry; or, Remarks Suggested by an Essay Entitled "The Four Ages of Poetry." In *Shelley's Poetry and Prose*, edited by Donald H. Reiman and Neil Freistat, 510–35. New York: W. W. Norton, 2002.

Turner, Steve. *The Beatles a Hard Day's Write: The Stories Behind Every Song.* New York: MJF Books, 1994.

Wordsworth, William. "Advertisement to *Lyrical Ballads* with a Few Other Poems." In *Wordsworth's Poetry and Prose*, edited by Nicholas Halmi, 8–9. New York: W. W. Norton, 2014.

———. "The Old Cumberland Beggar." In *Wordsworth's Poetry and Prose*, edited by Nicholas Halmi, 133–137. New York: W. W. Norton, 2014.

———. "Preface to *Lyrical Ballads.*" In *Wordsworth's Poetry and Prose*, edited by Nicholas Halmi, 76–96. New York: W. W. Norton, 2014.

———. *The Prelude.* In *Wordsworth's Poetry and Prose*, edited by Nicholas Halmi, 167–377. New York: W. W. Norton, 2014.

Chapter Seven

"When the Light that's Lost within Us Reaches the Sky"

Jackson Browne's Romantic Vision

Gary L. Tandy

In "Michael: A Pastoral Poem," William Wordsworth imagines "youthful Poets, who among these Hills / Will be my second Self when I am gone."[1] In his recent critical study, Andrew Bennett suggests that Wordsworth and the other British Romantic poets continue to have an impact on the poetry and poetic theory of our times: "Contemporary culture, indeed, is pervaded by developments in conceptions of poetry and art that are associated most fully with the Romantic period."[2] As Sayre and Löwy state, "Far from being a purely nineteenth-century phenomenon, Romanticism is an essential component of modern culture."[3] One contemporary musical artist who could justifiably be named a successor to Wordsworth (as well as other British Romantic poets) is the American singer-songwriter Jackson Browne. Beginning with his debut record in 1972, Browne has released twenty-three albums, consisting almost entirely of original music. He was honored with induction into the Rock and Roll Hall of Fame in 2004 and the Songwriter's Hall of Fame in 2007. I first encountered Jackson Browne's music as a university student, and his thoughtful, poetic, and honest lyrics captivated me and appealed to my English major critical sensibilities. The soothing tone of his voice and the folk-rock sound of his music were welcome antidotes to the turbulence in my teenage mind, and his images of yearning—for both romantic love and spiritual fulfillment—spoke to my confused and angst-ridden teenage heart. I was ushered into sleep many nights by the beautiful, melancholy melodies of the songs from his albums *Jackson Browne: Saturate Before Using* and *For Everyman.*

In graduate school as I delved deeply into the verse of the British Romantic poets—William Blake, William Wordsworth, Samuel Taylor Coleridge, Percy Bysshe Shelley, and John Keats—I began to recognize connections between Browne's lyrics and their poetry. As I would discover later, it was not just the singer-songwriter's words and images but also his worldview that led me to classify him as a Romantic lyricist. At the same time, I was impressed by Browne's artistry and craftsmanship as I discovered that not only did many of his song lyrics stand on their own quite well as poems, but also that each album had a unity of theme and imagery that reminded me of a book of poems or sonnets. In both of these aspects, I would suggest, Browne stands out from many rock and roll musicians and deserves to be considered in the same artistic ranks as other musical contemporaries, including Bob Dylan, Neil Young, and Bruce Springsteen.

Unlike Bob Dylan, Browne and his music have not received much in-depth literary/critical analysis. Outside of one book-length study by Mark Bego,[4] most critical commentary has appeared in the pages of *The Rolling Stone* where Browne has been called "one of America's most visionary and important songwriters"[5] and "rock's greatest confessional singer-songwriter"[6] and where his music has been described as "searching" and "intensely introspective."[7] While the music critics who write about Browne's lyrics in publications like *The Rolling Stone* have not connected him to the literary tradition of Romanticism, they have identified key themes essential to that worldview. For example, in a review of Browne's most recent album, *Standing in the Breach*, Anthony DeCurtis notes that the album's songs "play like conversations between lovers trying to reassure each other of their commitment in a world that devalues human connection of any kind in favor of profit,"[8] a statement that recognizes Browne's anti-capitalist stance. Earlier in the same review, the writer identifies the nostalgia for the past at the heart of Browne's Romantic vision, noting that in his early songs like "For Everyman," "Before the Deluge," "Running on Empty," and "The Pretender," Browne "took a hard look at why the values of the Sixties seemed to die for so many people when that decade passed."[9] DeCurtis goes on to acknowledge the essential unity of Browne's work, stating that his recent music is marked by a commitment to the same values—freedom, compassion, generosity—that informed his early works.[10]

Jackson Browne's lyrics demonstrate a worldview consistent with nineteenth-century British and European Romanticisms. While I will trace the Romantic themes and image patterns in Browne's body of songs to show their pervasiveness, I will also argue that Browne creates and sustains his own Romantic vision. While it is consistent with the characteristics of European Romantic movements, it is also unique to his artistry as a singer/songwriter and, of course, to the wider culture in which he exists as an artist. Or, stated another way, Browne uses the themes and imagery of the Romantic worldview but makes them his own, adapting them to fit his personal passions and his cultural milieu.

As both A. O. Lovejoy and M. H. Abrams note, the term "romanticism" has been defined in such varied ways by literary and cultural scholars that it is more accurate to talk about "romanticisms."[11] To be specific, then, for this analysis, I will follow the definition of Romanticism suggested by Michael Löwy and Robert Sayre in their article, "Figures of Romantic Anti-Capitalism," first published in 1984, and their book, *Romanticism Against the Tide of Modernity* (2001).[12] Sayre and Löwy describe Romanticism as a worldview that provides a specifically anti-capitalist critique of modernity. In what follows, I will present a description of Romantic characteristics from Löwy and Sayre, then identify theme and image patterns from Browne's lyrics corresponding to those characteristics. Since Löwy and Sayre identify multiple types, I will consider also how Browne's vision in his songs and albums aligns with a specific type of Romanticism.

A REJECTION OF CONTEMPORARY SOCIETY

The world is too much with us; late and soon,
Getting and spending, we lay waste our powers;—
Little we see in Nature that is ours;
We have given our hearts away, a sordid boon![13]
 —William Wordsworth

Löwy and Sayre note that Romantics often express disillusionment with contemporary society and that the source of this disillusionment is closely connected to their critique of modernity. Modernity, they suggest, refers to "modern civilization, which was engendered by the Industrial Revolution and in which the market economy prevails."[14] Ultimately, then, the Romantic worldview involves a "revolt against the civilization created by capitalism."[15]

One does not have to look far in Jackson Browne's lyrics to find expressions of disillusionment with contemporary society. In "From Silver Lake," a song from his first album,[16] the speaker addresses someone he calls "our brother" who has rejected society and sailed across the sea. The speaker contrasts that experience with his own situation in the industrialized, capitalist city, where the "skyline is shaking" and the "mechanical city was waking." The disoriented speaker runs out, away from the city, "stumbling, mumbling." At the conclusion of the song, the speaker imagines himself running after his brother someday, but the song ends without resolving the speaker's conflict. "Rock Me on the Water," from the same album, begins with an apocalyptic, prophetic warning: "Oh people, look around you / The signs are everywhere." These signs include walls that are burning and towers that are turning, and the speaker states his intention to leave the city and "get down to the sea somehow."

Browne's album, *For Everyman*,[17] continues the rejection of contemporary, capitalist society. At the beginning of the song "Our Lady of the Well," the speaker laments, "Across my home has grown the shadow of a cruel and senseless hand." His quest takes the speaker away from his home to a simpler, rural society where "the families work the land as they have always done," a decidedly non-capitalist vision. While in this simpler environment, the speaker continues to reflect negatively on his homeland: "It's so far the other way my country's gone," presumably referring to increasing mechanization, industrialization, and urbanization. In "Colors of the Sun," the speaker revels in his oneness with nature but contrasts his state with others from the urban, industrialized society as "dying men . . . Scuffle with the crowd to get their share / And fall behind their little bits of time." In a later line, Browne uses the term "disillusioned saviors" to describe divine or spiritual beings who want to show a better way to those consumed by capitalist society: "Disillusioned saviors search the sky / Wanting just to show someone the way." The speaker's overall motivation seems to be to find an idyllic setting far from the mechanized society of his home country. The title song of the album, "For Everyman," uses another apocalyptic setting and begins with a clear rejection of society: "They've seen the end coming down long enough to believe / That they've heard their last warning." Later the speaker expresses a longing to "give up the race / And maybe find something better," again rejecting capitalist pursuits.

Browne's 1974 album, *Late for the Sky*,[18] has been characterized as having as its "overriding theme the exploration of romantic possibility in the shadow of apocalypse,"[19] so it's no surprise the language of disillusionment and alienation continues. For example, in the song "Farther On," the speaker recognizes a disparity between his dreams and what he finds in the real world: "Now there's a world of illusion and fantasy / In the place where the real world belongs." The line recalls Georg Lukács's description of the Romanticism of disillusionment that is "characterized by an incommensurability between the soul and reality, in which 'the soul [is] larger and wider than the destinies which life has to offer it.'"[20] "Before the Deluge" once again turns to an apocalyptic setting. Its second verse mourns those who have traded the ideals of youth ("love's bright and fragile glow") for the material benefits of capitalism ("the glitter and the rouge"). The third verse, however, describes others who reject industrialized society because of its environmental damage: "Some of them were angry / At the way the earth was abused."

Perhaps Browne's *The Pretender* album[21] constitutes the singer/songwriter's most direct anti-capitalist statement, at least among his early works. The title song can be read as Browne's assessment of the state of the American Dream in the mid-1970s. The opening verse begins in an urban setting with the speaker declaring his intention to buy "a house in the shade of the freeway," to "pack his lunch in the morning and go to work each day." But by verse three the listener understands the speaker's words as deeply ironic, as he describes himself being "caught between the longing for love / And the struggle for the legal tender." It is not far from these lines to Wordsworth's "Getting and spending we lay waste our powers" and not impossible to imagine the songwriter might have had Wordsworth's sonnet in mind while composing "The Pretender." The tone of the song is markedly sad, and it becomes clear that the pretender symbolizes the failure of the Romantic imagination as it succumbs to a capitalist society. Thus, it is appropriate when the speaker asks us to "Say a prayer for the pretender / Who started out so young and strong / Only to surrender." And just in case the listener misses the point or the irony, the speaker refers to himself as one who struggles for the legal tender, a "happy idiot" who believes "in whatever may lie in those things that money can buy." Browne continues the ironic and the satiric tone in the song "Lawyers in Love," where the images of capitalist society include lawyers, designer jeans, TV trays, and political turmoil. The speaker in "Tender is the Night" expresses another disconnect, "Between a life that we expected / And the way it's always been." In a 2007 interview, Jackson Browne acknowledged the anti-capitalist bent of his artistic goals: "What I'm hoping to get to in my music is the quality of life, the quality of our existence, and whether it's getting better or not. That's very personal terrain, but our dreams seem relegated to the area of mass consumption."[22]

The above examples have been drawn from Browne's musical creations from the 1970s. His albums from the following three decades continue to employ the language of disillusionment with and alienation from late twentieth- and early twenty-first century U.S. culture. For example, the title song of the 1996 album *Looking East* opens with the speaker standing alone in the ocean looking east, a symbolic rejection of his own western society. The second verse describes the speaker's attitude toward the current state of his country: "These times are famine for the soul while for the senses it's a feast / From the edge of my country, as far as you can see, looking east." Characteristic of Browne's songs in the 1980s, 1990s, and beyond is the shift from naming what is wrong with contemporary capitalist society to considering what can be done to change the world through social activism. Beginning with his *Lives in the Balance* album (1986), the capitalism that Browne rejects is most often tied to other concerns like poverty, war, racial injustice, and the environment. Here Browne again follows the lead of the British Romantic poets—especially Blake, Wordsworth, and Shelley—who used their poetry to draw attention to areas of social injustice in England and Europe in the early nineteenth century.

NOSTALGIA FOR PARADISE LOST

> There was a time when meadow, grove, and stream,
> The earth, and every common sight
> To me did seem
> Apparelled in celestial light,
> The glory and the freshness of a dream.[23]
>   —William Wordsworth

When Bruce Springsteen inducted Jackson Browne into the Rock and Roll Hall of Fame in 2004, he contrasted two California musical sensations. The Beach Boys, Springsteen said, gave us paradise on the beach while Jackson Browne gave us paradise lost.[24] Springsteen's comment is perceptive, and with its allusion to Milton's epic poem about the Biblical myth of the garden captures some key aspects of Browne's musical universe. For example, the tone of Browne's musical creations is often melancholic and in that sense recalls a favorite attitude of the British Romantic poets including Wordsworth and, perhaps most notably, John Keats.[25] The speaker in Browne's songs often looks back nostalgically at some paradisaical time in the past—a time when life was simpler, easier, more free—more joyful even.

Löwy and Sayre note that for European Romantics, "Nostalgia for a lost paradise is generally accompanied by a quest for what has been lost. An active principle at the heart of Romanticism has often been noted in various forms: anxiety, a state of perpetual becoming, interrogation, quest, struggle."[26] The fact that Romantics look to the past does not mean they ignore present reality. In fact, another typical Romantic move is the attempt to rediscover paradise in the midst of bourgeois society. As Löwy and Sayre note, this attempt to find paradise in the present may take many forms, including a utopian experiment (for example, Coleridge's and Southey's youthful plans to establish an ideal community in Pennsylvania), the "creation of a community of like-minded individuals, or simply falling in love."[27] Finally, the ideal can also be sought in the "sphere of childhood, in the belief that the values that governed all adult society in a more primitive state of humanity—its 'childhood,' as it were—can still be found among children."[28]

While Browne's lyrics occasionally explore a desire for the "creation of a community of like-minded individuals," his efforts to locate a present paradise in the midst of the bourgeois society most often center around two other elements: falling in love and rediscovering the ideal in the state of childhood. Also, as we have seen in some of Browne's early songs like "Colors of the Sun" and "From Silver Lake," the speaker in the song considers the option of fleeing bourgeois society altogether. However, while this desire for flight is strong in some songs, it is far from being the predominant response to alienation in his music. The song "For Everyman," in fact, can be read as an indictment of the impulse to flee. As *Rolling Stone* writer Anthony DeCurtis notes:

> The title track of Jackson Browne's second album, *For Everyman*, was a response to the escapist vision of Crosby, Stills and Nash's *Wooden Ships*. As violence, fear and paranoia overtook Sixties utopianism, *Wooden Ships* imagined a kind of hipster exodus by sea from a straight world teetering on the edge of apocalypse. Browne wasn't giving up so easily.[29]

In fact, Browne's characteristic tendency (or to be exact, that of the persona in his songs) is not to flee, but to stay and search for utopia in the present world or, if not in the present, to hope for the eventual dawning of a utopia in the future, an impulse I will explore in the final section of this analysis. Browne's own description of "For Everyman" notes that the song arose from his nostalgia for the 1960s: "It's about the expectations we had, all the changes in the Sixties that had burned out by 1972, '73. It's meant to be an expression of the search for connection with others, for common purpose."[30]

The persona in Browne's lyrics frequently looks back to an idealized past, removed from the present. For example, in "From Silver Lake," the speaker tells of the quest of his "brother" who has left for some "ruin far away." In "For Everyman," everybody is looking for the one who can "lead them back to that place in the warmth of the sun / Where a sweet child still dances." Often the first-person narrator of the lyric looks back to his youth with nostalgia, a backward look typically occurring at the opening of the song. In "Looking into You," the speaker recounts returning to a house he once lived in "Around the time I first went on my own." Similarly, the opening of "The Barricades of Heaven" finds the speaker reflecting on his life at sixteen and his carefree days playing music with his friends in a van. Often these nostalgic looks at the past emphasize the simplicity and easiness of these youthful days. As another nostalgic speaker notes in "About My Imagination," "And it was so easy then to say what love could do / It's so easy when your world is new." The opening lines of "Off of Wonderland" strike a similar tone: "It was easy for me / Living off of Wonderland." While not all of Browne's songs should be interpreted autobiographically, we can safely assume that many of these nostalgic references come from Browne's experience, especially those that recall his life as a musician. It's also fairly common for Browne in his later songs to allude to his earlier ones, as he does in this song ("Living with an unknown band / Waiting there for Everyman"), further justifying an autobiographical reading in this case.

Related closely to Browne's mood of melancholic nostalgia is the expression of the experience of loss in his songs. One of Browne's earliest songs reflects on the state of being physically lost. The speaker of "A Child in these Hills" asks, "Who will show me the river and ask me my name?" and though he earlier states that it was his choice to leave the house of his father, he still mourns his lost condition: "I am alone." In "A Song for Adam," from the same debut album, the speaker reflects poignantly on the loss of a friend who committed suicide. In this song, it is the friend who represents the Romantic figure, who is a deep-thinking, melancholy loner: "He was alone into his distance / He was deep into his well," the speaker says of him.

As would be expected from a songwriter who often addresses romantic love, Browne's songs have their share of lost loves recalled with regretful tones. In the classic "These Days," written when Browne was sixteen, the speaker states, "I had a lover / It's so hard to risk another these days." And later, in a line that sounds like it was written by a sixty-year-old, not a teenager, the speaker makes a poignant request: "Don't confront me with my failures / I have not forgotten them." "Fountain of Sorrow" opens with a clever pun: "Looking through some photographs I found inside a drawer / I was taken by a photograph of you." But the tone quickly turns somber as the speaker notices the photo captures not just the subject's "childish laughter" but also the "trace of sorrow" in her eyes. Like Keats, whose poems often reflect the paradox of melancholy in the midst of happiness, the subject of Browne's song is loneliness that "seems to spring from your life / Like a fountain from a pool." The song also captures the Romantic theme of the impermanent and transitory nature of joy: "Now for you and me it may not be that hard to reach our dreams / But that magic feeling never seems to last." It would be easy to compare Browne's use of photographs in this song as a way of capturing and preserving an emotion to Keats's use of the Grecian urn in his famous ode.[31] Another song that mourns lost love as well as its impermanence is "Linda Paloma," which uses the image of wind favored by the British Romantics to capture a sense of loss: "Love will fill your eyes with the sight / Of a world you can't hope to keep."

Löwy and Sayre suggest that when Romantics seek paradise in the present, they often turn to childhood.[32] The British Romantics, especially Blake and Wordsworth, frequently featured children in their poetry. To mention one example among many, Wordsworth's "We Are Seven" contrasts the innocent faith of a child with the pragmatism of a worldly wise narrator, who comes off as cold and scientific in contrast to the loving and innocent girl.[33] Blake's poems about the chimney sweeps similarly contrast childlike faith with the greed and cruelty of the adults who exploit these children by employing them to perform difficult and health-damaging labor.[34] Additionally, a frequent notion for the Romantics, especially Wordsworth, is that children are closer to divine power and spiritual realities than are adults.

Browne, like the British Romantics, uses childhood to represent divinity and spirituality. In "Too Many Angels," Browne makes a connection between angels and children, a comparison that was natural for Wordsworth and Blake. Browne uses the motif of photographs of children "All in their silver frames / On the window sills and tabletops / Lit by candle flames." It is a scene that recalls a religious ceremony, a feeling that is reinforced when the speaker mentions the "angel faces" of the children. After noting that the photographs have preserved the children from the "ravages of time," the speaker contrasts the innocence and purity of the children/angels with the sorrow and sin of the adult world: "Too many angels / Have heard you lying." Wordsworth's poetry often makes a similar move, seeing children as more godlike or divine than adults. As he notes in his poem "Ode: Intimations of Immortality":

> Not in entire forgetfulness,
> And not in utter nakedness,
> But trailing clouds of glory do we come
> From God, who is our home. [35]

Often in Browne's lyrics children are more than symbols of innocence; they serve as representatives of the divine or spiritual, elements Romantics believe to be missing from a materialistic and industrialized society. In "Too Many Angels," Browne also returns to the Keatsian theme of art (represented by the photographs) giving permanence to impermanence.

Another song that features childhood is "Barricades of Heaven." The song opens with the speaker (presumably Browne himself) looking back on his childhood days when he was sixteen, carefree, and making music with his friends. The song's bridge then focuses on images of childhood: "Your face bathing me in light / Hope that never ends." While the images in this song are not as distinct as they were in "Too Many Angels," childhood seems to represent a spiritual experience that comes to the speaker in the night and is associated with other positive images ("voices of my friends" and "Hope that never ends"). Finally, "Your face bathing me in light," while an enigmatic image, carries with it some associations of religious, beatific visions. These examples show that Browne turns often to the imagery of childhood in his songs and that his symbolic use of childhood is consistent with that of the British Romantics, especially Blake and Wordsworth.

While many other examples could be cited, these should be sufficient to show a clear pattern of tone and imagery in Browne's music that expresses Romantic melancholic nostalgia for a lost paradise.

THE VISION OF PARADISE REGAINED

> I will not cease from Mental Fight,
> Nor shall my Sword sleep in my hand,
> Till we have built Jerusalem
> In England's green & pleasant Land. [36]
> —William Blake, *Milton*

Löwy and Sayre suggest that another strain of Romanticism does not find recovering paradise in present reality ultimately fulfilling or, in some cases, even possible. They note, "A third tendency holds the preceding solutions to be illusory, or in any event merely partial; it embarks on the path of authentic future realization."[37] As Löwy and Sayre point out, this orientation toward the future can also be found in other Romantic authors including Percy Bysshe Shelley, Pierre-Joseph Proudhon, William Morris, and Walter Benjamin, writers for whom the "recollection of the past serves as a weapon in the struggle for the future."[38]

Jackson Browne's lyrics provide numerous instances of this Romantic vision of the future. In fact, it is in his imaginative construction of this future vision connected with and empowered by social activism in the present that Browne makes his most original contribution to rock and roll music and the Romantic poetry of the late twentieth- and early twenty-first centuries. This orientation toward a future vision also means that Browne's specific type of Romanticism aligns most closely with what Löwy and Sayre name Revolutionary and/or Utopian Romanticism, defined as

> the nostalgia for a pre-capitalist past . . . projected into the hope for a post-capitalist future. It aspires . . . to see the abolition of capitalism and the creation of a utopian future possessing some traits or values of pre-capitalist societies.[39]

Browne's lyrical vision of a future paradise begins early in his songwriting career. Several songs from his first albums, including "Rock Me on the Water" and "For Everyman," use apocalyptic imagery and look forward prophetically to future events. Though some of the songs describe perilous and even destructive events, they also imply hope for a better future, a future at times portrayed with images of spiritual renewal and even salvation.

"Farther On" from *Late for the Sky* contains an explicit future vision, but it begins with the typical Romantic move toward the past. Looking back, the speaker recalls times of community and connection with the "gentle ones." Shifting his point of reference to the present, the speaker longs for paradise but admits, "Heaven's no closer than it was yesterday." Near the end of the song, the angels are introduced, and they are wiser than the speaker: "They know not to wait up for the sun." The angels also possess comprehensive vision. They look over the speaker's shoulder at "the vision of paradise contained in the light of the past." Thus the angels possess the Romantic ability to look toward the past but also envision the future. Presumably as a result of the guidance of the angels, the speaker is pictured at the end of the song with his "maps and my faith in the distance / Moving farther on." Here, as in "Rock Me on the Water," the exact nature of the paradisaical vision is not revealed, but it is clearly a vision of paradise located in the future.

"Before the Deluge," also from the *Late for the Sky* album, is another song with an apocalyptic setting. As the title indicates, the song looks toward some future time when a catastrophic event ("the deluge") will occur.[40] While the tone of most of the song seems to match the theme of desolation and destruction, the ending allows for optimism because a remnant survives the deluge, and the chorus strikes a positive note that the "music will keep our spirits high" and that creation will "reveal its secrets by and by / When the light that's lost within us reaches the sky."

A song from *The Pretender* album that follows a pattern similar to "Before the Deluge" is "The Fuse." It begins with an image reminiscent of a Coleridge conversation poem: "It's hard to say for sure / Whether what I hear is music or wind / Through an open door." The song continues on a largely pessimistic note climaxed by this exclamation regarding social injustice: "Oh Lord / Are there really people starving still?" The conclusion of the song presents another image of apocalypse but also envisions a better world to follow, where the singer will hear the sound "Of the waters lapping on a higher ground / Of the children laughing." Here Browne combines two of his favorite images—water and children—to present a vision of peace, joy, and salvation.

The title song of Browne's *World in Motion*[41] begins with a negative image, "Sun going down on the USA," and goes on to refer to social concerns including homelessness and income inequality. However, after a typical Romantic look backwards to an earlier, less troubled time, the speaker seems to be inspired with an optimistic vision for the future: "Things like hunger, greed and hatred / One way or another, gonna be eradicated." In a typical Romantic move, the speaker switches from a vision of the past to a positive vision of the future. Specifically, he transitions from the current world passing away ("Sun going down on the USA") to a vision of a new world order ("Sun coming up a hundred years away"), a world where hunger, greed, and hatred will be no more.

In "Don't You Want to Be There," from the same album, Browne invokes the future vision in the opening lines: "Don't you want to be there, don't you want to go? / Where the light is breaking and the cold clear winds blow." Wherever this "there" is, Browne's lyrics picture it as a place where forgiveness abounds. It is a time and place of reconciliation, where "those you have wronged, you know / You need to let them know some way." It is also, appropriately, a place of childlike innocence, "where the grace and simple truth of childhood go / Don't you want to be there when the trumpets blow?" The trumpets blowing suggest a celebration or perhaps even a second coming, and the trumpet metaphor continues through the anaphora of "Blow" in the next four lines. The people mentioned in these lines are those who have suffered poverty and injustice, but Browne's vision is of a time where all will be healed and the world will be as it was meant to be. The final stanza reinforces the paradisaical vision and returns to Browne's preferred angel imagery while emphasizing strength and love as contrasted with fear: "Don't you want to be where there's strength and love / In the place of fear."

"Far From the Arms of Hunger"[42] is another song that spins Browne's Romantic vision of a future utopia. In the first stanza he paints a picture of a world without hunger and without war, and the final line hints at the reason: it is "A world no longer ours alone." The next stanza expands on this theme describing a global attitude that recognizes as a brother the "face across the border / Across a sea of differences." The song's chorus envisions a future "Far from the world disorder / Beyond the reach of war." While the song acknowledges that change will have to occur for this new world to emerge (especially on the part of the United States), it expresses confidence that at some point in the future a global consciousness will emerge and along with it a world of unity and peace.

Browne's album *Standing in the Breach*[43] continues to explore a future vision. In the title song, the speaker sounds the call for social action on the part of the hearer. The "we" of the opening stanza sounds the Romantic call for community, for people to recognize their connectedness and common humanity. That recognition is one that leads to action, to "standing in the breach." He goes on, "And though the earth may tremble and our foundations crack / We will all assemble and we will build them back." Browne's choice of the verb form "will" is telling. It places the action in the future but it is not conditional (e.g., "should" or "could"). It speaks of confidence and hope, not uncertainty and despair.

This hope, however, is not achieved by ignoring difficult realities, as the second stanza makes clear with its focus on income inequality: "I will never understand however they've prepared / How one life may be struck down and another life be spared." The third stanza highlights the gap between this present reality and what the speaker (and the audience) knows this world could be. Though some doubt is expressed ("You don't know how it will happen now"), the speaker maintains hope because he knows the change the world needs already exists inside everyone. As with the choice of verb tense in the opening stanza, Browne's use of the second person ("You don't know"; "You know") is intentional and shows a progression in the songwriter's vision. Earlier songs casting the future vision like "Farther On" used the first person, focusing on the individual consciousness. "Standing in the Breach," by using the second person, seems to invite the listener to share the vision while stressing the common humanity that unites everyone. At the very least, it seems to invite anyone of good will who shares Browne's Romantic vision to stand with him. In a 2007 interview, Browne suggests the importance of having a future vision and how that future vision could influence present realities: "To imagine the world that you want to have is the most fundamental tonic we have, the thing that will actually produce the best food and the best art and the best solutions to the problems we're faced with."[44] In a 2014 review of *Standing in the Breach*, Anthony DeCurtis asserts that Browne has remained true to his vision: "But, like John Lennon, he's enough of an artist to understand that imagining the world as it should be is the first step in bringing that world about. However, the next step—doing something—is even more important."[45]

Typically, though, the songwriter must recognize the realistic obstacles that stand in the way of humanity's achieving the vision of paradise: "The unpaid debts of history / The open wounds of time / The laws of human nature always tugging from behind." Yet in spite of these obstacles, the speaker expresses hope, albeit conditional: he wants to think that the earth might heal and that people might still learn. Once again, Browne's grammatical choices are significant: "I want to think," "might still learn." In spite of experience and history, Browne simply must believe in a positive future vision. Browne's Romanticism is seen in his recognition, on the one hand, of the deeply flawed nature of the world and, on the other hand, his ability to maintain faith in the basic goodness of humanity embodied in his future vision of a better world. "Standing in the Breach," of all of Browne's future vision songs, seems to exemplify best the original nature of the singer/songwriter's contribution: his imaginative construction of a future vision connected with and empowered by social activism in the present. Browne himself underscored the importance of both vision and activism in a 2007 *Rolling Stone* interview:

> "You must be the change that you wish to see in the world" is another good one. If you're here, you're going to be part of what the world becomes. I don't have any confidence in surveillance systems or guards and the ways of preserving the disparity of wealth that I believe is at the heart of the policies of the right and the super-rich in this country. But the cataclysmic changes that we're staring at as a result of climate changes or famine or huge population migrations are going to lay them low too. They're in denial. They're asleep on the tracks and there's this train coming. It's in everybody's interest that we wake up and address these things.[46]

CONCLUSION

This analysis has focused not on proving influence but on identifying those elements of Browne's lyrics that demonstrate the continuity of his worldview with that of the European Romantic movement, specifically of the Revolutionary and Utopian type. Further, I suggest that Browne uses that shared worldview to construct a unique imaginative vision that stands as an original contribution to rock and roll music and to the Romantic poetry of the late twentieth and early twenty-first centuries. Finally, while this chapter has explored three major Romantic elements in Browne's lyrics, other themes and image patterns deserve attention. For example, like the British Romantics, Browne often uses his music to bring attention to a variety of social concerns like poverty, war, racial injustice, and the environment. Jackson Browne has been a keen observer of U.S. culture and has embodied his critique in poetry and music that yield pleasure and insight for his audience. His lyrics are worthy of close attention, an attention that will lead the critic to recognize Browne's poetic depth and artistic excellence as well as his Revolutionary and Utopian Romanticism.

NOTES

1. William Wordsworth, "Michael: A Pastoral Poem," lines 38–39, *The Works of William Wordsworth*, ed. Mark Van Doren (Roslyn, NY: Black's Readers Service Company, 1951), 430.

2. Andrew Bennett, *Romantic Poets and the Culture of Posterity* (Cambridge: Cambridge University Press, 1999), 264.

3. Robert Sayre and Michael Löwy, "Figures of Romantic Anti-Capitalism," *New German Critique* 32 (1984): 42.

4. Mark Bego, *Jackson Browne: His Life and Music* (New York: Citadel Press, 2005).

5. Anthony DeCurtis, "Jackson Browne: New World, Timeless Values," *Rolling Stone* 1220 (October 23, 2014): 58.

6. Bud Scoppa, "Jackson Browne: The Very Best of Jackson Browne," *Rolling Stone* 947 (April 29, 2004): 80.

7. John McAlley and Ted Drozdowski, "Performance," *Rolling Stone* 679 (April 7, 1994): 34.

8. Anthony DeCurtis, "Jackson Browne: New World, Timeless Values," 58.

9. Ibid.

10. Ibid.

11. M. H. Abrams, ed. *English Romantic Poets: Modern Essays in Criticism* (New York: Oxford University Press, 1960), 8.

12. Robert Sayre and Michael Löwy, "Figures of Romantic Anti-Capitalism," *New German Critique* 32 (1984): 42–92; Michael Löwy and Robert Sayre, *Romanticism Against the Tide of Modernity* (Durham, NC: Duke University Press, 2001).

13. William Wordsworth, "The World is too Much with Us; Late and Soon" lines 1–4, *The Works of William Wordsworth*, ed. Mark Van Doren (Roslyn, NY: Black's Readers Service Company, 1951), 536.

14. Löwy and Sayre, *Romanticism*, 18.

15. Ibid., 19–20.

16. Jackson Browne, *Jackson Browne: Saturate Before Using*, Asylum Records SD-5051, 1972, 33-1/3 r.p.m.

17. Jackson Browne, *For Everyman*, Asylum Records SD-5067, 1973, 33-1/3 r.p.m.

18. Jackson Browne, *Late for the Sky*, Asylum Records 7E-1017, 1974, 33-1/3 r.p.m.

19. Stephen Holden, Review of *Late for the Sky*, *Rolling Stone*, November 7, 1974, accessed January 13, 2016, www.rollingstone.com/music/albumreviews/late-for-the-sky-19741107.

20. Georg Lukács, *The Theory of the Novel* (Cambridge, MA: MIT Press, 1971), 112.

21. Jackson Browne, *The Pretender*, Asylum Records 7E-1079, 1976, 33-1/3 r.p.m.

22. Jackson Browne, quoted in Anthony DeCurtis, "Jackson Browne," *Rolling Stone* 1025–1026 (May 3, 2007): 134.

23. William Wordsworth, "Ode: Intimations of Immortality," lines 1–5, *The Works of William Wordsworth*, ed. Mark Van Doren (Roslyn, NY: Black's Readers Service Company, 1951), 541.

24. Bruce Springsteen, "Induction Speech for Jackson Browne, Rock and Roll Hall of Fame, 2004," October 22, 2010, accessed November 11, 2015, https://www.youtube.com/watch2v = 8yfyC6piz-k.
25. For Wordsworth, see "Sweet Was the Walk" and the "Lucy" poems; for Keats, see "Ode on Melancholy" and "Ode to a Nightingale."
26. Löwy and Sayre, *Romanticism*, 23
27. Ibid.
28. Ibid.
29. Anthony DeCurtis, *Rolling Stone*, quoted in Mark Bego, *Jackson Browne: His Life and Music* (New York: Citadel Press, 2005), 235.
30. Jackson Browne, quoted in David Fricke, "My Life in 15 Songs," *Rolling Stone* 1220 (October 23, 2014), 54.
31. John Keats, "Ode on a Grecian Urn," *John Keats: Complete Poems*, ed. Jack Stillinger (Cambridge, MA: The Belknap Press, 1978).
32. Löwy and Sayre, *Romanticism*, 23.
33. William Wordsworth, "We Are Seven," *The Works of William Wordsworth*, ed. Mark Van Doren (Roslyn, NY: Black's Readers Service Company, 1951).
34. William Blake, "The Chimney Sweeper," from *Songs of Innocence* and "The Chimney Sweeper," from *Songs of Experience, The Complete Poetry and Prose of William Blake*, ed. David V. Erdman (Berkeley, CA: University of California Press, 1982), 10, 22.
35. William Wordsworth, "Ode: Intimations of Immortality," lines 63–66, *The Works of William Wordsworth* ed. Mark Van Doren (Roslyn, NY: Black's Readers Service Company, 1951), 543.
36. William Blake, "Preface to *Milton*," lines 13–16, *The Complete Poetry and Prose of William Blake*, ed. David V. Erdman (Berkeley, CA: University of California Press, 1982), 95–96.
37. Löwy and Sayre, *Romanticism*, 24.
38. Ibid.
39. Ibid., 61.
40. Browne has stated that "Before the Deluge could be 'about the nuclear-power issue,'" see Anthony DeCurtis, "Jackson Browne," *Rolling Stone* 641 (October 15, 1992): 138.
41. Jackson Browne, *World in Motion*, 1984.
42. From Jackson Browne, *Time the Conqueror*, Inside Recordings (2) INR9231–8, 2008, compact disc.
43. Jackson Browne, *Standing in the Breach*, Inside Recordings (2) INR-14107–1, 2014, compact disc.
44. Jackson Browne, quoted in Anthony DeCurtis, "Jackson Browne," 134.
45. Jackson Browne, quoted in Anthony DeCurtis, "Jackson Browne: New World, Timeless Values," 58.
46. Jackson Browne, quoted in Anthony DeCurtis, "Jackson Browne," 134.

BIBLIOGRAPHY

Abrams, M. H., ed. *English Romantic Poets: Modern Essays in Criticism*. New York: Oxford University Press, 1960.
Bego, Mark. *Jackson Browne: His Life and Music.* New York: Citadel Press, 2005.
Bennett, Andrew. *Romantic Poets and the Culture of Posterity*. Cambridge: Cambridge University Press, 1999.
Blake, William. "The Chimney Sweeper." In *The Complete Poetry and Prose of William Blake*, edited by David V. Erdman, 10. Berkeley, CA: University of California Press, 1982.
———. "The Chimney Sweeper." In *The Complete Poetry and Prose of William Blake*, edited by David V. Erdman, 22. Berkeley, CA: University of California Press, 1982.
———. "Preface to *Milton a Poem*." In *The Complete Poetry and Prose of William Blake*, edited by David V. Erdman, 95–96. Berkeley, CA: University of California Press, 1982.
Browne, Jackson. *For Everyman*. Asylum Records SD-5067, 1973, 33-1/3 r.p.m.

————. *Jackson Browne: Saturate Before Using*. Asylum Records SD-5051, 1972, 33-1/3 r.p.m.

————. *Late for the Sky*. Asylum Records 7E-1017, 1974, 33-1/3 r.p.m.

————. *Lives in the Balance*. Asylum Records 60457–1–E, 1986, 33-1/3 r.p.m.

————. *Looking East*. Elektra 7559–61867–2, 1996, compact disc.

————. *Pretender, The*. Asylum Records 7E-1079, 1976, 33-1/3 r.p.m.

————. *Standing in the Breach*. Inside Recordings (2) INR-14107–1, 2014, compact disc.

————. *Time the Conqueror*. Inside Recordings (2) INR9231–8, 2008, compact disc.

————. *World in Motion*. Elektra 9–60830–1, 1989, 33-1/3 r.p.m.

DeCurtis, Anthony. "Jackson Browne." *Rolling Stone* 641 (October 15, 1992): 138.

————. "Jackson Browne: New World, Timeless Values." *Rolling Stone* 1220 (October 23, 2014): 58.

Fricke, David. "My Life in 15 Songs." *Rolling Stone* 1220 (October 23, 2014): 54.

Holden, Stephen. Review of *Late for the Sky*. *Rolling Stone*, November 7, 1974, accessed January 13, 2016, www.rollingstone.com/music/album reviews/late-for-the-sky-19741107.

Keats, John. "Ode on a Grecian Urn." *John Keats: Complete Poems*, edited by Jack Stillinger, 282–283. Cambridge, MA: The Belknap Press, 1978.

Löwy, Michael, and Robert Sayre. *Romanticism Against the Tide of Modernity*. Durham, NC: Duke University Press, 2001.

Lukács, Georg. *The Theory of the Novel*. Cambridge, MA: MIT Press, 1971.

McAlley, John, and Ted Drozdowski. "Performance." *Rolling Stone* 679 (April 7, 1994): 34.

Sayre, Robert, and Michael Löwy. "Figures of Romantic Anti-Capitalism." *New German Critique* 32 (1984): 42–92.

Scoppa, Bud. "Jackson Browne: The Very Best of Jackson Browne." *Rolling Stone* 947 (April 29, 2004): 80.

Springsteen, Bruce. "Induction Speech for Jackson Browne, Rock and Roll Hall of Fame, 2004," posted October 22, 2010, accessed November 11, 2015, https://www.youtube.com/watch2v=8yfyCópiz-k.

Wordsworth, William. "Michael: A Pastoral Poem." *The Works of William Wordsworth*, edited by Mark Van Doren, 429–442. Roslyn, New York: Black's Readers Service Company, 1951.

————. "Ode: Intimations of Immortality." *The Works of William Wordsworth*, edited by Mark Van Doren, 541–547. Roslyn, NY: Black's Readers Service Company, 1951.

————. "We Are Seven." *The Works of William Wordsworth*, edited by Mark Van Doren, 56–8. Roslyn, NY: Black's Readers Service Company, 1951.

————. "The world is too much with us. . ." *The Works of William Wordsworth*, edited by Mark Van Doren, 536. Roslyn, NY: Black's Readers Service Company, 1951.

Chapter Eight

"Swimming Against the Stream"

Rush's Romantic Critique of their Modern Age

David S. Hogsette

If we deny the artificial (and false) dichotomy between so-called literary high art and consumerist popular culture and then attempt to analyze the one in terms of the other, areas of signification, inquiry, and cultural criticism open up such that we can come to richer understandings of both and even begin to revise our critical assumptions. Specifically, by examining Rush in terms of Romanticism and, conversely, reviewing Romanticism in terms of Rush, we can appreciate Rush as contemporary Romantics, and we can revise our understanding of Romanticism as a visionary worldview that indeed began in the mid-to-late eighteenth century but did not end with the emergence of the Victorian era. What began in the mid-eighteenth century as diverse reactions to the dehumanizing consequences of industrialization, commercial capitalism, and political revolution manifests itself today through Rush as a sincere and at times earnest critique of modern society's tendency to stifle creativity, dehumanize the individual, and isolate the self from community. Much like the protagonist in Rush's song "2112" who uncovers the transformative potential of music in an ancient guitar, I discovered an instrument of beauty, truth, and power when I began listening to Rush as a teenager. By analyzing their music in relationship to Romanticism, we can better understand the Romantic worldview's enduring power to critique modernity and to offer hope for the potential of individual change that may lead to eventual societal transformation.

RESTLESS YOUNG ROMANTICS: RUSH AND THE ROMANTIC
CRITIQUE OF MODERN SOCIETY

Historians, literary scholars, and cultural critics have been struggling to define, classify, and explain Romanticism ever since a group of German poets
and thinkers in Jena referred to themselves as Romantics. Most scholars
define Romanticism as a literary and artistic movement possessing common
attributes that began in the late eighteenth century and lasted until the early to
mid-nineteenth century. Michael Löwy and Robert Sayre note that significant problems arise from such definitions that reduce Romanticism to a literary school identified by specific formal elements, because scholars tend to
focus on certain features they find peculiarly interesting, relying only on
empirical expressions of literary and cultural phenomena. Ultimately, various
unresolved contradictions emerge among different descriptions of Romanticism, and these definitions do not elucidate the artists' underlying cognitive,
spiritual, economic, social, and cultural motivations.[1] Instead of proliferating
idiosyncratic definitions or creating a definition based upon an extensive list
of observable artistic qualities and literary characteristics, what if we were to
see Romanticism as a critical worldview that began in the mid-eighteenth
century as a critique of modernity and that continues today exposing, con-
fronting, and addressing the dehumanizing aspects of current society using
contemporary modes of cultural expression? This definition of Romanticism
as a worldview allows us to examine contemporary manifestations of Romanticism in rock bands like Rush while also reexamining and clarifying our
current understanding of Romanticism.

 Löwy and Sayre lay a firm foundation for this conceptualization of Romanticism as a critical worldview. They define Romanticism not as a literary
era but as a critical perspective that examines modernity, critiquing its negative effects upon individuals and their social relationships. Modernity, according to Löwy and Sayre, is the society created by industrial capitalism and
sustained by the market economy. Romanticism, then, begins in the eighteenth century with the Industrial Revolution and continues in various forms
today, commenting on, reacting to, engaging with, and critiquing key ramifi-
cations of industrialism and market-driven social structures. Romanticism
confronts dehumanization, objectification of the human individual, and the
disruption of fundamental human relationships in pursuit of industrial growth
and market gains.[2]

 Marilyn Butler's historical analysis further reveals Romanticism to be an
enduring intellectual and artistic critique of modernism. Butler observes that
this critical social perspective pervaded late eighteenth-century thinking. It
was not spearheaded by a single writer or small group of writers; rather, the
critique resonated with readers because so many writers were engaging in it:
"Their works illustrate that outside the creative arts proper, the late eight-

eenth century was characterized first by its impulse to see society in a grand and simple historical perspective; second, by the tendency latent in the recourse to history, to find thoroughgoing fault with the contemporary world."[3] Primitivism, historicism, and criticism of modernity characterized this emerging Romantic vision. By recasting their present age within the confines of an historical and nostalgic perspective, these eighteenth-century writers created a critical worldview that examined the contemporary industrializing age against the backdrop of an idealized pastoral history. However, this form of social criticism is not unique to the late eighteenth and early nineteenth centuries; rather, it characterizes a Romantic worldview persistent even today, and we see this same nostalgic critique in Rush's contemporary Romantic vision, particularly in their epic fantasies, like "By-Tor and the Snowdog," "The Necromancer," and "The Fountain of Lamneth."

This critical Romantic worldview is often rooted in a relational, community-focused moral vision that seeks to move the audience of Romantic literature from subjective contemplation to ethical engagement of community and society. According to Laurence Lockridge, Romantic literature explores the ethical values and obligations associated with personal, public, and professional relationships. Romantics recognize that there are moral, ethical, and political issues that should be addressed in literature, because literature can encourage readers to reflect upon their own ethical positions and then consider how they might encourage moral progress and social change within their own spheres of influence and, ultimately, society at large. Thus, a Romantic worldview not only critiques modernity, but it also instructs readers on how they might individually address social concerns.[4] Similarly, Rush's Romantic vision encourages audiences to reflect personally upon the music's critical messages and to act locally within one's community while also recognizing the true challenges of the individual's ability to change the self and society within commercialized modernity.

One of the clearest representations of Rush's Romantic critique of modernity is their breakout hit "Subdivisions" from *Signals*.[5] North American rock radio stations continue to play this song regularly, and it is a perennial favorite at Rush concerts because it resonates with both original Rush fans and newer generations of contemporary fans. According to Chris McDonald, the reason for the enduring popularity of this song can be found in its cogent criticism of middle-class life that stifles imagination, discourages originality, and pressures conformity:

> "Subdivisions" fed directly into the dystopian myth of the North American suburb, describing the predictability, the cultural bleakness, the uneventful, unchanging landscape that endless residential neighborhoods provided for the North American middle class. This ambivalence seems strange given the comfort and relative affluence suburban postwar America enjoyed, but there re-

mained an uncomfortable in-between-ness here for some young suburbanites
who felt both a pull toward the conformity of North American middle-class
life and a revulsion from it.[6]

Indeed, the song focuses upon middle-class suburban experience, but the
concept of subdivisions serves as a wider metaphor for the various ways
modernity subdivides people's lives into dehumanized and alienated fragments. The song characterizes the suburbs or subdivisions as comfortable
borderlands insulating young minds from the garish lights of the city and the
mysterious darkness of the unknown. Subdivisions as a unique product of
contemporary modernity isolate individuals within a cocoon of perceived
safety and normalcy, shielding them from the dangers of the big city and the
uncertainty of diverse lands and experiences well beyond the tidy mundane
existence of suburbia. Although modern subjects are relatively safe within
the circumscribed zones of the subdivision, they also are denied the life-
enriching experiences of diverse others who dwell under the bright city lights
and in the "far unlit unknown."[7]

Moreover, the subdivisions of modern life force conformity, squelch the
creative imagination, and stifle the active yearnings of the idealistic dreamer.
Even if a few do manage to escape the conformist confines of the suburbs,
they will fall into another rat-race trap of modern life—the desire for getting
and spending. As Wordsworth warned in "The world is too much with
us . . . ," this commercial desire wastes their powers to see what is available
within nature that fuels their creative, imaginative capacities. As a result,
they dream of returning to the perceived peace and comfort of the very
suburbia they sought to escape: "Somewhere out of a memory / Of lighted
streets on quiet nights."[8] Rush's critique of the circuitous movement from
suburbia, to the city, and back again, recalls Wordsworth's nostalgic critique
of the urban. In such poems as "Composed Upon Westminster Bridge, September 3, 1802," "Lines Composed a Few Miles above Tintern Abbey," and
"The world is too much with us . . . ," Wordsworth juxtaposes images of the
new urban life wrought by an emerging industrial and commercial modernity
with nostalgic visions of the pastoral. The urban and all its industrial hard-
ship and commercial pressures must be tempered, even transformed, through
pastoral revisioning. Thus, we see a Romantic longing for natural landscapes
in the midst of urban expanses, veneration of pagan nature worship, and early
morning visions of cityscapes merging with natural landscapes.

However, these nostalgic visions are sadly ironic. For as much as Wordsworth dreams of urban London being transformed into a quiet and peaceful
pastoral landscape by its proximity to nature in the early morning mists, once
the urban day begins, London again becomes a bustling cityscape of industrial production and commercial exchange. Similarly for Rush, the ironic movement from suburbia to the city and back again is indeed bittersweet. Rush's

Romantic critique recognizes that modernity created the suburbs as an escape from urban life and its hectic pace, overcrowded conditions, expensive living, and escalating crime. Yet, this suburban haven forces conformity, squelches the imagination, and kills the dreams of individualism. Many will escape this suburban trap of modernity by flying like a moth to the bright lights of promise in the big cities, while in the process falling victim to the very urban pressures that suburbia was created to avoid. Ironically, they will consequently flutter back with singed wings to the suburban prisons of modernity from which they sought an escape, nostalgically (mis)remembering them as locations of comfort and tranquility.

REBELS AND RUNNERS: INDIVIDUALISM AS REACTION AGAINST MODERNITY

"Subdivisions" suggests there is no hope beyond the sad irony of modern suburbia's endless trap. However, Rush offers more than just ambivalent cyclical defeatism in the face of oppressive modernity. For Rush, individualism is the key to both critiquing modernity and overcoming its dehumanizing oppressiveness, and this emphasis on the sanctity of the individual acting freely within community is drawn directly from Romantic humanism. According to Löwy and Sayre, Romantic subjectivity is a reaction against modernity's dehumanization. Romanticism seeks to resist this dehumanization by developing the intellectual, spiritual, and imaginative uniqueness of each individual.[9] Rush celebrates the significant uniqueness of the individual in opposition to institutional oppression, human commodification, and market pressures that smother creative originality. As McDonald notes,

> Individualism provided Rush with a framework for making social critiques, and from 1975 to about 1985 individualism was one of the most important underpinnings for the critical, protest-oriented facet of Rush's repertoire. This led Rush, inevitably, to criticize just about anything threatening individuality, especially those ideas, social institutions, and circumstances that "massify" people.[10]

Because many Rush songs, particularly during the 1970s and 1980s, expressed an unabashed admiration of strong individualism and borrowed explicitly from the Objectivist writings of Ayn Rand,[11] some critics viewed Rush, at best, as naively obstinate right-wingers railing against socialism and unions, and, at worst, dangerous protofascists (even Nazis) spreading anti-collectivist hatred and right-wing oppression through their albums and live concerts.[12] Such critics failed to recognize the deeper cultural significance of Rush's individualist themes. As Robert Freedman explains,

> Peart's take on individualism, particularly in the early years, is a *moral* one. It's about the battle each of us faces as we wrestle with how to strike a balance in our own lives, whether to seize our sovereignty and be a leader or to let it wither on the vine while we allow ourselves to be led. We all think of ourselves as leaders of our own lives, but really in many small ways we prefer to abdicate responsibility for ourselves to others. [13]

Rush's commitment to the inalienable sovereignty of the individual and the responsibility of all people to make their own choices is at the heart of their Romantic critique of oppressive modernity.

Rush's exploration of individualism as Romantic critique is most vividly expressed in many of their science fiction songs. One musical epic serves as an excellent example: the aggressive "2112" from the eponymous album that would secure their creative independence. [14] "2112" is a twenty-minute Orwellian epic that borrows heavily from Ayn Rand's science fiction dystopian novel *Anthem*. The album's front cover displays a red star as the symbol of the oppressive Solar Federation that controls a number of planets, providing peace for fifty years. The back cover depicts a naked man with his hands held up in defiance against the red star icon that seeks to circumscribe him within boundaries of creative and expressive control. The cover art highlights the theme of the innocent individual resisting oppressive forms of totalitarian rule.

In this futuristic dystopia, stern technocrats, called Priests of the Temples of Syrinx, embrace computer technology with religious fervor and rule tyrannically over the people, bringing order, peace, and progress by imposing the "will" of the computers upon the masses. This theocratic government provides all things, controls all things, and even determines the very lives and destinies of its citizens. Deceived into thinking this world order provides happiness, the protagonist one day finds a curious object in a cave behind a waterfall: a guitar. This discovery introduces him to creativity and, by extension, individuality, because by learning to play the guitar, he realizes that he has his own creative voice and, thus, the ability to express his individual feelings in unique ways. In his naïve excitement, he shares this discovery with the Priests of Syrinx, who quickly reject his pursuit of music as a mere waste of time and dismiss his discovery of individuality as a danger to the collective harmony of the world order. The protagonist returns home a desperate and broken man, and he dreams of a world that encourages creative expression and celebrates individuality. He wakes from his dream even more depressed because he has glimpsed a world of free creative individuality that he thinks will never be present on his own planet. He resolves to commit suicide rather than live under an oppressive regime that stifles creativity and denies individuality. The song concludes ambiguously: some critics interpret the ending as defeatist and others as cynically ironic, because it seems that as the protagonist is dying, yet another oppressive force conquers his world.[15] Such interpretations indeed suggest a dark irony: the song clearly positions itself in favor of individual freedom and creativity, yet it (apparently) ends with the resurgence of totalitarianism, suggesting that in this world of expanding tyrannical theocratic governments, such freedom is impossible or highly unlikely.

However, according to Neil Peart, oppressive forces are not taking over; rather, a liberating power comes to end the rule of the Solar Federation and to usher in a new era of creative individuality. Many critics and listeners do not realize the protagonist's dream was actually a prophetic vision about the elder race who left the planet many years before to set up their own worlds where freedom is fostered, individuality is encouraged, and creativity is nurtured. At the end of the song, they have returned "Home to tear the Temples down / Home to Change."[16] Peart explains, "That's the good guys, that's the cavalry, you know, coming in at the end. So, it actually, to me, had a happy ending, as it were, that the Solar Federation was going to be shut down by the vision that our hero has of this other way of living. They're the people coming at the end. That's how I intended it."[17] This Orwellian vision of totalitarian oppression and collective conformity is destroyed, giving way to the eventual emergence of a new society in which individuals are free to pursue their unique dreams and to express artistically what is in their hearts and minds. Rush's Romantic humanism levels harsh criticism against totalitarian uniformity and locates the hope of liberation within ruling systems that foster creativity, individuality, and liberty.

ESCAPING THE CAVES OF ICE: QUESTS AS NOSTALGIC CRITIQUE OF MODERN CULTURE

Throughout the 1970s, both before and after the watershed album *2112*, Rush explored epic themes lyrically and musically, creating complex compositions that integrated fantasy quest narratives with progressive music and intermingling hard rock phrases with nostalgic, pastoral acoustic melodies. Such instrumental experimentation signifies Rush's Romantic critique of modernity. Because the Romantic worldview expresses a deep sense of loss over the dehumanizing elements of modern society and commercial pressures, one way a Romantic vision seeks to overcome this loss is through nostalgia for a preindustrial, precapitalist era. Löwy and Sayre argue, "The soul ardently desires to go home again, to return to its homeland, in the spiritual sense, and this nostalgia is at the heart of the Romantic attitude. What is lacking in the present existed once upon a time, in a more or less distant past . . . Romantic nostalgia looks to a precapitalist past, or at least to a past in which the modern socioeconomic system was not yet fully developed."[18] Butler identifies this Romantic nostalgia as a form of primitivism that seeks a more agrarian past in order to critique and escape the industrial present: "Perhaps alternatively these enthusiasms for the remote past are all aspects of primitivism, and have their roots in a more general principle still, a revulsion against sophisticated urban life in favour of a dream of the pastoral."[19] M. H. Abrams explains that many Romantic writers felt disconnected from their contemporary age and looked to ancient myths as a way to represent this alienation, seeking out legends as imaginative spaces in which to find alternatives to their contemporary reality. Narratively, these sentiments were often cast as poetic and narrative quests.[20] Similarly, Rush critiques modernity through grand quest narratives that express nostalgia for a forgotten past, lost truths, and authentic humanity that have been suppressed by dehumanizing elements of modernity, namely economic materialism and naturalistic determinism.

Many of Rush's Romantic quest narratives adopt elements of the mythopoeic fantasy genre, borrowing from J. R. R. Tolkien's *The Lord of the Rings* ("Rivendell" on *Fly by Night*) and alluding to *The Hobbit* ("The Necromancer" on *Caress of Steel*). Tolkien also appropriated a nostalgic Romantic worldview when subcreating Middle-Earth quest narratives, seeking to offer escape, recovery, and consolation.[21] Such mythopoeic fantasy is thoroughly Romantic in that it critiques the dehumanizing industrial world by offering escape into a pre-industrial mythic land. Through the various adventures and fantasy quests, readers vicariously recover truths and perspectives lost to a world shaped by commercial capitalism and dominated by naturalistic assumptions. Lastly, Tolkien's fantasy provides consolation through the joy of what he called eucatastrophe, the sudden and unexpected narrative turn of events from tragedy to an undeserved happy ending. By participating in this very same mythopoeic dynamic of escape, recovery, and consolation, Rush's epic narratives similarly offer a Romantic critique of contemporary society, presenting listeners with the hope of vicarious triumph and a rediscovery of lost truths that can be individually internalized and then used to reshape the wider world.

For example, "The Fountain of Lamneth" on *Caress of Steel*[22] is a twenty-minute mythic fantasy modeled after ancient Greek epics, like Homer's *Iliad* and *Odyssey*, and informed by Samuel Taylor Coleridge's "The Rime of the Ancient Mariner." This song also typifies Abrams's description of circuitous Romantic quests as moving from a state of innocence and unity, toward a fall into fragmentation and disunity, and culminating in a reunification of self and community.[23] Through such mythic quests, we see a Romantic critique of the modern age and a nostalgic desire for an idealized past metaphorically representing the world as it ought to be, at least from the perspective of a Romantic worldview disenchanted with its own age. The speaker in "The Fountain of Lamneth" narrates the epic of his own life, starting with his birth into carefree innocence and unbridled freedom.[24] Yet, as he matures, his soul longs for some unidentified object of desire. His quest to fulfill this unnamed desire takes him on an Odyssean journey in which his crew abandons him, and he is alone on his ship, like Odysseus or the Ancient Mariner, offering up supplications and crying out for divine intervention, but receiving none. He seeks meaning in sexual love and then in drunken revelry, but neither provides lasting satisfaction. The mere physical cannot satisfy the metaphysical cries of his heart. His journey continues and he finally reaches the mythic Fountain of Lamneth only to discover that the prize is located within the process of living a meaningful life motivated by a dream, sustained by hope, and fulfilled through faith: "Life is just a candle and a dream / Must give it flame."[25]

In a circuitous, Romantic fashion, "The Fountain of Lamneth" quest narrative comes full circle, ending with the same acoustic folk style of the song's opening phrases, suggesting a kind of rebirth into ultimate knowledge of one's own ontology. This knowledge that the purpose of life is fulfilled through the process of following a hopeful dream provides final consolation and reunification of self. This epic song provides listeners a fantastical escape from modern reality, entices them into a mythic land of adventure and soul searching, and provides consolation by reminding them that the meaning of life is not bound up in getting and spending but, rather, in living at peace with oneself. Clearly, Rush participates in a Romantic nostalgic critique of modernity through this circuitous, mythopoeic quest narrative.

Rush's mythopoeic critique of modernity indeed follows the creation, fragmentation, and eventual reunification of self through escape narratives, but Rush's Romantic music is not merely escapist, nor does it advocate separating the individual from community. The best example of Rush's anti-solipsistic Romanticism can be found in their epic song "Xanadu" from the album *A Farewell to Kings*.[26] In the preface to Coleridge's "Kubla Khan," Peart's literary source for this song, Coleridge creates a clever conceit that explains the artistic context for the poem. Coleridge claims to have consumed a medicinal mixture of alcohol and opium and settled in to read Samuel Purchas's *Purchas, His Pilgrimage*, a seventeenth-century travelogue exploring exotic lands and their various religions. As he was reading about the mystical lands of Mongolia and its powerful ruler, the Khan Kubla, Coleridge fell into a deep sleep and dreamed an entire poem about Xanadu. Upon awaking, Coleridge frantically began transcribing that majestic poem; unfortunately, a man on business interrupted him, and upon returning to the poem, Coleridge discovered to his artistic dismay that he had lost the vision. The poem can be interpreted as darkly ironic, simultaneously expressing a Romantic longing to escape the stifling oppressiveness of modern life into ancient realms of mystery, intrigue, and delight, along with frustration at not being able to achieve the desired escape due to unavoidable intrusions of modernity.[27]

Rush's adaptation of Coleridge's poem captures both the idealistic Romantic longing for escape and Romanticism's dark ironic frustration at artistic limitation and imaginative failure.[28] "Xanadu" begins with a five-minute instrumental introduction that functions like Coleridge's own preface to the poem, offering interpretive cues for the song proper and establishing a musical tone preparing listeners for the thematic shifts that come later in the song. The intro starts with a low drone note, reminiscent of Mongolian throat singing, as tranquil sounds of birds chirping, wood block percussion, and tinkling chimes are layered to provide meditative peacefulness. Alex Lifeson uses volume effects to blend soft, almost plaintive guitar notes that evoke a deep sense of longing, inviting listeners into this mystical and exotic sound(e)scape. Slowly, a low whooshing wind meanders in (much like the River Alph in Coleridge's poem), eventually whirling the listener into a crescendo of repeated guitar riffs and frenetic percussion, taking the listener from meditative solitude into a frenzied anticipation of adventure, thus ushering in the song proper.[29]

Much like Coleridge who sought to find in his dream the Xanadu described in *Purchas His Pilgrimage*, the speaker in Rush's "Xanadu" has taken a clue from an ancient book and longs to find Alph, the sacred river, "To walk the caves of ice / To break my fast on honeydew / And drink the milk of Paradise."[30] These lines are a direct allusion to "Kubla Khan," suggesting that the ancient text the speaker quotes may actually be Coleridge's poem. Whereas Coleridge's adventure is purely imaginative, taking place in his opium-induced dream, the speaker in the song embarks on an actual nostalgic quest, escaping the confines of modernity to seek artistic transcendence and material immortality in Xanadu. The fantastical, exotic musical style and the epic quest narrative are Romantic nostalgic escapism at its best, for listening to this song, especially with headphones, transports the listener to distant, ancient lands created as visions built on air, woven through lyrical incantations and instrumental magic.[31]

However, the song is not simply individualistic escapist fantasy, because it builds toward a dark irony that warns against escapism and solipsistic isolation. As the speaker ventures closer to finding the caves of ice, drinking the milk of paradise, and dining on honeydew—the food of the gods—he becomes anxious to achieve his goal of immortality. Sadly, his individualistic hubris is his undoing, for the very caves of ice that offer him visionary imagination and immortality become his eternal prison. Through this tragically ironic ending, Rush hints at another Coleridgean theme: creative hubris leads many to fear the visionary poet, leaving him isolated and excommunicated. This dark ending also communicates a Tolkienian vision of fantastical escape that warns against individualistic escapism. The purpose of the escape is to move outside the limitations of modernity into an imaginative, visionary realm that reveals lost truths and forgotten virtues, a quest that ultimately brings consolation for the ills of modernity. However, there must always be a return to community. Just as the hobbits must return to the Shire and restore the idyllic hobbit society using the knowledge gained from their quest, listeners of Rush's fantastical quest narratives are meant to enjoy the escape, but they should not become prisoners of escapism. They must find consolation in the musical escape and then return to the real world having drunk the milk of paradise and dined on honeydew, fully refreshed with the visionary and thus equipped to re-establish lost identities and to repair fractured community. That, at least, is the Romantic hope.

CONCLUSION: "HOME TO TEAR THE TEMPLES DOWN / HOME TO CHANGE"

In discussing Romanticism as a worldview that critiques modernity, Löwy and Sayre describe several typologies of Romanticism (for example, restitutionist, conservative, fascistic, resigned, reformist, revolutionary, and libertarian), and they locate various artists, writers, musicians, and philosophers since the eighteenth century within specific categories.[32] Of all these categories, Rush would most consistently fit libertarian Romanticism ("Anthem," "Beneath, Between and Behind," "2112," "Closer to the Heart," and "Red Barchetta"). However, we see through Rush's forty-year career as progressive rock Romantics that their critical vision is fluid, and these Romantic artists move beneath, between, behind, and beyond these various Romantic typologies. For example, early on, Rush wrote restitutionist Romantic songs characterized by nostalgic longings for a pre-industrial age as expressed through epic fantasy ("Rivendell," "The Necromancer," "The Fountain of Lamneth," "A Farewell to Kings," and "Xanadu"). At times Rush sounds like resigned Romantics, bemoaning the intractable advances of industrial capitalism ("Subdivisions," "Vital Signs," "Big Money," and "Middletown Dreams"). At other times, Rush seems to be reformist Romantics, seeking change while also expressing doubt in the justice and ambivalence in the efficacy of governmental reforms ("The Trees"). And sometimes, especially earlier in their career, they hold out brief hope in revolutionary and utopian Romanticism while also questioning that utopian vision through lyrical and musical irony. For example, in "Bastille Day" prisoners are freed, only to face new oppression, and the speaker in "Xanadu" found his mythic land and what he hoped would be utopian immortality, only to be trapped within the caves of ice to live an eternity in isolation. Rush's Romantic vision is not so easily classified, and they reveal aspects of different Romantic typologies over the course of their career. By examining their whole body of work, we can see how Rush participates in a variety of Romantic typographies as they critique modern, industrial, and consumerist experience while seeking possible resolutions to the different forms of contemporary dehumanization and alienation.

Rush's admirable longevity is a testament to their strong work ethic, devotion to their craft, and excellence in musicianship. But they remain relevant primarily due to their enduring Romantic vision, their exploration and critique of modernity, and their cautious optimism in the possibilities of individual change, relational restoration, and societal improvement. Throughout their career, they have expressed social critique and hope for change by shifting through the various typologies of Romanticism outlined by Löwy and Sayre while never being fixed within any one of them. We can see Rush as the Romantic harbingers of critique and change, the elder race of "2112" who have grown strong over the years and are returning home to tear down the oppressive temples of modernity. Rush's progressive music challenges commercial ideologies that have insinuated themselves in our hearts and minds, and it confronts restrictive corporate structures that stifle creativity and impose conformity. Rush's independent creative spirit and musical integrity have inspired many other bands, like Dream Theater, Symphony X, and Prototype, who resist corporate pressures to create market-driven, radio-friendly music. After forty years of rock, Rush continues to create music their own way, expressing their Romantic vision through song and by creative example. If we invite this vision into our imaginations, Rush just may come home to us and encourage change and consolation within ourselves that could be the impetus needed to provide recovery to an ailing modern world that, on so many levels, does not even recognize its own malady.

NOTES

1. Michael Löwy and Robert Sayre, *Romanticism Against the Tide of Modernity*, trans. Catherine Porter (Durham: Duke University Press, 2001), 3–5.

2. Ibid., 18–20.

3. Marilyn Butler, *Romantics, Rebels and Reactionaries: English Literature and Its Background, 1760–1830* (Oxford: Oxford University Press, 1981), 23.

4. Laurence Lockridge, *The Ethics of Romanticism* (Cambridge: Cambridge University Press, 1989), 16.

5. Rush, "Subdivisions," *Signals*, Mercury 810 0022–2, 1990, compact disc, originally released in 1982.

6. Chris McDonald, *Rush, Rock Music and the Middle Class: Dreaming in Middletown* (Bloomington, IN: Indiana University Press, 2009). *eBook Collection (EBSCOhost)*, EBSCO-*host* (accessed October 27, 2015), 3.

7. Rush, "Subdivisions."

8. Ibid.

9. Löwy and Sayre, *Romanticism Against the Tide of Modernity*, 25.

10. McDonald, *Rush, Rock Music and the Middle Class*, 84.

11. For discussions of Rush's reliance on Ayn Rand and their intellectual progression through varying degrees of libertarian thought, see Steven Horwitz, "Rush's Libertarianism

Never Fit the Plan," in *Rush and Philosophy: Heart and Mind United*, eds. Jim Berti and Durrell Bowman (Chicago: Open Court, 2011), 255–271; and Deena Weinstein and Michael A. Weinstein, "Neil Peart versus Ayn Rand," in *Rush and Philosophy: Heart and Mind United*, eds. Jim Berti and Durrell Bowman (Chicago: Open Court, 2011), 273–285.

12. For example, Barry Miles considers Rush to be far-right extremists expressing proto-fascism to unsuspecting listeners. He equates their views with Nazism by mischaracterizing their understanding of capitalism with the slogan "Work Makes Free" and then reminds readers this slogan was written atop the gate to the Auschwitz concentration camp. Miles likens another of Neil Peart's capitalist views to "Shades of the 1000 Year Reich." The allusions to Nazism are clear. Throughout this interview, Miles antagonizes the band with his own personal collectivist views and writes dismissively of Rush's perspectives, engaging in condescending mischaracterization and *ad hominem* attack. See Barry Miles, "Is Everybody Feelin' All Right? (Geddit. . . ?)," *New Music Express*, March 4, 1978, accessed October 27, 2015, http://www.2112.net/powerwindows/transcripts/19780304nme.htm. In a later *NME* interview with John Hamblett, Peart addresses Miles's interview, taking issue with his characterization of them as "nice-guy Nazis" and "fascist fanatics," and noting the biting irony of Rush apparently having "the world's first Jewish Nazi Bass Player." Peart states that the band was disappointed with Miles's "dishonest" article. Hamblett clarifies that Rush is not fascist, racialist, or nationalist, yet he does bemoan that they seem anti-unionist and reactionary (though Peart does attempt to address Hamblett's interpretation of "The Trees" as anti-unionist). See John Hamblett, "Rock against Right-Wing Rock Being Called Fascist," *New Music Express*, May 5, 1979, accessed October 27, 2015, http://www.2112.net/powerwindows/transcripts/19790505nme.htm. In a 2010 documentary, Alex Lifeson, the guitarist, recalls being deeply disappointed by Miles's writing the interview as if "we were Nazis, ultra right-wing maniacs." And Geddy Lee, the bassist, states, "Growing up as the son of Holocaust survivors, I found that just, you know, offensive." See *Rush: Classic Albums: 2112 & Moving Pictures* (New York: Eagle Rock Entertainment, 2010), DVD. For a more objective example of a critic noting that Rush is (unfortunately, for the critic) not so concerned with socialism and cultural revolution as some critics wish they were, see Roy MacGregor, "To Hell with Bob Dylan—Meet Rush. They're in it for the Money." *Maclean's*, January 23, 1978.

13. Robert Freedman, *Rush: Life, Liberty and the Pursuit of Excellence* (New York: Algora Publishing, 2014), 14–15.

14. Rush, "2112," *2112*, Mercury 314 534 626–2, 1997, compact disc, originally released in 1976.

15. See Weinstein and Weinstein, "Neil Peart versus Ayn Rand," 280, and Durrell S. Bowman, "'Let Them All Make Their Own Music': Individualism, Rush, and the Progressive/Hard Rock Alloy, 1976–77," in *Progressive Rock Reconsidered*, ed. Kevin Holm-Hudson (New York: Routledge, 2002), 198.

16. Rush, "2112."

17. *Rush: Classic Albums: 2112 & Moving Pictures* (New York: Eagle Rock Entertainment, 2010), DVD.

18. Löwy and Sayre, *Romanticism Against the Tide of Modernity*, 22.

19. Butler, *Romantics, Rebels and Reactionaries*, 20.

20. M. H. Abrams, *Natural Supernaturalism: Tradition and Revolution in Romantic Literature* (New York: W. W. Norton, 1971), 172.

21. J. R. R. Tolkien, *The Tolkien Reader* (New York: Ballantine Books, 1966), 75–87.

22. Rush, "The Fountain of Lamneth," *Caress of Steel*, Mercury 822 543–2, 1987, compact disc, originally released in 1975.

23. Abrams, *Natural Supernaturalism*, 182.

24. "Fountain of Lamneth" exhibits a Wordsworthian concern with individual *bildungsroman* and Romantic *kunstlerroman* as expressed in *The Prelude* and "Lines Composed a Few Miles above Tintern Abbey."

25. Rush, "The Fountain of Lamneth."

26. Rush, "Xanadu," *A Farewell to Kings*, Mercury 822 546–2, 1987, compact disc, originally released in 1977.

27. See David S. Hogsette, "Eclipsed by the Pleasure Dome: Poetic Failure in Coleridge's 'Kubla Khan,'" *Romanticism on the Net* 5 (1997), https://www.erudit.org/revue/ron/1997/v/n5/005737ar.html.
28. For discussions of Romantic irony, see Anne Mellor, *English Romantic Irony* (Cambridge: Harvard University Press, 1980) and David Simpson, *Irony and Authority in Romantic Poetry* (London: Macmillan Press, 1970).
29. For a musicological analysis of the intro to "Xanadu," see Bowman, "'Let Them Make Their Own Music,'" 202–203.
30. Rush, "Xanadu."
31. For discussions of how listening to Rush with headphones enhances the listener's experience of escape, see McDonald, *Rush, Rock Music and the Middle Class.*
32. Löwy and Sayre, *Romanticism Against the Tide of Modernity*, 69–80.

BIBLIOGRAPHY

Abrams, M. H. *Natural Supernaturalism: Tradition and Revolution in Romantic Literature.* New York: W. W. Norton, 1971.
Bowman, Durrell S. "'Let Them All Make Their Own Music': Individualism, Rush, and the Progressive/Hard Rock Alloy, 1976–77." In *Progressive Rock Reconsidered*, edited by Kevin Holm-Hudson, 183–218. New York: Routledge, 2002.
Butler, Marilyn. *Romantics, Rebels and Reactionaries: English Literature and Its Background, 1760–1830.* Oxford: Oxford University Press, 1981.
Freedman, Robert. *Rush: Life, Liberty and the Pursuit of Excellence.* New York: Algora Publishing, 2014.
Hamblett, John. "Rock against Right-Wing Rock Being Called Fascist." *New Music Express*, May 5, 1979, accessed October 27, 2015, http://www.2112.net/powerwindows/transcripts/19790505nme.htm.
Hogsette, David S. "Eclipsed by the Pleasure Dome: Poetic Failure in Coleridge's 'Kubla Khan.'" *Romanticism on the Net* 5 (1997), accessed October 27, 2015, https://www.erudit.org/revue/ron/1997/v/n5/005737ar.html.
Horwitz, Steven. "Rush's Libertarianism Never Fit the Plan." In *Rush and Philosophy: Heart and Mind United*, edited by Jim Berti and Durrell Bowman, 255–271. Chicago: Open Court, 2011.
Lockridge, Laurence. *The Ethics of Romanticism.* Cambridge: Cambridge University Press, 1989.
Löwy, Michael, and Robert Sayre. *Romanticism Against the Tide of Modernity.* Translated by Catherine Porter. Durham: Duke University Press, 2001.
MacGregor, Roy. "To Hell with Bob Dylan—Meet Rush. They're in it for the Money." *Maclean's*, January 23, 1978.
McDonald, Chris. *Rush, Rock Music and the Middle Class: Dreaming in Middletown.* Bloomington, IN: Indiana University Press, 2009. *eBook Collection (EBSCOhost)*, EBSCOhost. Accessed October 27, 2015.
Mellor, Anne. *English Romantic Irony.* Cambridge: Harvard University Press, 1980.
Miles, Barry. "Is Everybody Feelin' All Right? (Geddit. . . ?)." *New Music Express*, March 4, 1978, accessed October 27, 2015, http://www.2112.net/powerwindows/transcripts/19780304nme.htm.
Rush, "2112." In *2112*, Mercury 314 534 626–2, 1997, compact disc. Originally released in 1976.
———. "Anthem." In *Fly by Night*, Mercury 314 534 624–2, 1997, compact disc. Originally released in 1975.
———. "Bastille Day." In *Caress of Steel*, Mercury 822 543–2, 1987, compact disc. Originally released in 1975.
———. "Beneath, Between and Behind." In *Fly by Night*, Mercury 314 534 624–2, 1997, compact disc. Originally released in 1975.

————. "Big Money." In *Power Windows*, Mercury 314 534 635–2, 1997, compact disc. Originally released in 1985.

————. "By-Tor and the Snowdog." In *Fly by Night*, Mercury 314 534 624–2, 1997, compact disc. Originally released in 1975.

————. "Closer to the Heart." In *A Farewell to Kings*, Mercury 822 546–2, 1987, compact disc. Originally released in 1977.

————. "Farewell to Kings, A." In *A Farewell to Kings*, Mercury 822 546–2, 1987, compact disc. Originally released in 1977.

————. "Fountain of Lamneth, The." In *Caress of Steel*, Mercury 822 543–2, 1987, compact disc. Originally released in 1975.

————. "Middletown Dreams." In *Power Windows*, Mercury 314 534 635–2, 1997, compact disc. Originally released in 1985.

————. "Necromancer, The." In *Caress of Steel*, Mercury 822 543–2, 1987, compact disc. Originally released in 1975.

————. "Red Barchetta." In *Moving Pictures*, Mercury 800 048–2, 1987, compact disc. Originally released in 1981.

————. "Rivendell." In *Fly by Night*, Mercury 314 534 624–2, 1997, compact disc. Originally released in 1975.

————. "Subdivisions." In *Signals*, Mercury 810 0022–2, 1990, compact disc. Originally released in 1982.

————. "Trees, The." In *Hemispheres*, Mercury 314 534 629–2, 1997, compact disc. Originally released in 1978.

————. "Vital Signs." In *Moving Pictures*, Mercury 800 048–2, 1987, compact disc. Originally released in 1981.

————. "Xanadu." In *A Farewell to Kings*, Mercury 822 546–2, 1987, compact disc. Originally released in 1977.

Rush: Classic Albums: 2112 & Moving Pictures. New York: Eagle Rock Entertainment, 2010. DVD.

Simpson, David. *Irony and Authority in Romantic Poetry*. London: Macmillan Press, 1970.

Tolkien, J. R. R. *The Tolkien Reader*. New York: Ballantine Books, 1966.

Weinstein, Deena, and Michael A. Weinstein. "Neil Peart versus Ayn Rand." In *Rush and Philosophy: Heart and Mind United*, edited by Jim Berti and Durrell Bowman, 273–285. Chicago: Open Court, 2011.

Chapter Nine

Wordsworth's "Michael," the Georgic, and Blackberry Smoke

Ronald D. Morrison

Applying genre labels from literary studies to popular music is neither a common nor an uncomplicated gesture. Still, considering how often rock music reflects both Romantic ideals and rhetorical strategies, exploring connections between the ways in which rock music and Romanticism make use of genre categories can nevertheless be fruitful—especially since rock and Romanticism often deliberately blur the lines separating genre classifications. In this chapter, I explore how the form of the georgic—especially as reconceived by contemporary ecocritical theory—provides helpful insights into both rock music and Romanticism. As case studies, I focus on Wordsworth's "Michael" and the songs of the American Southern rock band Blackberry Smoke. Ultimately, I argue that both Wordsworth's poem and many of the songs of Blackberry Smoke should be considered as revitalized versions of the georgic that are focused on nuanced meanings of the term "environment," including human-created environments and culture. Teasing out the significance of the use of georgic elements in both Wordsworth's "Michael" and the music of Blackberry Smoke offers an opportunity to explore the significance of how recent environmental approaches to literary study have contributed to our understanding of Romantic literature. In particular, such an analysis suggests that reconsidering the conventional emphasis upon the pastoral and rediscovering an emphasis on the georgic might reveal some intriguing tensions in Wordsworth and in Romantic literature as a whole.

Wordsworth frequently went out of his way to challenge conventional genre distinctions inherited from the eighteenth century and earlier. The most basic example can be found in the provocative title of *Lyrical Ballads*, a collection in which he undermines the traditional hierarchy of poetic forms by elevating the brief lyric, the ballad, and the pastoral, a form that he found particularly tantalizing during these early years. Undoubtedly, his most famous pastoral is "Michael," which first appeared in the expanded second edition of *Lyrical Ballads* published in 1800, and which took the place originally intended for Coleridge's unfinished "Christabel" as the collection's final poem.[1]

Together, Wordsworth and Coleridge determined that "Christabel" represented too great a departure from other poems in the new volume especially since, as David Fairer articulates it, at this time Wordsworth regularly "turned his mind to pastoral."[2] Notably, Wordsworth labeled five of the poems in the new volume as pastorals through their subtitles.[3] Coleridge recognized the significance of his friend's fascination with the pastoral, and in a letter from May 1800 he related to Southey that "Wordsworth publishes a second Volume of Lyrical Ballads, & Pastorals."[4] As Stephen Parrish reminds us, "By 1802 the title page of the collection read *Lyrical Ballads, with Pastoral and Other Poems.*"[5] Furthermore, to underscore the significance of "Michael," Wordsworth determined that the poem would receive its own separate title page within the larger volume.[6]

Since the poem's original publication, Wordsworth's subtitle for "Michael" has often tended to narrow discussions of the poem, as critics have focused on the ways in which "Michael" conforms to or deviates from conventions of the pastoral. But at the same time, critics have also had to reconsider the features of the pastoral in order to account for Wordsworth's (largely) realistic descriptions of the actual lives of rural people caught up in powerful economic and political forces resulting from the Industrial Age. As one editor puts it, "The subtitle shows Wordsworth's modification of the term 'pastoral' from aristocratic make-believe to the tragic suffering of people in what he called 'humble and rustic life.'"[7] Wordsworth himself seems to have recognized that he was moving beyond the normally idyllic elements of the pastoral, as we see in his letter to Charles James Fox (accompanying a copy of the second edition), emphasizing that "Michael" and "The Brothers" demonstrate how a "little tract of land" could represent for small landowners "a kind of permanent rallying point for their domestic feelings."[8] In the same letter, Wordsworth laments that the class of "small independent *proprietors* of land" was disappearing.[9]

If Wordsworth seems dissatisfied with the limitations of the traditional pastoral, the georgic emerges as a productive alternative to describe "Michael." Even at first glance, "Michael" fits neatly into this genre focused on the practical aspects of farming and rural life. While Wordsworth offers what might be considered a sentimentalized description of Michael and Isabel and their "life of eager industry" (1.124),[10] he nevertheless manages to detail their working lives in more realistic fashion than one typically finds in a traditional pastoral poem. In fact, Wordsworth's poem addresses lingering problems that have plagued farming communities for two centuries or more: burdensome mortgages, the out-migration of rural young people, the loss of family farms, and the steady erosion of traditional rural customs and values. Although the pastoral tradition has received considerably more attention than its more realistic and practical counterpart, a few scholars have recognized that the georgic also has had a long-term influence on British literature. For example, W. J. Keith, writing about the rural tradition in British prose (including writers such as Gilbert White, William Cobbett, and Richard Jefferies), concludes that the georgic shaped rural prose writings in the nineteenth century far more profoundly than did the more familiar pastoral.[11] Bruce Graver, one of a handful of scholars who have studied Wordsworth's longterm interest in the georgic, offers convincing evidence that Wordsworth "translated, retranslated, combined, and finally adapted in [his] poetry" various sections of Virgil's famous poem—especially early in his poetic career.[12] Graver concludes that Virgil's *Georgics* should be considered a major influence on Wordsworth's poetry as a whole.[13] Writing specifically about "Michael," Graver asserts that the poem displays the influence of Virgil's *Georgics*, asserting that "Michael" should be considered a "generic hybrid: a georgic pastoral."[14] As Fairer has recently pointed out, Graver's interpretation of the poem sets up an attractive but perhaps oversimplified binary opposition—pastoral *otium* versus georgic *labor*—that might call into question georgic values altogether. But Fairer's alternative method of reading the poem suggests that georgic values simply need to be sustained, which the georgic form allows since it typically contains, as he claims, "resourceful continuities."[15] As Fairer argues, even when Michael's and Isabel's land eventually passes into a "Stranger's hand" (l.484), there remains hope for "a flourishing future for another family."[16] Michael, Isabel, and their cottage might be gone, but the land and its almost limitless potential remain.

Contemporary ecocriticism offers additional insights into the potential significance of the georgic as a literary form. Although in his influential *Romantic Ecology* Jonathan Bate never goes so far as to label "Michael" a georgic poem, he concludes that "Michael" is a "new kind of pastoral, stripped of the Schillerian 'sentimental,' the sophisticated and self-conscious."[17] Furthermore, Bate argues that an ecocritical re-conception and revitalization of the pastoral is highly desirable. Bate observes that for much "modern criticism, . . . pastoral poetry is historically and socially specific"[18] in ways that ignore the importance of the natural environment; moreover, Bate claims that an environmentally inflected criticism has its own valuable perspectives to offer, including an emphasis on the effects of the Industrial Age upon both natural and created human environments. Approaching the pastoral with an environmental awareness helps to counter claims by critics such as Roger Sales, who complain that "Pastoralism should be divested of its silver-tongued language and myths of the golden age."[19] Even so, it is striking that Bate does not develop more fully the significance of the georgic elements in Wordsworth's poetry and how they might be connected to history, culture, and the environment.

In his well-received introduction to ecocritical theory, Greg Garrard offers the georgic as one of several literary forms that exemplify the larger trope of "dwelling." While Garrard acknowledges that historically the georgic has often been co-opted by powerful ideological forces that exploit both the earth and those who labor upon it, he nevertheless sees considerable potential for the georgic, especially as it has been adapted by contemporary writers such as Wendell Berry, whose works exemplify an evolving modern georgic tradition promoting environmentally responsible uses of land and respect for agrarian culture. For Garrard, "dwelling" is "not a transient state; rather, it implies the long-term imbrication of humans in a landscape of memory, ancestry and death, of ritual, life and work."[20] This rich description captures key thematic elements in Wordsworth's "Michael" (as well, perhaps, as many other poems in *Lyrical Ballads*). The pastoral, as Keats describes it figuratively in "Ode on a Grecian Urn," is "cold," or frozen in time. The georgic, in contrast, constantly displays an awareness of the relentless pressures of time and of human toil. In what Fairer describes as Wordsworth's new versions of pastorals, "georgic demands" are typically revealed through "changes of weather, economic pressures, physical toil, above all the duty of husbandry."[21] From an ecocritical perspective, the georgic invites readers to reconsider the long-term sustainability of farming practices and, more generally, of rural culture as a whole. As fewer and fewer people directly work the land, rural culture assumes an even greater significance—in Wordsworth's day as well as our own—as an important link to the land and to traditions associated with an agricultural past quickly slipping away.

One important aspect of "the manners of rural life," as Wordsworth describes it in his 1800 preface,[22] is religious belief and practice in rural locations. Despite all of the biblical resonances in "Michael" (the Abraham and Isaac story and the parable of the Prodigal Son are only two of the most obvious), the poem seldom refers to religion in specific terms.[23] Instead, Wordsworth appears more broadly focused on rural culture, with religion—especially Evangelical belief—as an important part of this culture. Wordsworth could certainly be intrigued by Evangelical practice, as he is in *Peter Bell*, originally composed at the same time as *Lyrical Ballads* but not published until 1819. Mary Jacobus observes that *Peter Bell* exhibits the unmistakable influence of the "Methodist conversion-narrative—almost a popular art form in its own right."[24] Richard E. Brantley argues, more broadly, that "the most distinctive features of Wordsworth's literary practice can best be understood in terms of his pervasive Evangelical idiom."[25] Brantley never offers a fully developed reading of "Michael," but he nevertheless claims that, following the birth of Luke, Michael experiences a profound spiritual awakening that has parallels to a religious conversion experience.[26]

Still, more often than not, Michael's religious views are distinctly secular versions of Evangelicalism, as we see in what we might call Michael's "religion of work." The value of hard work is central to Evangelical culture and, in a telling moment, Wordsworth emphasizes that Isabel and Michael lead a life not just of "eager industry" (l.124) but "endless industry" (l.97). Although Michael invokes Heaven in blessing Luke (l.407) and in asking forgiveness if he errs in sending his son to the city (l.390), Michael typically conflates work and morality in relatively simplistic terms—as when he says to Luke "let this Sheep-fold be / Thy anchor and thy shield" (ll. 417–18).[27] The sheepfold may hold rich symbolic possibilities, but it also literally represents a building project that Michael hopes will bind his son to the land—and to his promise to secure it. As Graver insightfully notes, it is a major "failure" that Michael provides his son with such a "joyless education."[28] From such a perspective, it seems understandable that Luke abandons the life of "endless industry" laid out for him by his parents; and, predictably, the source of Luke's eventual disgrace is that he begins to "slacken in his duty" (l.452), which leads to his flight from England—and ultimately his flight from family obligations and the unbending religion of work.

Turning from Wordsworth's poetry to the songs of an American country-rock band may initially seem incongruous, but there are some rather striking connections to explore. First, however, some background is in order. In the spring of 2015, Britain's *MOJO* magazine proclaimed that Atlanta's Blackberry Smoke has become "the hottest hard rock band on the planet,"[29] and the band has been touring relentlessly over the past decade and a half in America and Europe to earn this praise, building along the way a fiercely devoted fan base and selling out mid-sized venues across the U.S. and parts of Europe. Nevertheless, Blackberry Smoke and its music defy easy categorization and might be considered a generic hybrid—a "crossover" act that has never settled into just one category.[30] In certain respects, the band both deserves and embraces the "Southern Rock" label that links it to the Allman Brothers, Lynyrd Skynyrd, Little Feat, and the Black Crowes, groups with which it shares a number of stylistic features, including harmonized lead guitar lines, the frequent use of slide guitar, and New Orleans-influenced piano and organ passages, as well as elements of gospel and rhythm and blues. But the band's music also includes many of the features of modern country music as well, and in fact studio versions of a number of songs make use of pedal steel, fiddle, and mandolin.

As a result, the band has enjoyed considerable success on modern country radio and on Country Music Television, and the band's last four albums have appeared simultaneously on both country and rock charts.[31] Blackberry Smoke's British classic rock influences also remain strikingly evident, and in live shows the band offers convincing covers, in whole or in part, of songs by Led Zeppelin, the Rolling Stones, and Black Sabbath. In 2015, Blackberry Smoke contributed cover songs to two tribute albums—a version of Led Zeppelin's "The Rover" on *Physical Graffiti Redrawn* and a version of Lynyrd Skynyrd's "Workin' for MCA" on *One More for the Fans*.[32] These two iconic bands probably represent two of the most important influences on the band, although there are certainly others.

In solo venues, Charlie Starr, the band's primary songwriter and vocalist, has identified specific autobiographical elements in various song lyrics, but I believe it is best to approach Blackberry Smoke's songs as a series of interconnected monologues (a feature which often parallels Wordsworth's approach in *Lyrical Ballads*) that collectively present a complex vision of twenty-first-century Southern working-class culture. Even though it proves stylistically awkward at times, I refer to these songs as having speakers rather than searching for autobiographical connections that might be challenging or impossible to document. It is true that Blackberry Smoke songs do not focus on agriculture *per se*, but they nevertheless use elements of the georgic tradition both to celebrate Southern culture and to question its sustainability. Blackberry Smoke songs include many references to the simple pleasures and natural beauties of Southern life, but there is also the bittersweet acknowledgement that poverty, lack of employment opportunities, extreme narrowness, and drug and alcohol abuse stand as severe threats to the long-term sustainability of this culture. Thus, the music of Blackberry Smoke has much in common with a revised conception of the georgic that recent environmental criticism allows us to see in Wordsworth.

Many of Blackberry Smoke's songs capture an essential part of Southern working-class culture by utilizing metaphors explicitly linked to Evangelical culture. To echo Brantley's conclusions about Wordsworth's poetry, the lyrics of Blackberry Smoke songs indeed often make use of a "pervasive Evangelical idiom"—although in an admittedly different manner from Wordsworth's poetry. Many of the songs offer a gentle, insider's parody of Evangelical belief, practice, and rhetoric, while at the same time utilizing this idiom to capture essential truths about secular culture as a whole. The idiom of Evangelical culture permeates *The Whippoorwill* in particular, right down to the artwork, which includes a photograph of a river baptism early in the twentieth century. Not surprisingly, several of Blackberry Smoke's songs utilize elements of the Evangelical conversion-narrative, although the "conversion" might lurch toward the ironic or the comic. One excellent example is "Six Ways to Sunday," which opens *The Whippoorwill*. Throughout the song, the speaker describes his plans for making love to a woman, hoping that he will soon hear her "speaking in tongues."[33] Later in the song the speaker claims he is willing to "pick up the snakes and drink the strychnine too,"[34] referring to the practice in some Evangelical churches of handling poisonous snakes or drinking poison in order to show one's faith. He will brave these dangers, he claims, "As long as I get a chance to lay my hands on you,"[35] playfully referencing the concept of the "laying on of hands" in such churches.

Similarly, in the song that concludes the same album, "Shakin' Hands with the Holy Ghost," the speaker compares singing, dancing, and falling in love to something akin to an ecstatic religious experience, proclaiming that he "Feel[s] like I'm singing with the Heavenly Host"—and, in a striking turn of phrase, he declares he feels as though he is "shakin' hands with the Holy Ghost."[36] Although these songs can display a wry and raucous sense of humor, the references to Evangelical culture are neither snide nor mean-spirited nor even necessarily comic. Instead, the lyrics use an Evangelical idiom to capture the ways in which love and sex are profound, transcendent experiences that need to be described through religious metaphors. "Sanctified Woman," which appears in two distinct versions on both *Bad Luck Ain't No Crime* and *Little Piece of Dixie*, represents another example of this idiom.[37] In Evangelical parlance, a "sanctified woman" is a woman who has given herself entirely to God and through whom a mate or spouse might also find salvation. Given the playful and ambiguous tone of the lyrics, when the speaker cries out that he needs redemption "from that sanctified woman,"[38] it is unclear whether she will provide this redemption, or whether the speaker needs to be relieved of the burden of dealing with this volatile woman. Still, the song suggests that love offers profound hope of redemption, however temporary or imperfect. In these songs, love itself is not the idealized and sexless version typically presented in the pastoral world but a harsher, more fragile kind of experience that connects it to the more resilient georgic. Love affairs may inevitably fail, but new possibilities are always just around the corner. In "Testify" (from *Bad Luck Ain't No Crime*) the lyrics again use an Evangelical idiom to describe the strange and wondrous vicissitudes of love that might drift from the morally profound to the comic and back again without warning in a "redneck bar" and other places and situations familiar to a working-class audience: "[I] wanna testify about the things I've seen / Wash my hands but they never come clean."[39]

Also following the tradition of the georgic, the songs of Blackberry Smoke acknowledge both the enduring value and soul-crushing weight of work. So, for example, "Leave a Scar" (from *The Whippoorwill*) might best be remembered for its rousing chorus of "I may not change the world, but I'm gonna leave a scar."[40] Still, much of the song serves as a heartfelt tribute to a working-class Southern upbringing in a small town or rural area. The speaker relates that his father, whom he describes as a "good man," taught his children how to work and to fight, and he "Told me about the good Lord and when to use a gun / Made me very proud of where it is that I come from."[41] In its basic message, "Leave a Scar" shares key elements with

Wordsworth's "Michael" about the significance of family bonds and the transmission of rural values. Michael has, in effect, left a scar of sorts in Green-head Ghyll with the unfinished sheepfold that Wordsworth describes early in the poem. But, just as we see in "Michael," the overwhelming pressures of work and family commitments can create nightmarish obstacles for young people in particular. In the poignant "One Horse Town" (also from *The Whippoorwill*), work and family obligations in a "little bitty town" have a painful and predictable influence on the young people born there.[42] It may seem anachronistic to use a Blackberry Smoke song to explore key values articulated in "Michael," but lines such as the following illustrate that the core values of "Michael" and twenty-first-century rural America remain strikingly similar: "You grew up doin' what your daddy does. / You don't ask questions. You do it just because."[43] While the song describes some of the self-imposed psychological factors that keep young people in such towns, "Bottom of This" (from *Little Piece of Dixie*) realistically details the effects of a life dominated by "the boss, the bank, the box full of bills / empty gas tank, and it's all uphill."[44] "Normaltown" (from *Bad Luck Ain't No Crime*) presents an even bleaker portrait of the enforced conformity and narrowness of small town life that eventually creates a "living hell" since everything in Normaltown "is square or is round."[45]

If Blackberry Smoke's music explores the curse of hard work and the weight of family commitments, several songs describe in jubilant fashion the temporary escape *from* work, as we see in the band's concert staple "Good One Comin' On" from *Little Piece of Dixie*. The song starts out by describing the preparations for the weekend as "No chance of stayin' sober. / I can feel a good one comin' on."[46] And with a tank full of gas and supplies of beer, tequila, and cigarettes, the speaker sets out for fun and romance on a warm Alabama night, in what might be considered as a lighthearted version of what eventually happens to Luke in Wordsworth's poem. More serious is "Freedom Song" (from *Little Piece of Dixie*), which describes the speaker triumphantly leaving the working world behind: "I been walkin' the line a long time. / I need a change."[47] Whereas in "Michael" work provides the shepherd with a stable sense of identity (which Luke eventually comes to reject), in "Freedom Song" work erodes basic identity and must be escaped rather than embraced. But the desire for escape is also fraught with various dangers. Several songs from the band's catalog express serious concerns about the forms of addiction and dependence that plague small towns in America. For example, "Lesson in a Bottle," from *New Honky Tonk Bootlegs*, has a certain tongue-in-cheek quality, but it is also deadly serious about "white lines and wild times" that render the speaker "passed out cold and left behind."[48] The speaker declares unabashedly that he has been "a winner, and a loser, sloppy drunk and drug abuser," and that he now finds himself "a long, long way from where I was goin'."[49] But the "Lesson in a Bottle" is never learned. To choose a more recent example, in "Too High," which appears on *Holding All the Roses*, there are references to "pills and meth" being the "kiss of death," and the music video for the song portrays two lost little girls apparently rescued by a man cooking meth in a rural shed.[50] In stark contrast to "Good One Comin' On," this song directly acknowledges the difficulty but crucial importance of maintaining sobriety and escaping addiction.

One of the most memorable Blackberry Smoke songs is "The Whippoor-will" from the album of the same name. Although the lyrics are minimalist, the speaker suggests that he has drifted from his most profound and enduring cultural values. The lyrics refer obliquely to a female relative—perhaps a grandmother—who originally put the speaker on "the Jericho Road" and who provided various life lessons—some followed and some now forgotten.[51] The speaker seems haunted by the whippoorwill's song, which is mimicked by lead guitar lines. The song also includes references to bougainvilleas and honeysuckle, items from the natural world which, along with the whippoor-will, seem to stand as emblematic for the speaker of family traditions and rural values, rather like Michael's anchor and shield. But in this case, they have been lost or discarded, and the song becomes an elegy to their memory. Perhaps the most striking song in the Blackberry Smoke catalog is "No Way Back to Eden" from *Holding All the Roses*, which seems to chronicle moral, cultural, and environmental decay with its refrain of "There's no way back to Eden / From what I've seen."[52] Although the speaker is haunted by "things I left behind," he also knows that he has "Come too far to turn back."[53] The pastoral world has been wholly subsumed by the georgic. As Fairer comments, the georgic necessarily must go "East of Eden,"[54] a statement that fits this particular song perfectly. The band's signature song—the song that closes out most live performances—is "Ain't Much Left of Me," which describes a spectacular yet never fully articulated "fall from grace."[55] While Starr dedicates the song to "divorced people" on the live version on *Leave a Scar: Live in North Carolina*,[56] the lyrics might just as well describe a religious crisis, drug addiction, or any other form of failure or error—and this essential ambiguity makes the song applicable to a wide range of experiences and types of loss. But despite this calamity the speaker remains unbowed and defiant. In the spirit of the georgic (and perhaps the blues, which shares much with the georgic), he proclaims: "I'm still holding on and there ain't much left of me."[57]

And thus the music of Blackberry Smoke remains resilient, good-natured, and forward-looking—even in the face of loss, disappointment, and disillu-sionment. Rather than celebrating an idealized pastoral world frozen in time, the music of Blackberry Smoke embraces a georgic view that acknowledges the difficulties of the present but which still looks hopefully to the future. Ultimately, the music of Blackberry Smoke opens up new possibilities for considering Southern rock itself as closely connected to the georgic form as reconceived by ecocriticism. Garrard's concise description of the modern georgic not only applies to a poem such as "Michael," but its emphasis on "memory, ancestry and death, of ritual, life and work" remains a poignant description and definition of what constitutes contemporary Southern rock music. In describing the contrast between the ecological visions of British and American literary traditions, Bate emphasizes the British focus on "localness" in contrast to an American awareness of the "vastness" of nature.[58] But just as Wordsworth focuses on the local features of the Lake District in "Michael," Southern rock focuses squarely on the local aspects of the Southern environment, including the significance of a secularized Evangelical culture and the joys and sorrows of work. Ultimately, the georgic becomes one way of making sense of what constitutes Southern rock, and the songs of Blackberry Smoke help us to make some unique observations about the rural culture described in Wordsworth's poetry. Moreover, the extended case study presented here also provides some new ways of approaching Wordsworth through the lens of contemporary ecocriticism. While traditional discussions of Romantic poetry have emphasized the significance of the pastoral form, this unusual case study also provides an initial reassessment of the importance of the georgic form, which also seems to undergird much of Wordsworth's early poetry. Never entirely content with the idyllic and unrealistic form of the conventional pastoral, Wordsworth more typically embraced a view of humans and their environment that is more in line with the themes of the georgic, a form that retains its power and its poignancy to this day.

CODA: *LIKE AN ARROW*

As this volume was moving through the publication process, Blackberry Smoke released its fifth studio album, *Like an Arrow*, which in many respects continues the successful formula that the band has followed. This album, like the others before it, illustrates the ways in which elements of the georgic might be applied to their music. Charting in the top five on both Billboard's rock and country charts, this album also charted #1 on the newly established Billboard Americana chart, which, in fact, may be the most accurate way of labeling the band's music.[59] Most of the previous elements remain present here. Following themes established on earlier albums, "Workin' for a Workin' Man" describes the grinding, humiliating realities of working for a living: "I got to shuck and jive just to even survive / It ain't workin' for a workin' man."[60] Similarly, "Let it Burn" is an up-tempo number in much the same vein as "Freedom Song," although with a slightly darker edge, as the speaker imagines himself burning down his house along with his problems before making his escape from his oppressive home town.

But there is also a maturity and wisdom evident in several new songs. For example, "The Good Life" might be considered a re-imagining of "Michael," with the mature son voicing his appreciation for his gruff father's positive influence on his life. Despite the fact that the speaker's father "was not the kind of man / That would walk you to school hand in hand," the father has nevertheless provided lasting practical advice, and he has always encouraged his son to remember "the good life."[61] Ultimately, the album looks beyond the narrowness of the "One Horse Town" from *Little Piece of Dixie* and imagines, in the words of "Sunrise in Texas" "There's a world goin' on / Outside the world that I'm in."[62] While the ominous "Waiting for the Thunder," the darkest, heaviest song on the album—probably in the entire Blackberry Smoke catalog—describes an apocalyptic scene caused by "the money and the war and religion,"[63] there remains considerable hope in most of these songs. One notable example is "Ain't Gonna Wait," which declares that time waits for no one, as the speaker maintains he will overcome his past and move on to other opportunities and experiences, once again exemplifying the resilient spirit of the georgic.

NOTES

1. James Butler and Karen Green, eds., *Lyrical Ballads, and Other Poems, 1797–1800*, Cornell Wordsworth (Ithaca: Cornell University Press, 1992), 30.

2. David Fairer, "The Pastoral-Georgic Tradition," in *William Wordsworth in Context*, ed. Andrew Bennett (Cambridge: Cambridge University Press, 2015), 112.

3. See Butler and Green, 26. In addition to "Michael," the poems identified as pastorals include "The Brothers," "The Oak and the Broom," "The Idle Shepherd-Boys," and "The Pet Lamb."

4. Earl Leslie Griggs, ed., *Collected Letters of Samuel Taylor Coleridge*, vol. 1, 1785–1800 (Oxford: Clarendon Press, 1956), 585.

5. Stephen M. Parrish, *The Art of the* Lyrical Ballads (Cambridge: Harvard University Press, 1973), 159.

6. Butler and Green, 252n.

7. Stephen Greenblatt, gen. ed., *The Norton Anthology of English Literature*, 9th ed., vol. 2 (New York: Norton, 2012), 320n.

8. Quoted in Butler and Green, 401.

9. Ibid., Wordsworth's emphasis.

10. All quotations from Wordsworth's poetry are taken from Butler and Green. All citations appear in the text by line numbers.

11. W.J. Keith, *The Rural Tradition: A Study of the Non-Fiction Prose Writers of the English Countryside* (Toronto: University of Toronto Press, 1974), 5.

12. Bruce E. Graver, "Wordsworth's Georgic Beginnings," *Texas Studies in Literature and Language* 33, no. 2 (1991): 138.

13. Ibid., 137.

14. Bruce E. Graver, "Wordsworth's Georgic Pastoral: *Otium* and *Labor* in 'Michael,'" *European Romantic Review* 1, no. 2 (1991): 119.

15. Fairer, 115.

16. Ibid.

17. Jonathan Bate, *Romantic Ecology: Wordsworth and the Environmental Tradition* (New York: Routledge, 1991), 104.

18. Ibid., 18.

19. Roger Sales, *English Literature in History 1780–1839: Pastoral and Politics* (Boston: St. Martin's Press, 1983), 77.

20. Greg Garrard, *Ecocriticism*, 2nd ed., New Critical Idiom Series (New York: Routledge, 2012), 117.

21. Fairer, 114.

22. Butler and Green, 743.

23. See Butler and Green for a helpful overview of criticism on Wordsworth's engagement with biblical narratives (401–402).

24. Mary Jacobus, *Tradition and Experiment in Wordsworth's* Lyrical Ballads *(1798)* (Oxford: Clarendon, 1976), 266.

25. Richard E. Brantley, *Wordsworth's "Natural Methodism"* (New Haven: Yale University Press, 1975), xi.

26. Ibid., 136.

27. The phrasing here corresponds to no specific passage in the Bible, although the anchor and shield are common metaphors in various parts of the Old and New Testaments.

28. Graver, "Wordsworth's Georgic Pastoral," 128.

29. *"Physical Graffiti* Redrawn," *MOJO*, April 2015, 6.

30. A t-shirt offered for sale on the band's website captures the point succinctly: "Too rock for country / Too country for rock."

31. *Billboard Artist Chart History*: Blackberry Smoke, www.billboard.com/artist/289123/blackberrysmoke/chart?f=408.

32. The first compact disc was included in the April 2015 issue of *MOJO*; Lynyrd Skynyrd [and Various Guest Artists], *One More for the Fans*, Loud and Proud Records LNP022, 2015, 2 compact discs.

33. Blackberry Smoke, *The Whippoorwill*, Southern Ground Artists SGA 012, 2012, compact disc. Because the lyrics on album notes and the band's website contain a number of inconsistencies (generally restricted to capitalization and punctuation), I have silently introduced minor revisions to improve clarity for a reading audience.

34. Ibid.

35. Ibid.

36. Ibid.

37. Blackberry Smoke, *Bad Luck Ain't No Crime*, BamaJam Records BJAM 01004, 2003, compact disc; Blackberry Smoke, *Little Piece of Dixie*, BamaJam Records 01001, 2009, compact disc.

38. Ibid.

39. *Bad Luck Ain't No Crime*.

40. *The Whippoorwill*.

41. Ibid.

42. Ibid.

43. Ibid.

44. *Little Piece of Dixie*.

45. *Bad Luck Ain't No Crime*. This song stands in sharp contrast to "Woman in the Moon" from *Holding All the Roses*. In this song, a celebration of creativity and originality, the speaker describes his way of seeing the world as "A little off-kilter, just left of center / Bent just a little out of round" (Blackberry Smoke, *Holding All the Roses*, Rounder Records 11661–36160–02, 2015, compact disc).

46. *Little Piece of Dixie*.

47. Ibid.

48. Blackberry Smoke, *New Honky Tonk Bootlegs*, BamaJam Records 01005, 2003, compact disc.

49. Ibid.

50. *Holding All the Roses*.

51. *The Whippoorwill*.

52. *Holding All the Roses*.

53. Ibid.

54. Fairer, 113.

55. *The Whippoorwill.*
56. Blackberry Smoke, *Leave a Scar: Live in North Carolina*, 3 Legged Records 3LG03, 2014, compact disc.
57. *The Whippoorwill.*
58. Bate, 39.
59. *Billboard Artist Chart History.*
60. Blackberry Smoke, *Like an Arrow*, 3 Legged Records 3LG05, 2016, compact disc.
61. Ibid.
62. Ibid.
63. Ibid.

BIBLIOGRAPHY

Bate, Jonathan. *Romantic Ecology: Wordsworth and the Environmental Tradition.* New York: Routledge, 1991.
Billboard Artist Chart History: Blackberry Smoke. www.billboard.com/artist/289123/black-berry-smoke/chart?f=408.
Blackberry Smoke. *Bad Luck Ain't No Crime.* BamaJam Records BJAM 01004, 2003, compact disc.
———. *Holding All the Roses.* Rounder Records 11661–36160–02, 2015, compact disc.
———. *Leave A Scar: Live in North Carolina.* 3 Legged Records 3LG03, 2014, compact disc.
———. *Like an Arrow.* 3 Legged Records 3LG05, 2016, compact disc.
———. *Little Piece of Dixie.* BamaJam Records 01001, 2009, compact disc.
———. *New Honky Tonk Bootlegs.* BamaJam Records 01005, 2003, compact disc.
———. *The Whippoorwill.* Southern Ground Artists SGA 012, 2012, compact disc.
Brantley, Richard E. *Wordsworth's "Natural Methodism."* New Haven: Yale University Press, 1975.
Butler, James, and Karen Green, eds. *Lyrical Ballads, and Other Poems, 1797–1800.* Ithaca: Cornell University Press, 1992.
Fairer, David. "The Pastoral-Georgic Tradition." In *William Wordsworth in Context*, edited by Andrew Bennett, 111–118. Cambridge: Cambridge UP, 2015.
Garrard, Greg. *Ecocriticism.* 2nd ed. New Critical Idiom Series. New York: Routledge, 2012.
Graver, Bruce E. "Wordsworth's Georgic Pastoral: *Otium* and *Labor* in 'Michael.'" *European Romantic Review* 1, no. 2 (1991): 119–134.
———. "Wordsworth's Georgic Beginnings." *Texas Studies in Literature and Language* 33, no. 2 (1991): 137–159.
Greenblatt, Stephen, gen. ed. *The Norton Anthology of English Literature.* 9th ed. Vol. 2. New York: Norton, 2012.
Griggs, Earl Leslie, ed. *Collected Letters of Samuel Taylor Coleridge.* Vol. 1 (1785–1800). Oxford: Clarendon, 1956.
Jacobus, Mary. *Tradition and Experiment in Wordsworth's* Lyrical Ballads *(1798).* Oxford: Clarendon, 1976.
Keith, W.J. *The Rural Tradition: A Study of the Non-Fiction Prose Writers of the English Countryside.* Toronto: University of Toronto Press, 1974.
Lynyrd Skynyrd [and Various Guest Artists]. *One More for the Fans.* Loud and Proud Records LNP022, 2015, 2 compact discs.
"Physical Graffiti Redrawn." *MOJO* Magazine. April 2015: 6–7.
Parrish, Stephen M. *The Art of the* Lyrical Ballads. Cambridge: Harvard University Press, 1973.
Sales, Roger. *English Literature in History 1780–1830: Pastoral and Politics.* Boston: St. Martin's 1983.
Various Artists. Physical Graffiti *Redrawn.* MOJO *Magazine* April 2015, compact disc.

Chapter Ten

Wordsworth on the Radio

Rachel Feder

Is it too late to write about *The Prelude*? Or, more precisely, what is *The Prelude*'s relationship to lateness, delay, refusal? If Wordsworth has proven a stalwart friend to readers and critics insofar as his works remain perpetually open to interpretation and, by extension, to new interpretations of interpretation, then nowhere is this phenomenon more palpable than in the case of *The Prelude*, that infinitely porous, reverberating river of blank verse that promises to be, or to build up, the mind of the poet itself. But a sense of delay or lateness when it comes to writing about *The Prelude* has less to do with a deconstructive model that views the poem as a process of dynamic projection and shift, and more to do with the poem's forms of refusal, the poetics of what it *won't* do . . . or, at least, *won't* do *yet*.

In the past, when I've tried to think about *The Prelude*, I've tended to summon John Locke, whose understanding of infinity as accumulative or accretive was particularly important for Wordsworth. With its accumulation of line upon line, we might understand *The Prelude*'s blank verse to approximate a Lockean enumerative framework in which repetition leads to a limited but real belief in selfhood and in what transcends it. If, as Locke argues, the "endless *addition* . . . of numbers . . . is that . . . which gives us the clearest and most distinct idea of infinity[,]" and, by extension, "the identity of the same *man* consists . . . in nothing but a participation of the same continued life, by constantly fleeting particles of matter, in succession vitally united to the same organized body[,]" then *The Prelude* might be said to function as an adding up—the growth of a poet's mind, one line, one memory at a time. [1] But beyond this simple application of Lockean theory, we might understand *The Prelude*'s enumerative form as an act of delay, procrastination, or refusal. At once the preface to an unrealized epic and a Romantic fragment poem, the poem refuses to begin and refuses to end. The blank verse line—or, rather, the accretion of line upon line—is its form of refusal.

As "preparatory poem" and "Ante-chapel" to Wordsworth's unfinished epic, *The Recluse*, *The Prelude* piles blank verse line upon blank verse line, delaying the beginning of the poem to which it ostensibly lays the foundation. This is true when we read biographically—*The Prelude* occupied Wordsworth intermittently for forty years, enacting a never-ending quality in its very composition.[2] A sense of not-yet-ness and too-late-ness also permeates the poem's aesthetics, from the "dejection," the "deep and genuine sadness" that follows when a group of travelers learn that they "have crossed the alps" without climax, epiphany, or sublimity,[3] to the "meditation[s]"[4] and "darkness" or "blank desertion"[5] that arise in the mind following particularly intense experiences of nature, partial afterimages, signs of the mind changed. Turning from its potential epicality, we might also situate *The Prelude* in the tradition of Romantic fragmentation—the text is, after all, unfinished, at least in some sense, no matter how extensive or over-edited it might be. Indeed, when the poem concludes with the promise that "what we have loved / Others will love, and we may teach them how[,]"[6] it not only suggests that the text might serve a pedagogical function—perhaps a function whereby the sometimes tedious formal acts of attention that make up the poem activate a mechanism of love—but also implies a pedagogical function in the poem's *futurity*, that what might have been accomplished in the poem's thirteen or fourteen books (depending on which version you prefer) lies still ahead. The poem will teach something, not yet, but soon. Not to its explicit audience (Coleridge, Dorothy) but to "others." The poem thus encodes its own repetitions, enacts its own afterlife, even as it refuses, one blank verse line at a time, to end or to begin.

Brandon Brown's collection *Top 40* (2014) takes up this conceit. Its forty poems, each structured around a song from one week's pop music chart, expand the form of the blank verse line—long, unrhymed—to one-sentence, prose paragraph stanzas. For example, from "Lana Del Rey, *Summertime Sadness*":

> Wordsworth writes in "The Prelude," that his concern is with "The very world which is the world of / all of us the place on which, in the end, / we find our happiness or not at all."
>
> Happiness is tied to contingency and doomed to ephemerality, this is what makes it possible but impossible to savor, fragile as finance.
>
> Some say that Lana Del Rey was born in a manger behind a burrito shop in Weed in order to wage war against temporariness.

> In the history of ideas about happiness, people are basically divided about
> whether happiness is transient or lingering.[7]

Not only the run-on verse paragraphs but also the central trope encode, in
Top 40, a sense of too-lateness, of a self-rejuvenating ephemeral. Brown
writes: "That's part of what lends a countdown its particular suspense; you
can't tell the future. / But I'm not listening to the Top 40 in one extended
sitting, instead I stray, revisit, lurch forward and backward across its span,
walking to the train, waiting for the bus, little crystal rhomboid serenading
me."[8] Brown claims that "America's Top 40 attempts to draw a matrix of
collective attention to the present"[9] and that "[t]he structure of the Top 40 is
not seismically safe, it cannot survive unagitated longer than one week."[10]
The top 40 functions as a bizarre spot of time, a personal glimpse into a
cultural body that will and won't recycle. Dated, as Brown notes, by the time
the book is finished and by the time the reader encounters it, the collection is
quintessentially too late in a way only responses to popular culture can be.
On this topic, Brown writes:

> I wrote a poem comparing Amanda Bynes to Socrates, Alli was like who is
> Amanda Bynes?
>
> Her point I guess was that I rely too much on the endlessly substitutable icons
> of pop culture as catalysts for my writing, which could instead model itself
> after the timeless.
>
> It's true that by the time I finish my book, much less by the time you're
> reading it, there will be an entirely new Top 40.
>
> Cellular refiguration marked by rapid morphological mutation.[11]

The connection between the Wordsworthian and the pop cultural, at least in
terms of what Brown deems "everyday time travel,"[12] is explicit in *Top 40*.
Throughout the volume, Brown conceptualizes himself as participating in a
Wordsworthian, or, more precisely, preludian project. For example:

> You know how in *The Prelude*, Wordsworth rows a boat out onto a moonlit
> pond, awed by the susurrations of cattails in the lunar lit breeze and the poem
> latently suggests this experience was formative to his later development as a
> poet?
>
> Well, for me it was just like that, only I wore headphones and there was
> nothing "natural" anywhere in sight.[13]

And, later:

> You know how in *The Prelude*, Wordsworth rows a boat out onto a moonlit
> pond, awed by the susurrations of cattails in the lunar lit breeze and the poem
> latently suggests this experience was formative to his later development as a
> poet?
>
> Well for me it was just like that, dragging a mower, churning up snipped grass,
> mosquitoes drinking my blood, flipping off my dad when he frowned at my
> careless lines in the grass, playing N.W.A.'s *Straight Outta Compton* over and
> over and over.[14]

In addition to these moments of alignment, Wordsworth crops up throughout
the volume as a way of thinking, a way of being poetic without doing or
having done anything much, yet. To be Wordsworthian, or preludian,
emerges as a way of being in relation to what is popular where popular
means ephemeral, repetitive, unrealized, perpetual. In a poem on Miley Cyrus, Brown writes, "I had a real Wordsworth moment in there, looking around
the bath and my body and the little pieces of leaves, suddenly even my
beloved bathtub became a hall of pain, me all wet in there, crying out *was it
all for this*? / Not that I've ever had to do anything really. / Not that Miley
Cyrus has ever had to do anything."[15] Referring to Taylor Swift, Brown
writes, "Taylor, perhaps more than anyone since Wordsworth, has famous
powers of almost immediate reflective tranquility, although she is much less
hysterical than Wordsworth."[16] Or, referring to a sick day in a poem about a
Justin Timberlake song: "The extra two hours we slept in were like whole
years in the life of Wordsworth, while he walked around Wales freaked out
about the sudden appearance of a full moon on a leafy dale or whatever. /
The whole day was permeated by 18th century laziness."[17]

Returning to Locke, we might note that Brown's eighteenth-century laziness has something to do not only with the countdown, but also with counting. In "Lorde, *Royals*," Brown writes, "I count minutes down near the wane
of every work day. / I count strokes, breaths, and laps when I swim. / I count
sentences in my book *Top Forty*."[18] In the poem "Daft Punk ft. Pharrell
Williams, *Get Lucky*," Brown focuses on the song's repetitiveness and ultimately brings his interpretation to bear on a meditation on gambling, addiction, and boredom. Brown argues that "*Get Lucky* suggests that repetition is
endurance's strategy[,]"[19] and, in a parallel construction, that "counting is
addiction's constant praxis."[20] Let's think this back to *The Prelude*: repetition and counting become the tangible forms of addiction and endurance, the
poem's method of honoring its obsessions and casting itself forward. To
refuse to begin is to refuse to end.

At the end of his poem about *Get Lucky*, Brown offers the following self-
corrective:

I shouldn't let this poem turn into a discursive substitute for a months-long argument I've been having in my head with Sophie about *Get Lucky* being boring or not.

For some reason I let it hurt *my* feelings, like she meant *I* was boring.

Ugh.

What I should have done instead is compare *Get Lucky* to a poetic form, it is in one after all, about counting and pattern, how counting and pattern war against boredom in form. [21]

But at this point, the poem is written, and it's too late, so Brown wraps up with a joke about sestinas.

Is it possible to read the form of *The Prelude* as a battleground on which counting wars against boredom? In some ways, this formulation feels familiar; the "vacant," "pensive" mood broken in Wordsworth's "I wandered lonely as a cloud" by the seemingly endless crowd of daffodils "flash[ing] upon th[e] inward eye" offers a scene of numerousness overcoming vacancy, the poem pushing back with its formal and imagistic patterns. [22] Perhaps we can bring this into conversation with *The Prelude*'s closing lines: what others will be taught in futurity, after all, has to do with "how the mind of man becomes / A thousand times more beautiful than the earth / On which he dwells." [23] So in addition to conjuring the mind grown, the mind changed, *The Prelude* promises to change minds in the future, to make them more beautiful or to help them recognize their own beauty. In this way, *The Prelude*'s delay and refusal is for us, whoever *we* are.

In the volume's penultimate poem, Brown rethinks the ephemerality of popular culture in just this vein:

> Because pop songs are for us, because they're for reiteration in our mouths and in our keys, because they're made for us to gather together and sing with each other, because they're meant to condition and inflect how we reflect on our own indeterminate and affective experiences, it hardly matters who the "you" is in something like *Love Somebody*.

> The substitutability of the definite 2nd person pronoun and the indefinite 3rd person pronoun depends on the site of our performance, who we dream of is somebody, anybody, whoever, or whether we speak to you.

> You are the last word in the syntagm "I love you."

> You are what binds us in the sentence, the one we're dancing around and singing with.

But the future of the sentence can never be known.[24]

Echoes, here, of *The Prelude*'s closing promise: that what we have loved, others will love; that we may teach them how. A preludian jump from the immediate audience—the beloved, the circle of friends—to what Brown terms the "you all."[25] It is not the "we" or the "others" or the "you" that is relevant, but the act of love itself, or, rather, the form and focus of that love. *The Prelude*'s forms of refusal extend the act of love endlessly, without ever quite putting it in service of anything or anyone. The repetition is a type of teaching. By refusing to end, the poem attempts to encode "the future of the sentence."

The link between enigmatic, multivalent audiences and the poem's futurity underscores another recent response to popular music, or, at least, to a popular musician, Lauren Ireland's *Dear Lil Wayne* (2014). The volume is composed of letters/prose poems that figure Lil Wayne as their recipient but that linger, for the most part, in a realm of general personal expression unspecific to Lil Wayne. For example:

August 6 2010

Dear Lil Wayne,

Today the corner of morning breaks around this battered island. There's a pine sisken. Don't worry—I'm not collecting things. I'm taking a responsible vacation in the salt marshes of despair. There's things that crawl and things that attach. Where are you? Someone told me I don't look like a poet. Well, good. There's salt drying on my shoulders. I'm sending you.[26]

In an introductory note to the volume, Ireland explains, "I sent these letters to Lil Wayne during and after his incarceration. He never wrote back." One of the ensuing letters/prose poems elaborates, describing these texts as open, both figuratively and literally: "I've been imaging that you don't open my letters. You can't. They are postcards. Ha ha! and anyway you're not there."[27] Beyond revealing that it might have been impossible to write back to these unsigned postcards, Ireland thus reverses the dichotomy between the immediate and future audiences, what Brown calls the "you" vs. "you all,"[28] by rendering the explicit audience abstract and unreachable and conjuring an actual audience that might be "there" but that is, nonetheless, much less specific. That the future audience implied by publication is more tangible, more real, than the present audience entextualized in the dated missives speaks to a broader concern with temporal shifts. When, in a letter/prose poem dated July 26 2010 and published in 2014, Ireland writes, "Do you know I suspect this is not just for you[,]" past and future both become present.[29] Might we understand this as another form of delay, fast-forward, refusal?

Dear Lil Wayne is obsessed with time, and with all the little temporal unrealities our idioms make possible. The volume pleads for time and creates time, using poetry to activate everyday time travel. Ireland writes: "how about we ride into a time that hasn't been invented yet";[30] "Could you please give me back my time";[31] "Bats, ocean, cessation of time";[32] "All I want is for everything to stop moving for a minute so I can think";[33] "In 8 million years everyone will be dead";[34] "I just want a bus and all the time in the world";[35] "No one is ever going to be this happy, ever again";[36] "Have you ever wanted to be someone else for a little while?";[37] "I feel better when I tell you things. For a minute";[38] "I'm not myself lately";[39] "More later, I'm sure."[40]

In *The Prelude*, Wordsworth describes "spots of time, / Which with distinct preeminence retain / A renovating virtue, whence, depressed / By false opinion and contentious thought, / Or aught of heavier or more deadly weight / In trivial occupations and the round / Of ordinary intercourse, our minds / Are nourished and invisibly repaired[.]"[41] The timeless moment, in other words, can help you out at any time. So is it a neo-Romantic formation when Ireland writes, "Lil Wayne, I am inviting you to all my future parties?"[42] The celebrity here functions as a sort of memory, as a form of self-projection into a future that is, somehow, better.

Celebrity also functions as an alternate form of memory in Sarah Blake's *Mr. West* (2015), another book-length poetic experiment that takes a pop musician as its central concern. In *Mr. West*, Blake meditates on celebrity as mythos and divine mystery, explaining that "Kanye is Horus, or another Egyptian god. / He is a merman, a centaur, the Minotaur[,]"[43] describing how "Kanye almost died in a car accident, / so he became a star[,]"[44] and proclaiming, "Bring forth Kanye according to his kind."[45] At the same time, the book tenderly sets forth its elective affinity with the celebrity, aligning the poet's pregnancy and loss of a grandfather with the lives of Kanye and Donda West. For example, Blake writes, "While swallowing a prenatal vitamin before bed, I'm watching an / MTV interview / with Rick Ross about how / you taught him to see music in colors"[46] and "Donda made it seem easy in her memoir. / To love Kanye. To unconditionally love him. / She even knew he was a boy. In utero. / My son remains my mystery."[47] Such moments of alignment take more intense forms, as well, with Kanye playing the role of the invisible in expressions of faith:

I think Kanye's like me,
and I think it's incomprehensible.
I think he and I and my mother and Donda West

are easily moved.

> We enter into discourse thinking first,
> *love*.[48]

The musician shines forth, in Blake's writing, as an imagined community, a distant *thou*. In one line that cuts through the volume like a beating heart, Blake laments, "Kanye, if only I could write a poem for you and not about you."[49]

Kanye's lyrics are boxed out throughout the volume, an absence glossed in the book's back matter, which functions as its own index poem, with the explanation, "See lyrics blacked out throughout the book because permission to print could not be gained."[50] The result is a sort of quasi-dialogic, found-poem aesthetic, an aesthetic that reaches crises in two poems composed almost entirely of hate speech from Internet comments. On first or second read, these poems, one titled "Hate for Kanye," the other "It's Hard Not To Be Moved," seem unfair insofar as they commit racist vitriol to university press paper. "Hate for Kanye" contains neither gloss nor explanation, while "It's Hard Not To Be Moved" concludes with a perhaps overly simple reaction, the poet and her husband in front of the screen together: "We're both still surprised at the racism and violence and hate. / We're full of fear // but that's not what fearsome means."[51]

What do these poems *do*? Or, to think with *The Prelude*, what do they *refuse* to do? And what do they remember? From the first pages of *Mr. West*, Blake includes references to her American Jewish identity:

> In the chorus of one of my favorite songs are three throat-clearing sounds—
> sometimes depicted as *Ha Ha Hum*
> on lyrics websites such as azlyrics.com, lyricstime.com, and anysonglyrics.com.
>
> A sound we make when we talk with the mouths of Jews.
> *Channukah, l'chaim, chutzpah.*
> Voiceless fricative.[52]

This poem ends with the line, "The mouths we speak with are hidden by our other mouths[,]"[53] a line echoed, a few poems later, in Blake's statement that "The past pushes us."[54] This past, I argue, is indelibly linked to the hate speech Blake reproduces elsewhere in the book. Across the pages of *Mr. West*, celebrity emerges as an alternative to memory. Celebrities—and their very public, very large lives—might provide us, after all, with a different way to consume memory. The crucial and miniscule moments in the life of Kanye—a car crash, a cruel internet comment—become memories we consume, spots of time that alter our perception of our personal and collective history without demanding that we go through the pain (or any of its many opposites) in our own skin. Memory comes from the inside and from the outside. The volume's opening poem addresses Kanye and the poet's unborn son as follows: *"The two of you, tied to this week in my life."*[55] Thus, according to Blake's work, not every memory comes from personal experience. Memory can be consumed, and it can change you. Compare Wordsworth: "what we have loved / Others will love, and we may teach them how[.]"[56]

Thus arises the volume's employment and deployment of pop music (crossed out) and celebrity culture (deified, reified, internalized) to motivate an examination of Holocaust memory. This examination takes as axiomatic the conflation and juxtaposition of Kanye's life with the details of Jewish identity as a received or inherited practice: "My grandfather believed. He looked at the stars as proof / long after he stopped going to synagogue. // Kanye understood his belief—'I think 50% because it was instilled in me. That's what we call on'";[57] "We sometimes burn a *yahrzeit* candle. It burns for 24 hours, or 26, or 3 days, more. It's white and burns in a tall glass so you don't have to worry about leaving an open flame overnight . . . You spent the nights around the anniversary of your mother's death on a stage that looked like the universe."[58] Within the framework of Holocaust memory, anonymous hate speech becomes a memory approached obliquely, a memory overheard. It's hatred that isn't directed at you but that's reaching you; and, much like Lauren Ireland's poems to Lil Wayne, it's reaching you *instead*. In the poem "Hate is for Hitler," Blake writes, "my mother used to tell me . . . My grandmother used to say it . . . I wonder if Kanye's mother said it too."[59] Holocaust memory, in Blake's hands, involves identifying as a past and potential victim, even while identifying oneself as relatively safe. Along these lines, Blake complicates her poetic treatment of her own privilege: "A white Jewish woman has privilege until she's traveling in France . . . A white Jewish woman gets privilege from her mother's Irish married name."[60]

White Jewish privilege, for Blake, is transient, conditional. To ingest celebrity culture is to remember trauma experienced at a distance, trauma that nonetheless informs one's sense of self, trauma that it's too late to experience first hand, to do anything about. In "I Want a House to Raise My Son In," Blake confesses:

> I have made Noah promise he will save me over the boy
> if it came to that.
>
> I've told no one this.
>
> It is my one non-maternal act, my one feeling
> that reminds me of the selfish child I was
> when I thought how I would have spit and peed
> on the Torah if I'd been a child in the Holocaust,
> if it would have saved me,
> which, only as an adult do I understand,
> could not have saved me.[61]

The poem goes on to invoke Adorno: "Can I write anything after that? / Can the poem continue?"[62]

The possible world of the inherited memory changes with time, a childhood solution dissolving into a holistic understanding. Yet time, for Blake, collapses, the trauma distant but also intimately close: "In the Holocaust the barrel of a gun was shoved up the vagina of a white pregnant Jewish woman and her baby was shot and so she was. / Is 70 years a long time?"[63] In the concluding notes that function as a sort of wrap-up poem, Blake revivifies this traumatic intimacy, offering a note of hope, or something like it:

> "Gaze": See my father-in-law, born before the end of World War II. See his mother, choosing to get pregnant and bring a Jewish child into this world at a time when Jews were being killed by the millions. See, I imagine, an incredible amount of faith in herself as a mother, in her ability to provide. See how she was right. See how that's incredible. If she hadn't, I wouldn't have my husband or my son.[64]

If, as I'm suggesting, *Mr. West* is a book about grappling with Holocaust memory, then it offers celebrity culture as an alternate site of memory, a place to put memories that are too painful or too complicated to live in the day-to-day. Kanye's lyrics wafting over the radio waves become a sort of shared attic in which collective memories can be stored without being forgotten. The memories we consume via celebrity culture become, within this framework, a safe alternative, a stand-in. The lyrics are an epic.

These lyrics don't appear, of course, in *Mr. West*. Their absence begs the question: what is the future of the sentence that's crossed out? What is the future of the sentence that belongs to everyone, that's easily accessed, but that can't be reprinted, reproduced? In *Top 40*, *Dear Lil Wayne*, and *Mr. West*, pop music functions as a vehicle of memory and futurity, a preludian thinking back into the past and casting into the future. In these recent works of contemporary poetry, the music of the moment encodes the poem's repetitions. The poems can't stop; they won't stop.

While I was writing about *Top 40*, mutual acquaintances put me in touch with Brandon Brown, and we exchanged a few emails about his book and about Wordsworth. In our conversation, Brown wrote that "[the] vocational influence of the natural world [on Wordsworth] rhymed with something that was important to me in thinking about pop and poetry, not just the autobiographical fact of my being influenced by song and (especially) rap prosody (being an autobiographical fact, it is sort of meaningless) but the connection of melody with wisdom, *sophos* right?"[65]

In Plato's *Symposium*, philosophy is portrayed as a kind of love coming out of lack. One loves wisdom because one does not fully possess it; therefore, one seeks wisdom. Within this framework, *The Prelude*'s closing promise, that "what we have loved / Others will love, and we may teach them how[,]"[66] defines a philosophical project. If the poem teaches us how to love, then it teaches us how to lack. By teaching lack, it moves from "we" to "others," out over the radio waves of time, a pop-song longing, just personal enough to belong to you. Catchy, no?

NOTES

1. John Locke, *An Essay Concerning Human Understanding*, ed. Roger Woolhouse (New York: Penguin Books, 2004), 198.
2. See Jonathan Wordsworth, M. H. Abrams, and Stephen Gill's preface to *The Prelude* as well as Wordsworth's 1814 preface to *The Excursion*, both in *The Prelude, 1799, 1805, 1850*, ed. Jonathan Wordsworth, M. H. Abrams, and Stephen Gill (New York: W. W. Norton and Company, 1979), ix–xiii, 535.
3. Ibid., 216.
4. Ibid., 460.
5. Ibid., 50.
6. Ibid., 482.
7. Brandon Brown, *Top 40* (New York: Roof Books, 2014), 105–106.
8. Ibid., 29.
9. Ibid., 44.
10. Ibid., 57.
11. Ibid., 17.
12. Ibid., 70.
13. Ibid., 48.
14. Ibid., 81.
15. Ibid., 110.
16. Ibid., 57.
17. Ibid., 97.
18. Ibid., 46.
19. Ibid., 84.
20. Ibid., 86.
21. Ibid., 86.
22. William Wordsworth, "I wandered lonely as a cloud . . .," in *William Wordsworth: The Major Works*, ed. Stephen Gill (New York: Oxford University Press, 2008), 303–304.
23. Wordsworth, *The Prelude*, 482.
24. Brown, *Top 40*, 129.
25. Ibid., 35.
26. Lauren Ireland, *Dear Lil Wayne* (Northampton: Magic Helicopter Press, 2014), 14.
27. Ibid., 37.
28. Brown, *Top 40*, 35.
29. Ireland, *Dear Lil Wayne*, 5.
30. Ibid., 1.
31. Ibid., 10.
32. Ibid., 15.
33. Ibid., 17.
34. Ibid., 19.
35. Ibid., 20.
36. Ibid., 40.
37. Ibid., 52.
38. Ibid., 53.
39. Ibid., 57.
40. Ibid., 21.
41. Wordsworth, *The Prelude*, 428–430.
42. Ireland, *Dear Lil Wayne*, 30.

Rachel Feder

43. Sarah Blake, *Mr. West* (Middletown: Wesleyan University Press, 2015), 88.
44. Ibid., 23.
45. Ibid., 25.
46. Ibid., 11.
47. Ibid., 47.
48. Ibid., 68.
49. Ibid., 15.
50. Ibid., 103.
51. Ibid., 66.
52. Ibid., 5.
53. Ibid., 6.
54. Ibid., 8.
55. Ibid., 2.
56. Wordsworth, *The Prelude*, 482.
57. Blake, *Mr. West*, 35.
58. Ibid., 50.
59. Ibid., 67.
60. Ibid., 89–90.
61. Ibid., 46.
62. Ibid., 46.
63. Ibid., 91.
64. Ibid., 105.
65. Brandon Brown, email message to author, April 6, 2015.
66. *The Prelude*, 482.

BIBLIOGRAPHY

Blake, Sarah. *Mr. West*. Middletown, CT: Wesleyan University Press, 2015.
Brown, Brandon. *Top 40*. New York: Roof Books, 2014.
Ireland, Lauren. *Dear Lil Wayne*. Northampton: Magic Helicopter Press, 2014.
Locke, John. *An Essay Concerning Human Understanding*. Edited by Roger Woolhouse. New York: Penguin Books, 2004.
Wordsworth, William. *The Major Works*, edited by Stephen Gill. New York: Oxford University Press, 2008.
———. *The Prelude, 1799, 1805, 1850*, edited by Jonathan Wordsworth, M. H. Abrams, and Stephen Gill. New York: W. W. Norton and Company, 1979.

Chapter Eleven

The *Scapigliatura* and *Poètes Maudits* in the Songs of Piero Ciampi (1934–1980)

Lorenzo Sorbo

The "*Scapigliatura*," whose members were called "*scapigliati*" (literally meaning "disheveled"), was an artistic and literary movement which developed in Italy from 1860 to 1880.[1] This movement mostly protested against the bourgeois society of Milan, which was at the time the economic and cultural center of the Italian bourgeoisie and therefore also the ideal center of the movement. The *Scapigliatura* was first mentioned in the novel *The Scapigliatura and February 6th* (1861) by Cletto Arrighi. The term is a free translation of the French "*bohème*," a word that makes reference to the disorderly and nonconformist lives of the Parisian artists described in Henri Murger's novel *Scenes de la vie de bohème* (1851). Other notable exponents of the "disheveled" school were Vittorio Imbriani, Giovanni Camerana, Iginio Ugo Tarchetti, Carlo Dossi, Arrigo Boito, Antonio Ghislanzoni, and Emilio Praga.

The *scapigliati* were animated by a spirit of rebellion against a traditional and bourgeois culture, leading unconventional lives so that their debates often appeared in political, ethical, and literary discourse. In politics, the *scapigliati* accused the bourgeoisie of betraying *Risorgimento*[2] ideals of freedom, justice, and equality by enslaving and oppressing the masses. In ethics, they denounced the lies and hypocrisies of conventional morality, from which came their taste for provocation, their will to offend at all costs through the desecration of traditional values, and the excesses of their lives. Their controversy especially targeted Alessandro Manzoni, the symbol of Romantic ideology repudiated by the *scapigliati*.

In literature, the *scapigliati* rejected either the moralizing and patriotic aspects of early Italian Romanticism—which was often pompously emphatic—or the themes of later Italian Romanticism, which they viewed as languid and sentimental. In their perception of the gap between European and Italian contemporary literature, the *scapigliati* supported the new principle of the artist's absolute creative freedom and took it to an extreme, while in their view Italian Romanticism stood still, adhering to backwards, moderate, and provincial positions. Therefore, they proposed to create a new poetry and to be in tune with the avant-garde movements of European culture.

The poetry of the *scapigliati* railed against Romanticism and rediscovered a fundamental principle: opposition to the "artificial" poetry of Classicism. In fact, the Italian Romantic poet and novelist Manzoni always saw reality enlightened by Providence while the *scapigliati* instead saw reality in its naturalness and even in its turbidity, in the manner of *The Flowers of Evil* by Charles Baudelaire. Expanding the horizon of their art, the *scapigliati* anticipated the motifs and forms of two literary movements: *Verismo*[3] and Decadentism.[4] Under the influence of French Naturalism, they anticipated Realism, which conceptualizes art as an impersonal and objective representation of the surrounding culture's true social and moral aspects, capturing even its more starkly realistic and gruesome features. Therefore, the *scapigliati* upheld the concept of poetry as inner insight, capable of expressing even murky and morbid feelings. Their aesthetics ranged from Realism to Decadentism; although their literary styles were different, they oscillated between the use of a rough, unkempt language and a precious and refined language. Their importance to the history of Italian costume and literature in general was remarkable. On a literary level, in fact, their importance lies in the fact that they broke (or at least tried to break) with the tradition of Italian Romanticism, which was still anchored in patriotic and civil themes especially in the first Romantic generation. Sayre and Löwy (2001) highlight how in Italy "the early impulse is primarily nationalist (opposition to foreign occupiers or support for national unification), and in the absence of a significant bourgeois element it is often directed against a decadent local aristocracy."[5] Reacting to both early and late Romanticism, the *scapigliati* strived to make Italian literature less provincial by opening it to the influence of avant-garde art and culture of the most advanced European countries, introducing Poe, Baudelaire, Heine, and others.

TRACES OF *SCAPIGLIATURA* AND BOHÈME IN CIAMPI'S LYRICS

In the preface of the novel *Scenes from the Life of Bohème* (1851), Murger describes three types of bohemians: unknown, amateur, and real.[6] According to Murger, the first are amateur artists and "inveterate dreamers" who do not seek fame but believe that it will come since "a bare sight of a masterpiece throws them into a fever." They are poor and often die from this condition, and they remain unknown because "unknown Bohemia is not a thorough-fare; it is a *cul-de-sac*."[7] As for artists belonging to the second type of bohemian, "amateurs" are essentially bourgeois who decide to become bohe-mian out of habit, seduced by a life "full of attraction for their minds." These ones often end up bored and go back to being bourgeois by giving up "the game before long" as they "scamper back in hot haste to the paternal roast, marry their little cousin, set up as notaries in some town of thirty thousand inhabitants."[8]

Finally, true bohemian artists enjoy success, "which quite definitely de-termines that all ways are good." Despite this, they give up everything just to be able to continue living in their extravagant lifestyles, their economic prob-lems "continually solved by audacious feats of mathematics."[9] In other words, the true style of bohemian life is inherent to their adventurous way of life since "[r]ain or dust, shadow or sun, nothing brings these bold adventur-ers to a stand." For this reason they are eternal wanderers, since they "cannot take ten steps on the Boulevard without meeting a friend, and thirty, no matter where, without encountering a creditor."[10] Following Murger's taxon-omy, there is no doubt that Ciampi belongs to the third kind of bohemian, the most authentic kind, as he lived this way with an absolute militancy. In order to justify that classification, however, I need to review Ciampi's life, which is in fact rich with official and legendary anecdotes often reconstructed from his friends and associates.

Piero Ciampi was born in 1934 in Livorno, a small town in Tuscany with a lively port where ships departed and arrived laden with goods and adven-turous sailors. His father Umberto was a leather trader. Piero was the son of a second marriage. Soon after high school, Ciampi joined the faculty of Engi-neering which he left after passing a few exams.[11] Together with his brothers Paolo and Roberto he formed a trio in which he was the lead singer. Mean-while, he worked in a firm selling lubricating oils to earn his living until joining the military. While on leave, he formed a band playing in small clubs with three of his fellow soldiers, including Gianfranco Reverberi.[12] His *maudit* character peremptorily emerged because of Ciampi's quarrelsome character. He did not mind occasional heavy drinking and brawling. He recited poems to friends, and through his verses he even made the daughter of his commander fall in love with "letters even Cyrano couldn't have done better."[13] Back in Livorno, Ciampi played the double bass in small bands, but he felt restless and dissatisfied, so that in 1957 he dropped by Genoa to see Reverberi. Announcing his departure for Paris as described by the same Reverberi, "he had a guitar, a shirt and a one way ticket . . . He said that he had to live these experiences personally; only in this way he would write his poems with sincerity."[14] Here, once again, can be noticed some similarities with the *poètes maudits* who had chosen Paris as a cultural and spiritual capital, the right place to set many of their novels or poems. It was a dark, mysterious Paris full of gloomy alleys and suspicious characters. Not the glitzy city of lights and entertainment, but the one Baudelaire masterfully described: "O swarming city, city full of dreams, / Where in full day the spectre walks and speaks; / Mighty colossus, in your narrow veins. / My story flows as flows the rising sap."[15]

A century after Baudelaire, Paris also seduced Ciampi, who immediately began to lead a bohemian life performing as a *chansonnier* and writing fragmentary poetry on napkins without having any money and even meeting—at least according to a legend—other members of the *disheveled* such as Céline. In 1957 he returned to Italy after finishing his "artistic education," and he met again his friend Reverberi, who invited him to Milan to work with him for the record company *Ricordi*. So in 1963, Ciampi released his first album, titling it *Piero Litaliano* after his Parisian nickname "litaliano," written without the apostrophe. However, the album was unsuccessful except in the judgment of Natalia Aspesi, who commented, "in his lyrics there is something quite poetic . . . incomprehensible to lovers of pop ditties."[16] Ciampi moved to Rome and in the meantime wrote songs for others, but he did not have a breakthrough. Ciampi's experience of the sixties are often characterized by continuous aimless wanderings in Sweden, Spain, England, Ireland, and Japan. Meanwhile, he married a young Irishwoman, Moira, whom he met in Italy, but after only one year of marriage she ran away with their son Stefano because of her turbulent relationship with Ciampi.

In these years Ciampi's dependence on alcohol deepened, and he was often spotted drunk on the street. Later, Ciampi had an affair with another woman—Gabriella—leading to a daughter, but that relationship also ended due to quarrels and misunderstandings. The two women, Moira and Gabriella, and their children were to be constant figures within the songs of Ciampi, becoming for him a literary *topos*. After all, the theme of the difficulty of a long-term relationship with a woman is also a common theme in the lives and works of many *scapigliati*.[17] Ciampi was eternally restless, so his affective instability had a direct impact on his wandering life, carried out always in search for places and people to crowd the universe of his lyrics. In this regard, another French *maudit* poet, Tristan Corbière (1845–1875), who belonged to Verlaine's circle, seems to provide a perfect portrait of Ciampi.[18]

Ciampi's musical production consists of only five albums produced between 1963–1975, several singles and collections, different unpublished songs, and many other songs written for other singers. He was assisted by Gianni Marchetti (1933–2012), a composer, arranger, and author of numerous soundtracks. Marchetti was able to provide the right musical arrangements for Ciampi's difficult and challenging texts, which often consisted of long, blank verse lyrical compositions. Ciampi's work was part of an Italian

musical scene characterized by different currents. In the 1960s, popular singers like Domenico Modugno, Gianni Morandi, and Adriano Celentano
emerged. In these years also arose the so-called "schools of songwriters"
who were more engaged and influenced by the model of French *chansonniers* in cities like Genoa and Milan (Gino Paoli, Bruno Lauzi, Luigi Tenco,
Enzo Jannacci, and Giorgio Gaber). In the 1970s, songwriting touched upon
political, social, and existential themes thanks to Fabrizio De André and
Francesco De Gregori, parallel with the rise of many pop, rock, and prog-
rock bands.

In this scene, Ciampi is placed in a transverse position: he cannot be
defined as a pop or rock figure in the strict sense, but he is certainly influenced on various fronts. Ciampi developed a personal style drawing on both
the French song and the melodic style of the early 1960s. One can rather
affirm that his artistic choices are similar to that of rebel and nonconformist
rock stars.

Even the death of Ciampi, or should I say, the style of his death, could not
be more *maudit* if one considers that he died at only forty-six years old and in
poverty, expressing last wishes consistent with his lifestyle: "A flower and a
glass of wine." In an important essay on *Scapigliatura*, the Italianist Rosa
Giovanna highlights that their disheveled narrative style focuses on a "hyper-
trophied ego" enhancing "the solitude of the self-centered author" with many
references to their existential dimension, where "the focus of disheveled
production is placed within the sphere of private intimacy, full of existential
torments."[19] The protagonists of disheveled novels are always obsessed with
their passions and stories because, as Tarchetti writes, "the novel is the story
of the human heart that recounts troubles and gives voice to man's concerns."[20] Similarly, Ciampi's lyrics enact his own ego because his stories are
based on firsthand experience. In other words, Ciampi identifies his life with
his art without delimiting a boundary. In fact, his life, based on self-destruc-
tion, elevated him to a symbol of non-conformism. His career, like his private life, was marked by artistic achievements. In his songs one can find the
same themes of the *poètes maudits*.

The song "He Has All It Takes" represents the manifesto of a misunder-
stood artist who rejects societal values, leading a provocative, dangerous,
anti-social, or self-destructive lifestyle. In this song, Ciampi seems to list the
requirements needed to be a true artist, at least according to a disheveled
aesthetic: "He is melancholic / drinks like an Irishman."[21] Ciampi embeds his
life in the song, which describes his condition as an artist among other artists.
Yet he is a lonely artist who hates working, and he admits to living his life
badly but loves it as it is with no illusions. According to him, the only
condition for being an artist in the eyes of ordinary people appears to be
"selfishness." This song-manifesto touches on topics similar to Scapigliatura's manifesto contained in the preface to *The Scapigliatura and February*

6th. In it, the author Arrighi describes the typical disheveled artist: "Individuals of both sexes, between twenty and thirty-five, not more; always full of wit; more advanced than their time; independent as an eagle of the Alps; ready for good as for evil; restless, troubled, turbulent . . . for some terrible contradictions between their condition and their status—that is, between what they have in mind and what have in their pockets."[22] Arrighi's portrait of the perfect member of the disheveled seems to give a close-up of Ciampi, and it is impressive to see how this literary description resembles him so much: "A haggard, furrowed, cadaverous face; on it are the imprints of nights spent guzzling and gambling, overshadows the secret of an infinite pain . . . tempting dreams of an unattainable happiness and tears of blood, tremendous distrust and the final despair."[23]

Continuing in the vein of desperation, another famous song by Ciampi is "The Wine," a hymn to Dionysian intoxication and to the euphoria of a lonely man as well. Its lyrics describe Ciampi lying in a ditch, perhaps after an accidental fall, but surely due to intoxication. Ciampi is lying down and does not complain; indeed, he takes the opportunity to contemplate the stars and reflect on the brevity of life. The pretext of the wine is transformed into a philosophical reflection on the beauty of his life lived without any compromise. Baudelaire's poem "Be Drunken" immediately comes to mind as it describes a very similar scene:

> Drunken with what? With wine, with poetry, or with virtue, as you will. But be drunken. And if sometimes, on the stairs of a palace, or on the green side of a ditch, or in the dreary solitude of your own room, you should awaken and the drunkenness be half or wholly slipped away from you, ask of the wind, or of the wave, or of the star, or of the bird, or of the clock, of whatever flies, or sighs, or rocks, or sings, or speaks, ask what hour it is.[24]

The concept of drunkenness as the inebriation felt because of a life lived to the fullest is similarly described in the songs of Ciampi. However, the scene contained in the line "I am in a ditch" resembles "on the green grass of a ditch" by Baudelaire. Was Ciampi likely to have read Baudelaire? Probably so. Judging from the evidence, his friends described him (in moments of sobriety) as an educated man, a lover of literature, and capable of amazing quotations in public despite his wandering and homeless life.[25] If the wine is omnipresent in Ciampi's life, it primarily represents a metaphor in his songs. It is directly quoted or shown as a magnificent metaphor as in "Go Walk and Work," a song-monologue against the mechanisms of a capitalistic and mechanical society where Ciampi ironically proclaims his slogan: "The wine against the oil!"

In the eyes of the *scapigliati*, a lasting relationship, even a marriage, represents nothing more than an old bourgeois model in decline or simply a condition incompatible with that of being an artist. Therefore the whole disheveled narrative is populated with unhappy, fleeting, passionate but never enduring loves. Yet the woman is idealized as the main engine of artistic creation both in Ciampi's work and that of the *scapigliati*, as summarized in the aphorism by Giovanni Faldella, a wealthy but somewhat disheveled intellectual, that "the genius without a woman is like a coal gas before the approaching flame: you cannot see it, you can only smell the stench: put a woman nearby, a match, poof! It becomes a star of light!"[26] Another example of a conflicting relationship can be seen in the novel *Fosca* (1869) by Iginio Ugo Tarchetti, focused on the crazy Fosca's feeling (an ugly and sick woman) for Giorgio, a young officer who loves another woman instead. The passage where Tarchetti writes, "I had two great loves, two loves differently felt, but equally fatal and formidable. It is with them that my youth died out; it is because of them,"[27] is remarkably similar to Ciampi's line in the song "He Has What It Takes": "He so loved two women, / they were beautiful, blond, tall, slender. / But to him they do not exist anymore." Yet Ciampi sings always about love. While it is not happy and long-lasting, he still recognizes that it makes life worth living. *His* love is not the languid sentiment of many pop songs of the 1960s, but an all-encompassing love of life itself.

In fact, in a rare television appearance in 1977 Ciampi explains his idea of love, once again in a poetic way: "And what is love? Love comes from below, from the statues. Because of this, I sing to my children. How many do I have? I do not know. For me they are all the same. I love all of you, humanity, everybody!"[28] Many of Ciampi's songs deal with failed love affairs, regrets, and nostalgia often narrated without denying personal responsibility. A striking example is the inscription on the cover of his first album, *Piero Litaliano* (1963): "I wrote these twelve songs for a woman that I loved and lost. These twelve memories are the Bastille of my heart. For my woman I did greater things than these songs, but those things are now lost. Now remain only twelve songs."[29] For Ciampi, the love affair is essentially a meeting of two solitudes. To understand it one can just look through the titles of songs like "Miserere," "What Remains," "Asking Forgiveness Is Not a Sin," "You by Your Head, Me by My Heart. " In each of his songs there is at least one memorable line condensing its symbolism in a poetic image through linguistic inventions worthy of the best of the avant-garde.

In "Barbara is Not Here," the absence of an umpteenth woman who ran away is described through an empty and desolate interior full of objects still recalling her. The lightning line, "all her shoes are here. / My love is barefoot," carries the brilliant metaphor of a love without shoes and therefore devoid of an emotional content. Another song about loneliness and love gone away is "The Absence is a Siege." Its Italian title, *"L'assenza è un assedio,"* represents itself as a minimalist poem through the use of assonance and condensation of the poetic image recalling the famous *"M'illumino d'immenso*" (I enlighten myself of immense) by Giuseppe Ungaretti, master of hermeticism.[30] Moreover, Ciampi has always declared himself a pure poet rather than a singer, using similar hermetic techniques such as short verses and assonances such as these:

> Cara.
> La tua mano
> è così piccola
> mi sfuggirà
> sempre.[31]

> Darling.
> Your hand
> is so small
> to slip me
> always.

The image of a small and delicate hand, symbol of female innocence and sanctity, is also found in a poem by Verlaine which witnesses the poetic communion with Ciampi, surely a *maudit* poet but able to evoke innocent and effective images:

> Her hand, so little and so light,
> A humming bird within it could not hide,
> Captures, without hope of flight,
> The heart in secret, short of pride.[32]

However, in Ciampi's lyrics, as in those of the *scapigliati* and *poètes maudits*, it is always a desperate, restless love, full of conflicts in which Ciampi, as opposed to his partners, is essentially an unreliable and unbearable man. Ciampi's letters to his first wife Gabriella are full of impossible and never kept promises. One reads phantom promises of riches and many never returned loan applications, regular demands for money, promises to change his attitudes, and admissions of guilt and separations.[33]

There are two songs which best represent these themes. The first is, "I'll Show You Who I Am," a perfect scene of a bohemian, penniless couple living in an unhealthy home; she wants a middle-class life, and he makes a thousand promises that never come true. Here as elsewhere, Ciampi uses his typical "*recitativo*" in the sense that he declaims a text, often improvised, based on well-arranged music by Marchetti. The text depicts the interior of a slum where he promises a house with fourteen rooms and even a lion fur. In his megalomania, Ciampi wants to fix a "vulgar" problem of their miserable cohabitation by asking her for money for the taxi. Here Ciampi's hypertrophic ego reaches its peak when he states that the house is no longer enough, so he promises a submarine and then an ocean liner to generate envy in the neighbors. The "spoken song" ends with a claim of ownership, obviously returning to Ciampi's constant fear of losing a love because of his total unreliability.

Ciampi was chronically selfish and cruel in his hedonism, but unlike other Italian *chansonniers*, he was the only one to mix so much life and art as to disorient his listeners and drag them into the mud of his emotional slum. One of Ciampi's last songs, entitled "Adius" and published in 1976, disrupts the image of a romantic, tormented, and suffering love always at the center of Italian pop songs of the era. In context, in 1976 one of the best-selling singles in Italy was the song "One Cannot Die Inside" by Gianni Bella, which describes an ended love affair. In short: when he leaves her, she replies to him, "one cannot die inside." But a year later he despairs because he really feels he has lost an important love. In contrast, in "Adius" Ciampi completely reverses the concept "she leaves him, he despairs" to "she leaves him, he does not care." Indeed he sends her literally to hell singing an unequivocal "fuck you" never dared before in reassuring Italian songs of the seventies. This word is shouted and reiterated to an unrequited love, all the more shocking if one considers the social and cultural context of bourgeois Italy of those years. After "Adius" is published, Ciampi grants his last interview, stating he "has played down the departure of every love song: everybody cries and I don't give a damn."[34]

The interview represents a wonderful portrait of the character-artist Ciampi. The interviewer's questions hide a subtle moralizing: even the subtitle in bold reveals, "He claimed the title of poet also on his passport." Ciampi, obviously drunk, replies contemptuously, and all his *maudit* themes emerge as he describes his relationship with his audience, whom he often insulted during concerts, his hometown Livorno, and his concept of love. The interviewer provocatively asks, "But what has a guy like you to do with Italian song?" Ciampi's witty answer is, "It is the one Italian song which has nothing to do with me, if anything." The need to be defined as a poet, not a singer, is crucial to Ciampi, and his bohemian attitude is certainly not pretense when he states that in order to feel "rich," he lacks only "so many things: fried onions, a glass of wine, hot coffee, and a taxi to the door. I never had all these things together." His hedonism reaches its climax when he says, "it is death that makes me especially angry, because I cannot fool it," providing another excuse for a flaming, final jab: "I am truly the greatest of all because I can take from three hundred thousand to half a million lire for each evening and send another to sing for me. After all who knows Piero Ciampi?"

CONCLUSION

Ciampi's poetics draw from both the *Scapigliatura* and *poètes maudits*; however, he cannot be purely defined as a member of the "disheveled." Literary

criticism aimed at identifying the *Scapigliatura* as "a landlocked rebellion . . . hopelessly enclosed in the bourgeois world or rather within the same
world from where it started"[35] needs to take into account that, in fact, almost
all *scapigliati* were born to wealthy families, and their rebellion was realized
in late-Romantic Italian literary forms rather than anti-Romantic ones, even
if they consistently lived up to their image to the point of succumbing to
consumption (as in the case of Tarchetti and Praga) or suicide (Pinchetti).
The common aspects of *scapigliati* found in Ciampi are seen in the rejection
of a bourgeois life and critique of the dominance of money and existential
mechanization, but in Ciampi's lyrics political controversy or social criticism
is not to be found. He assimilates *poètes maudits* through the equation "art
equals life" in the belief that poets are absolutely disconnected from the
social, emotional, and political conditioning of the time in which they live.
He has a Romantic view of love in the literary sense, but his poems are in
many ways completely anti-academic and anti-Romantic. To Ciampi, the
poet is the artist who puts his life in verse, not an ideal hero, but his poetry
does not strive to be idealistic and moralistic. As he ironically states, "Once a
poet is dead, another one will be born."[36]

NOTES

1. Unless otherwise noted, all Italian quotations and lyrics are translated by the author.
2. The "Risorgimento," literally "The Rising," means the movement for Italian unification
and independence, which was achieved in 1861.
3. "*Verismo*" means "Realism," from the Italian "*vero*," meaning "true." It was an Italian
literary movement occurring between 1875 and the early 1900s. Giovanni Verga and Luigi
Capuana were the main exponents and authors of *Verismo*'s manifesto.
4. "Decadentism" was an Italian artistic style based mainly on the Decadent movement in
the arts in France and England around the end of the nineteenth century. The main Italian
decadent authors were Antonio Fogazzaro, Italo Svevo, Giovanni Pascoli, and Gabriele
D'Annunzio.
5. Michael Löwy and Robert Sayre, *Romanticism Against the Tide of Modernity.* Translated by Catherine Porter (Durham, NC: Duke University Press, 2001), 51–52.
6. Henry Murger, "Preface," in *Bohemians of the Latin Quarter* (London: Vizetelly & Co.,
1888), http://www.gutenberg.org/files/18445/18445–h/18445–h.htm.
7. Henry Murger, "Preface," in *The Latin Quarter ("Scènes de la Vie de Bohème")*, trans.
Ellen Marriage and John Selwyn (London: Grant Richards, 1901), XXI-XXII-XXVII. https://
archive.org/details/latinquartersc00murguoft.
8. Ibid., XXVII–XVIII.
9. Ibid., XXIX.
10. The portrait of the typical bohemians strolling in the city was finely analyzed in Walter
Benjamin, *Charles Baudelaire: A Lyric Poet in the Era of High Capitalism* (London: Verso,
1997), 36–37. Benjamin describes the figure of the *flâneur* strolling under the "glass-covered,
marble-paneled passageways" Arcades of Paris feeling that "he is much at home among the
façades of houses as a citizen is in his four walls."
11. Ciampi's adversarial relationship with formal education is a feature common to some
scapigliati such as Antonio Ghislanzoni (1824–1893) and Olindo Guerrini (1845–1916), who
were both expelled in adolescence from a seminar for irreverent behavior. A similar attitude of

inconstancy or rejection of studies is also found in the cursed French poets Paul Verlaine, Arthur Rimbaud, Mallarmé, and Marceline Desbordes-Valmore.

12. Gianfranco Reverberi (1934), musician, composer, and author of soundtracks and many songs from the 1960s.

13. Enrico De Angelis, *Piero Ciampi Tutta l'opera* (Milano: Arcana Editrice, 1992), 21.

14. Ibid., 22.

15. Charles Baudelaire, "The Seven Old Men," in *The Flowers of Evil*, ed. James Huneker (New York: Brentano's Publishers, 1919), http://www.gutenberg.org/files/36287/36287–h/36287–h.htm#THE_SEVEN_OLD_MEN.

16. Enrico De Angelis, *Piero Ciampi Tutta l'opera* (Milano: Arcana Editrice, 1992), 22.

17. Giovanna Rosa, "Senza famiglia"in *La narrativa degli scapigliati* (Roma: Laterza, 1997), 228, https://www.liberliber.it/mediateca/libri/r/rosa/la_narrativa_degli_scapigliati/pdf/rosa_la_narrativa_degli_scapigliati.pdf.

18. Tristan Corbière, "Paria" in *Les amours jaunes*, http://www.paradis-des-albatros.fr/?plaquette&poeme=corbiere/paria.

19. Giovanna Rosa, "Solitari egocentrici," in *La narrativa degli scapigliati* (Roma: Laterza, 1997), 222, https://www.liberliber.it/mediateca/libri/r/rosa/la_narrativa_degli_scapigliati/pdf/rosa_la_narrativa_degli_scapigliati.pdf.

20. Iginio Ugo Tarchetti, "Idee minime sul romanzo," in *Tutte le opere*, ed. Enrico Ghidetti (Bologna : Cappelli, 1967), 530–531.

21. Lines 3 and 4 of the opening song *Ha tutte le carte in regola* (Ciampi/Marchetti) in the album *Io e te abbiamo perso la bussola*, published by the Label "Amico" (Catalogue number : DZSLF 55133) in Milan, 1973. The translation is mine and the original Italian lines are: "Ha un carattere melanconico, / beve come un irlandese."

22. Cletto Arrighi, "Introduzione" in *La Scapigliatura e il 6 febbraio* (Milano: Tipografia di Giuseppe Radaelli, 1862), 7.

23. Ibid., 8–9.

24. Charles Baudelaire, "Be Drunken," in *Baudelaire, His Prose and Poetry*, ed. Thomas Robert Smith (New York: Boni and Liverlight, 1919), 57, https://archive.org/details/baudelairehispro00baudiala.

25. Giuseppe De Grassi, *Maledetti amici* (Rome: Rai Eri, 2001), 101–102.

26. Giovanni Faldella, *Il male dell'arte* (Milan: Luigi Beuf, 1874), 53.

27. Iginio Ugo Tarchetti, *Fosca* (Milan: Edoardo Sonzogno, 1874), 10.

28. "Piero Ciampi No!", last modified Sept. 2013, https://www.youtube.com/watch?v=cx9f0Tijn9A.

29. The Storming of the Bastille on July 14th, 1789, impressed many English Romantic writers not only for political reasons but as a symbol of the power of ideas and words. In Ciampi's meaning, "Bastille" probably represents a defeat of his love strongly barricaded by wrong values and therefore overcome through the separation of his two women.

30. "Hermeticism" was an Italian literary movement developed in the 1920s mainly thanks to Eugenio Montale and Giuseppe Ungaretti. The hermetic poets pursued the ideal of "pure poetry," free not only from the traditional and rhetorical verse forms, but also from any didactic and celebratory purposes. The central theme of hermetic poetry was the sense of desperate loneliness of modern man who has lost faith in the old values, in myths of romantic and positivistic civilization, and no longer has any certainties to anchor the self or its beliefs firmly.

31. Enrico De Angelis, *Piero Ciampi Tutta L'opera* (Milano: Arcana Editrice, 1992), 202

32. Paul Verlaine, "All Grace and All Light," in *Paul Verlaine, His Absinthe-tinted Song, a Monograph on the Poet, with Selections from His Work*, trans. Bergen Applegate (Chicago: The Alderbrink Press, 1916), 92.

33. Enrico De Angelis, *Piero Ciampi Tutta L'opera* (Milano: Arcana Editrice, 1992), 301–305.

34. Lina Agostini, "Sono il più bello il più bravo e non perdono," *Radiocorriere Tv* n. 25 (Roma: Editore Rai, 1976), 28–29.

35. Lina Bolzoni and Marcella Tedeschi, *Dalla Scapigliatura al Verismo* (Roma-Bari: Editori Laterza, 1990), 7.

36. "Piero Ciampi No!", last modified Sept. 2013, https://www.youtube.com/watch?v=
cx9f0Tijn9A. Ciampi transforms a famous Italian proverb, "Morto un *papa* se ne fa un altro"
into "Morto un *poeta* se ne fa un altro," meaning that nobody is indispensable.

BIBLIOGRAPHY

Agostini, Lina. "Sono il più bello il più bravo e non perdono." *Radiocorriere Tv*, n. 25. Roma:
Editore Rai, 1976.
Arrighi, Cletto. *La Scapigliatura e il 6 febbraio.* Milano: Tipografia di Giuseppe Radaelli,
1862.
Baudelaire, Charles. "Be Drunken." In *Baudelaire, His Prose and Poetry*, ed. Thomas Robert
Smith. New York: Boni and Liverlight, 1919, accessed December 12, 2017, https://
archive.org/details/baudelairehispro00baudiala.
Baudelaire, Charles. *The Poems and Prose Poems of Charles Baudelaire with an Introductory
Preface by James Huneker*, edited by James Huneker. New York: Brentano's Publishers,
1919, accessed July 11, 2017, http://www.gutenberg.org/files/36287/36287–h/36287–h.htm.
Benjamin, Walter. *Charles Baudelaire: A Lyric Poet in the Era of High Capitalism.* London:
Verso, 1997.
Bolzoni, Lina, and Marcella Tedeschi. *Dalla Scapigliatura al Verismo.* Roma-Bari: Editori
Laterza, 1990.
Ciampi, Piero. *Io e te abbiamo perso la bussola.* Amico DZSLF 55133, 1973, 33⅓ rpm.
Corbière, Tristan. *Les amours jaunes*, edited by Paradis des Albatros, accessed July 11, 2017,
http://www.paradis-des-albatros.fr/?plaquette&poeme=corbiere/paria.
De Angelis, Enrico. *Piero Ciampi Tutta l'opera.* Milano: Arcana Editrice, 1992.
De Grassi, Giuseppe. *Maledetti amici.* Roma: Rai Eri, 2001.
Faldella, Giovanni. *Il male dell'arte.* Milano: Luigi Beuf, 1874.
Löwy, Michael, and Robert Sayre. *Romanticism Against the Tide of Modernity.* Translated by
Catherine Porter. Durham, NC: Duke University Press, 2001.
Murger, Henry. *Bohemians of the Latin Quarter.* London: Vizetelly & Co., 1888, accessed July
11, 2017, http://www.gutenberg.org/files/18445/18445–h/18445–h.htm.
———. *The Latin Quarter* ("Scènes de la Vie de Bohème"). Translated by Ellen Marriage and
John Selwyn. London: Grant Richards, 1901, accessed July 11, 2017, https://archive.org/
details/latinquartersc00murguoft.
Rosa, Giovanna. *La narrativa degli scapigliati.* Roma: Laterza, 1997.
Tarchetti, Iginio Ugo. *Tutte le opere.* Edited by Enrico Ghidetti. Bologna: Cappelli, 1967.
———. *Fosca.* Milan: Edoardo Sonzogno, 1869, 1874.
"Piero Ciampi No!" YouTube, accessed July 11, 2017, https://www.youtube.com/watch?v=
cx9f0Tijn9A .
Verlaine, Paul. *Paul Verlaine, His Absinthe-tinted Song, a Monograph on the Poet, with Selec-
tions from His Work.* Translated by Bergen Applegate. Chicago: The Alderbrink Press,
1916.

Index

About the Editor and Contributors

Dr. **James Rovira** received his Ph.D. from Drew University and is chair and associate professor of English at Mississippi College. Dr. Rovira's monograph *Blake and Kierkegaard: Creation and Anxiety* was published by Continuum in 2010. Since then, he has published reviews and scholarship in *Blake: An Illustrated Quarterly, European Romantic Review, Journal of Eighteenth-Century Studies, College English, Romantic Circles Reviews and Receptions*, and elsewhere. He has also published poetry and short fiction, and he has one book chapter about music and masculinity in *Guardians of the Galaxy* and the Marvel Cinematic Universe soon to appear in *Assemble: Essays on the Modern Marvel Cinematic Universe*, forthcoming by McFarland, and another about Blake, Kierkegaard, and the Socratic tradition in the forthcoming *Kierkegaard, Literature, and the Arts* (Northwestern UP). His research interests include William Blake, British Romanticism, Kierkegaard, Continental philosophy, literature and psychology, literature and religion, and their intersections with popular culture studies in music and film. He has presented at conferences for the Modern Language Association, the North American Society for the Study of Romanticism, the American Society for Eighteenth-Century Studies, the International Society for Eighteenth-Century Studies, the International Conference on Romanticism, the College English Association, and others. He lives in the greater Jackson, Mississippi, area with his wife Sheridan and his children Penn, Grace, and Zoë.

Dr. **David Boocker** is dean of the College of Arts and Sciences at the University of Nebraska at Omaha. Dean Boocker's teaching specializations include Renaissance and Early Modern Literature; Milton and his influence; and English literature. He has published numerous articles on the work and influence of John Milton, including "Milton after 9/11," in *Milton and Popu-*

171

lar Culture, "Milton and the Woman Controversy," in *A Search for Meaning: Critical Essays on Early Modern Literature*, and "'Women are indebted to Milton . . .': Milton and Woman's Rights in the Nineteenth Century," in *Arenas of Conflict: Milton and the Unfettered Mind* (winner of the Milton Society of American Irene Samuel Award for the best multi-author collection of essays).

Dr. **Lisa Crafton** is a professor of English at University of West Georgia where she teaches British Romanticism (specifically Romanticism and revolution and a seminar on William Blake) and British women writers as well as interdisciplinary courses in media and celebrity studies. Her most recent book, *Transgressive Theatricality, Wollstonecraft, and Romanticism*, was published by Ashgate in 2011. She is the author of numerous articles on British Romanticism and women's literature as well the editor of the volume *The French Revolution Debate in English Literature and Culture*. Her life-long interest in the music of U2 and Leonard Cohen has informed her teaching courses on music and literature as well as contemporary media studies.

Dr. **Rachel Feder** is assistant professor of British Romantic literature at the University of Denver. Her work has appeared in *ELH* and *Studies in Romanticism*. With David Ruderman, she is currently editing a special issue of Romantic Circles Pedagogy Commons focused on teaching the Romantic with the contemporary. Her current book project, *Infinity in Crisis: Romanticizing Environmental Calamity*, recuperates Enlightenment and Romantic-era debates about the nature and reality of infinity in order to historicize environmental humanities.

Dr. **David S. Hogsette** is professor of English at Grove City College, where he serves as Writing Program Director. His major teaching and research concentrations include Romantic period literature, Gothic literature, science fiction, fantasy literature, and college composition. He has published articles on reader-response in Margaret Atwood, cultural reception of Samuel Taylor Coleridge, the transatlantic Gothicism of William Godwin and Charles Brockden Brown, and philosophical perspectives on nineteenth-century science in Mary Shelley. He has also published a composition textbook titled *Writing That Makes Sense: Critical Thinking in College Composition* and a book on basic Christian apologetics titled *E-mails to a Young Seeker: Exchanges in Mere Christianity*. He is currently completing his next book project titled *Exploring the Ethics of Elfland: Fantasy Literature and the Mythopoeic Voice of Reason*.

Dr. **Nicole Lobdell** is a visiting assistant professor of English at DePauw University. Her research interests include nineteenth-century literature, material culture, science fiction, and women writers. She has published previously on Mary Shelley and Margaret Fuller, and her longer projects include a new edition of H. G. Wells's *The Invisible Man* (forthcoming from Broadview Press, Spring 2018) and a book on hoarding in nineteenth-century literature and culture.

Dr. **Ronald D. Morrison** is professor of English at Morehead State University, where he teaches courses in Romantic and Victorian literature and literary theory. He is co-editor, with Laurence W. Mazzeno, of *Victorian Writers and the Environment: Ecocritical Perspectives* (Routledge, 2017) and (also with Mazzeno) *Animals in Victorian Literature and Culture: Contexts for Criticism* (Palgrave 2017). He has published on a variety of nineteenth- and twentieth-century authors in such journals as the *CEA Critic*, the *CLA Journal, Critique: Studies in Contemporary Fiction, The Hardy Review, Nineteenth-Century Studies*, and *Victorians: A Journal of Culture and Literature*. In his younger years, he played guitar in rock and country bands, and he remains an avid guitarist.

Dr. **Douglas T. Root** is assistant professor of English at Claflin University. He served from 2003 to 2005 as a graduate teaching assistant at Florida State University while earning his master's degree. From there he moved on to the University of Georgia, where he was a graduate teaching assistant until earning his doctorate in May 2010. He remained at the University of Georgia as a postdoctoral fellow and instructor. After a brief stint in Cincinnati at the two-year college level, he returned to the four-year setting at Georgia Southern University. In August 2015 he was hired by Claflin University where he is currently up for pre-tenure. His research interests include eighteenth-century British literature, early American literature, and popular culture works on professional wrestling and music.

Dr. **Lorenzo Sorbo** obtained a Ph.D. in musicology at the University of Milan in 2015. In 1997 he also obtained a diploma in violin at the Conservatory "G. Martucci" of Salerno, and in 2000 he earned a diploma in experimental composition at the Conservatory "S. Pietro a Majella" in Naples. In 2009, he graduated with an M.A. in modern literature at the University "Federico II" of Naples with a dissertation on the Neapolitan composer Andrea De Simone (1807–1874) after conducting research on his unpublished and undiscovered manuscripts. He has been teaching music in primary school since 2000 and has performed in many concerts. His research interests include music from the seventeenth century to the present.

Dr. **Gary L. Tandy** is professor of English and chair of the English and Theatre Department at George Fox University. He has published essays and reviews on the works of C. S. Lewis and Christian spirituality in *The Bulletin of the New York C. S. Lewis Society*, *The Christian Chronicle*, *Christianity and Literature*, *Sehnsucht: The C. S. Lewis Journal*, and *Christian Feminism Today*. His book, *The Rhetoric of Certitude: C. S. Lewis's Nonfiction Prose*, was published by Kent State University Press in 2009. Dr. Tandy has taught writing and literature for twenty-three years at three universities.

Janneke van der Leest has an M.A. (2001) in comparative arts with a specialization in music and literature from Radboud University, Nijmegen (the Netherlands). In 2011 she obtained her M.A. in theology at the same university and worked as subject librarian in the fields of theology and religious studies at University Library Nijmegen. Currently she is curriculum developer and assistant head at the Institute for Education for Elderly People in Nijmegen, which organizes educational programs at an academic level for retired people. Since January 2015 she has been an external Ph.D. candidate at Radboud University, writing a dissertation on "The remembrance of the moment of inspiration in English and German romantic poetry and its relevance to modern identity." In addition to her passion for Romanticism, she is a music lover and plays guitar in a rock band.

Dr. **Luke Walker**'s research frequently revolves around the relationship between Romanticism and subsequent countercultural movements. His doctoral thesis, "William Blake in the 1960s: Counterculture and Radical Reception," was completed at the University of Sussex in 2015. Published articles and book chapters cover the influence of Blake and Wordsworth on Allen Ginsberg, the relationship between the American Beat movement and British postwar poetry, and other elements of the literary history of the 1960s. A further research interest involves the intersections between Blake's poetry and four centuries of children's literature. Currently teaching in London at the University of Roehampton, he has previously worked at the University of Chichester and the University of Sussex.